RISING

RISING
30 Women Who Changed India

KIRAN MANRAL

RUPA

Published by
Rupa Publications India Pvt. Ltd 2022
7/16, Ansari Road, Daryaganj
New Delhi 110002

Sales Centres:
Allahabad Bengaluru Chennai
Hyderabad Jaipur Kathmandu
Kolkata Mumbai

Copyright © Kiran Manral 2022

The views and opinions expressed in this book are the author's own and the facts are as reported by her which have been verified to the extent possible, and the publishers are not in any way liable for the same.

All rights reserved.

No part of this publication may be reproduced, transmitted, or stored in a retrieval system, in any form or by any means, electronic, mechanical, photocopying, recording or otherwise, without the prior permission of the publisher.

ISBN: 978-93-5520-191-1

First impression 2022

10 9 8 7 6 5 4 3 2 1

The moral right of the author has been asserted.

This book is sold subject to the condition that it shall not, by way of trade or otherwise, be lent, resold, hired out, or otherwise circulated, without the publisher's prior consent, in any form of binding or cover other than that in which it is published.

CONTENTS

Introduction   ix
A League of Their Own

1. Sushma Swaraj   1
   A People's Politician
2. Sheila Dikshit   8
   Madam Chief Minister
3. M. Fathima Beevi   15
   Lady Justice
4. Mahasweta Devi   21
   Mother of the Dispossessed
5. Amrita Sher-Gil   29
   On Her Own Terms
6. Amrita Pritam   37
   I Will Meet You Again
7. Sonal Mansingh   45
   Against All Odds
8. Lata Mangeshkar   59
   Nightingale of India
9. Anita Desai   68
   The Writer in the Family
10. M.S. Subbulakshmi   76
    The Veena in Her Throat

11. Harita Kaur Deol — 83
    Flying High
12. Madhuri Dixit — 90
    The 'Dhak Dhak' Girl
13. Bachendri Pal — 98
    Climbing More Than Mountains
14. Rekha — 106
    A Life Lived Unapologetically
15. Chhavi Rajawat — 114
    The Village Sarpanch
16. Karnam Malleswari — 122
    Fighting Iron with Iron
17. Shailaja Teacher — 133
    Virus Slayer
18. Hima Das — 141
    Wings on Her Feet
19. Naina Lal Kidwai — 147
    Smashing the Glass Ceiling
20. Shakuntala Devi — 165
    More Than a Human Calculator
21. P.T. Usha — 174
    Payyoli Express
22. P.V. Sindhu — 183
    Racket Girl
23. Ekta Kapoor — 190
    The Queen of the Screen
24. Kiran Bedi — 198
    Crane Bedi

25. Mary Kom 206
    Magnificent Mary

26. Menaka Guruswamy 216
    By the Constitution

27. Tessy Thomas 232
    The Missile Woman of India

28. Aparna Sen 239
    From in Front of the Camera to Behind It

29. Kiran Mazumdar-Shaw 247
    Power Lister

30. Maharani Gayatri Devi 265
    The Queen of Hearts

Acknowledgements 273

INTRODUCTION

A LEAGUE OF THEIR OWN

How does one begin to write about the lives of women who have lived so magnificently that they have become, by the dint of their lived experiences, icons for future generations? It is a daunting task to encapsulate in a few thousand words the sheer breadth of a life lived as a path-breaker. More importantly, what does one take away from their journeys so that we too can, in some way, forge our own paths ahead as they did in a blaze of determined glory?

The aim of this book is not to eulogize these powerful women or to put them on a pedestal. They probably wouldn't care for something as pedestrian as pedestals anyway; they shine wherever they are, regardless of spotlights. The aim rather is to tell their stories, through what we know of them, from information available in the public domain or from first-hand accounts given by those who were gracious enough to spare some time to tell us about their journey. This is an attempt to give the readers an insight into what went into their struggles, what were the crucibles that moulded them, what broke them and how they became stronger in the broken places. It is a salute to their lives, their trials, their struggles and their achievements. Through their lives they teach the women who come after them that they too must shine bright and that they do not need anyone's permission to do so.

Leadership comes in different forms. It sometimes comes cloaked in a distinctive blue Kanjeevaram saree, with a strand of fragrant flowers securely pinned around a bun—unassuming and gentle—with glittering diamond nosepins that catch the rays of sunlight as the wearer enthrals listeners with her voice. In others, it wears a police officer's uniform, commands respect and enforces the law. In others still, it mesmerizes on the silver screen, making us laugh, cry and smile in adoration. Leadership is an inspiring journey in entrepreneurship that starts from a garage and goes on to become a self-made billionaire. Leadership walks graciously into a boardroom, draped in a classic, traditional silk and a strand of pearls, negotiating high-level deals that make the headlines. Leadership gives up life in the lap of luxury for one fraught with uncertainties to pursue a passion for dance to the exclusion of all else. Leadership makes space for itself in politics, heading the national capital as a chief minister for multiple terms, in a Cabinet berth of vital importance. Leadership takes different paths to reach the zenith, and all these paths—whether from a small village in the backwaters of Kerala or the heights of Uttarkashi to the traffic-laden streets of our metropolises—have forged individual destinies that have made a difference to the lives of those around them.

It indeed has been a long journey for women to prove themselves in a world that continues to remain unjustly skewed in favour of men. From the pervasive gender disparity in pay, unequal representation in the House of Parliament and escalating gender violence rates globally, to the immensity of the #MeToo movement, and the basic denial of nutrition and education to the girl-child, women are still fighting their battles though they hold up half the sky, as Chairman Mao Tse-tung once famously proclaimed.

The women featured in this collection of essays have all, in their own way, shattered glass ceilings, battled formidable odds, made difficult life choices, and faced multiple obstacles and censure. Yet, they continued doing what they were destined to: break records, achieve milestones and create new benchmarks, all the while refusing to settle for anything less. Some of them are known feminist icons, some relatively unknown, a few may have courted controversy at certain points in their lives, but what binds them together is that in some way or the other, they have shattered gender barriers and have renegotiated the boundaries that women have been confined to.

Every woman featured in this collection is a path-breaker, some are household names such as Lata Mangeshkar, Rekha and Madhuri Dixit, while others are quiet super-achievers such as Dr Tessy Thomas and Menaka Guruswamy. Some are no longer with us, but have, through their lives, left a legacy: Maharani Gayatri Devi, M.S. Subbulakshmi, Shakuntala Devi, Mahasweta Devi, Sheila Dikshit and Sushma Swaraj, to name just a few. Yet others continue to chart out their successes such as Mary Kom, P.V. Sindhu and Hima Das.

Every story is replete with takeaways, lessons to be learnt, not just professionally but otherwise too. These women have lived life on their own terms, becoming a beacon of hope to many others, women and men alike. If after learning about these inspirational women, a young girl, anywhere in the country, thinks to herself, *That could be me! If she can do it, so can I*, this book would have served its purpose.

1

SUSHMA SWARAJ

A PEOPLE'S POLITICIAN

On 6 August 2019 when the news trickled in, the entire nation was engulfed in a wave of shock and grief. Sushma Swaraj—former minister of External Affairs in the Narendra Modi-led government, stalwart politician from the Bharatiya Janata Party (BJP), former Delhi chief minister and former Lok Sabha Speaker—had passed away from a massive cardiac arrest. She was only 67.

Hundreds gathered outside her home and the BJP headquarters to pay their last respects. Draped in the Indian Tricolour and a red saree, with a red bindi adorning her forehead, she looked quite at peace. It had been a troubled few years for her. Plagued by ill health, she wasn't able to contest the 2019 general elections. Perhaps she knew that the end was near.

She was born in Ambala (Haryana) on 14 February 1952. Her family was steeped in nationalism. Her father, Hardev Sharma, was a Rashtriya Swayamsevak Sangh (RSS) leader as was her grandfather. Her early education was at Ambala, and she majored in Sanskrit and Political Science, going on to study law at the Panjab University.[1]

Her oratory skills, which earned her much acclaim, possibly had their origins when she was barely five. In an interview with NDTV, she spoke about the *Chhath ka Mela*, where the RSS Shakha had held an Antakshari programme featuring patriotic songs and poems. When it was their team's turn, they had to recite a poem beginning with the consonant 'tha'. The young Sushma knew one such poem and she tugged at her father's sleeve nudging him to allow her to recite it. He gave her a go-ahead. She recited the poem confidently, this was her *'manch pravesh'* (initiation to the stage).² At university, she won the best Hindi speaker award for three consecutive years.

She was a politically active student in college, holding dharnas and rallies and opposing Prime Minister Indira Gandhi's policies. When the opposition parties merged together to form the Janata Party, she joined the campaigning team. She was barely 23 when she started campaigning for stalwarts such as Atal Behari Vajpayee, George Fernandes and Madhu Limaye, to name just a few. The social reformist Jayaprakash Narayan was instrumental in getting her formally inducted into electoral politics. In 1977, when she was barely 25 years old, she contested the state elections and became a Member of the Legislative Assembly (MLA) and Cabinet minister in the Devi Lal government in Haryana. She served two terms during which she was given the position of Minister of Labour and Employment, and then of Education, Food and Civil Supplies in the state government.

It was politics that brought her together with her future life partner, Swaraj Kaushal, then an advocate at the Supreme Court. He was associated with George Fernandes, a noted socialist leader. Sushma, who had joined the Supreme Court as an advocate back in 1973, joined Fernandes on his legal team. Cupid struck, and Swaraj and Sushma were married on 13 July 1975.

She was elected to the Rajya Sabha in 1990 and was successful in winning a seat in the Lok Sabha from South Delhi six years later, which resulted in a brief stint in the short-lived, 13-day Vajpayee-led government, in May–June 1996. She was sworn in as the Union Cabinet Minister for Information and Broadcasting, but her term, unfortunately lasted barely

13 days before the government fell. Her turn would come again in 1998, when she was re-elected to the 12th Lok Sabha from the South Delhi parliamentary constituency for a second term, in March that year under the second Vajpayee government. She was then sworn in as Union Cabinet Minister for Information and Broadcasting with an additional charge of the Ministry of Telecommunications. She held this position from 19 March to 12 October 1998. This time, she herself resigned from the Cabinet minister-rank position to take up the position of Delhi's chief minister, becoming the first woman to hold this post. This post too was short lived, from mid October to early December, and she took a call to return to national politics.

She contested against Sonia Gandhi, Congress national president, from Bellary in Karnataka, a Congress stronghold, in the 1999 elections. She led a spirited campaign, addressing voters in their native language, Kannada, and winning their hearts, but unfortunately lost the elections. In 2000, she returned to Parliament as a member of the Rajya Sabha from Uttar Pradesh and then was reallocated to Uttarakhand when the new state was formed. She was appointed the minister of Information and Broadcasting, a position she held from September 2000 to January 2003 in the National Democratic Alliance (NDA) government, and was then reassigned to the Health and Family Welfare and Parliamentary Affairs portfolios in January 2003, positions she held till May 2004.

As Union Minister of Health, she set up six of the All India Institute of Medical Sciences (AIIMS)—at Bhopal, Bhubaneshwar, Jodhpur, Patna, Raipur and Rishikesh. In 2004, when the Congress-led United Progressive Alliance (UPA) came to power after the general elections, Swaraj was in the limelight for a sensational piece of news. She had retained her Rajya Sabha seat at the time and had threatened to shave her head and wear white, symbols of widowhood, if Sonia Gandhi were to become the prime minister of India. Mrs Gandhi, however, chose to stay out of the Cabinet. Later, when asked by a journalist if she would have indeed shaved off her head if Mrs Gandhi had become the prime minister, Swaraj replied in the affirmative. Two years later, in April 2006, she was re-elected to the Rajya Sabha from Madhya Pradesh and served as the leader of the Opposition. In 2009, she won a seat in the Lok Sabha by a staggering margin of over 400,000 votes and became the leader of the Opposition in the Lok Sabha.

Her speeches have gone down as some of the fieriest speeches delivered on the floor of the House. Among them, the speech she delivered on 11 June 1996 was perhaps her most powerful speech. The fabled 1996 speech was in response to the no-confidence motion that saw the nascent Vajpayee government fall:

> Yes, Mr Speaker, we are communal, because we advocate the singing of Vande Mataram. Yes, we are communal, because we fight for the respect of the national flag, we are communal, because we want to abolish Article 370, we are communal, because we want to put an end to discrimination based on caste and creed in this country, yes, we are communal, because we want to get the Uniform Civil Code (Saman Nagrik Samhita) implemented in this country. Mr Speaker, we are communal, because we want the voices of the Kashmiri refugees to be heard.[3]

In 2014, she won the Lok Sabha polls by a great margin, and was an integral part of the BJP's landslide victory when it formed the first Narendra Modi government. She was appointed as the minister for External Affairs and for Overseas Indian Affairs in the Modi Cabinet. She was the second woman to hold this important portfolio after Mrs Indira Gandhi. To quote Modi:

> In any ministerial duty she held, Sushma Ji brought about a marked change in the work culture there. One would conventionally associate the MEA with protocol but

Sushma Ji went a step ahead and answered the people's call, making the Ministry people-friendly. There was a time when there were hardly 70 passport offices in the country. Now, there are over 500 passport offices in the country.[4]

Her spearheading of Operation Raahat, a mammoth air-evacuation exercise by the Indian Air Force and Air India which brought back over 4,000 Indians stranded in Yemen during the Syrian crisis during the military intervention by Saudi Arabia and its allies in 2015 was commended. Her role in bringing back Geeta, a hearing-and-speech impaired girl who was stuck in Pakistan for 15 years and Uzma Ahmed, who was trapped in an abusive marriage and had sought shelter at the Indian High Commission in Islamabad, were among the cases that received much international attention. Her helping Gurpreet, who escaped from an abusive marriage only to find herself and her eight-year-old daughter in a German refugee camp, return to India, earned her much goodwill.

It is interesting to note that Sushma Swaraj managed her own social media accounts. One of her tweets that made the Twitterverse chuckle was this response to someone who had tweeted to her about his refrigerator, 'Brother, I cannot help you in matters of refrigerator. I am very busy with human beings in distress.'[5] She did not hesitate to take a dig at herself, calling John Kerry, the then US Secretary of State, who was very tall, and herself, tiny as 'the long and short of diplomacy'.

In fact, in 2018, she became the most followed foreign minister on Twitter, with over 11 million followers.[6] Her immediate accessibility and responses on Twitter to pleas for help from Indian citizens abroad endeared her to the nation. In fact, it became a known fact that Indian diplomats in overseas missions could no longer switch their phones off when they went to sleep while she was Minister of External Affairs, because she was known to call unmindful of time difference. To quote her from a press conference, 'I do not sleep. I do not let Indian envoys sleep.'

Swaraj was a firm proponent of gender equality, and even suggested that men should take up home science to be equipped to manage the home. She encouraged girls to take up martial arts, and was an enthusiastic supporter of the Women's Reservation Bill, advocating all political parties to support it.

Her health issues began with an infection which required her to get a kidney transplant. She insisted on having her surgery done at New Delhi's AIIMS even though doctors there advised her to travel abroad for her surgery. She had said, according to her husband Swaraj Kaushal, that if she went abroad for her surgery, people would lose faith in our doctors and hospitals. 'She fixed the date of her surgery and asked Dr Mukut Minz, "*Doc Sab, aap sirf instruments pakadaiye, Sri Krishna meri surgery karenge* (Doc saab, just hold the instruments, Lord Krishna will perform my surgery)".'[7]

She announced that she would not be contesting the 2019 general elections. With this, her role as a definitive player in the politics of the nation ended. She was awarded the Padma Vibhushan posthumously in January 2020.

Diminutive and sparkly eyed with a strong voice and a warm heart, Sushma Swaraj redefined what it meant to be a minister in a country where power and position elevate a person making them inaccessible. Her accessibility to the common man, her humility and the willingness to serve the nation made her great and carved her legacy.

NOTES

1. Sushma Swaraj, https://www.britannica.com/biography/Sushma-Swaraj. Accessed on 13 January 2022.
2. Sreenivasan Jain, 'I'd like to make BJP more disciplined: Sushma Swaraj', NDTV, 15 February 2021, https://www.ndtv.

3. com/india-news/id-like-to-make-bjp-more-disciplined-sushma-swaraj-569171. Accessed on 13 January 2022.
3. 'Sushma Swaraj's Famous Five Speeches', *Live Mint*, 9 August 2019, https://www.livemint.com/politics/news/sushma-swaraj-s-famous-five-speeches-1565334153412.html. Accessed on 13 January 2022.
4. https://twitter.com/pmoindia/status/1161264453280763910. Accessed on 13 January 2022.
5. Rekha Dixit and Mandira Nayar, 'Sushma Swaraj, the minister who brought a human touch to MEA', *The Week*, 1 June 2019, https://www.theweek.in/news/india/2019/06/01/Sushma-Swaraj-the-minister-who-brought-a-human-touch-to-MEA.html. Accessed on 13 January 2022.
6. 'Sushma Swaraj: The Politician Who Transformed the Foreign Ministry', *Feminism in India*, 8 August 2019, https://feminisminindia.com/2019/08/08/sushma-swaraj-former-external-affairs-minister-and-bjp-leader-passes-away-at-67/. Accessed on 13 January 2022.
7. Uttam Kumar, 'Just hold the scalpel...': What Sushma Swaraj told docs right before surgery', *Hindustan Times*, 5 November 2019, https://www.hindustantimes.com/india-news/just-hold-scalpel-what-sushma-swaraj-told-docs-just-before-surgery/story-qGrIqYnfEVZWz0qBVLRrTP.html. Accessed on 13 January 2022.

2

SHEILA DIKSHIT
MADAM CHIEF MINISTER

She wasn't tall but commanded a room when she entered. Understated in her trademark traditional weaves, Sheila Dikshit never called attention to herself, but her measured words and tempered responses did. The longest-serving chief minister of Delhi, with a commendable term of 15 years, from 1998 to 2013, she held onto the capital for the Congress party for three consecutive electoral victories, before being voted out in favour of the Aam Aadmi Party's (AAP) Arvind Kejriwal.

How did a young girl, with absolutely no family background in politics, emerge as one of the leading political figures on the Indian political landscape? This is a story that has love, duty and happenstance as its crux.

Born on 31 March 1938 in Kapurthala (Punjab) into a Punjabi Khatri family, Sheila was educated at the Convent of Jesus and Mary and did her master's from Miranda House, Delhi University. Her father was a colonel in the Indian Army. In college, she fell in love with Vinod Dikshit, the only son of the former West Bengal and Karnataka governor Uma Shankar Dikshit, a highly respected Independence activist from Unnao, and a former Union minister in the Indira Gandhi Cabinet.

She writes in her autobiography, *Citizen Delhi: My Times, My Life*:

He was one among the twenty-odd students in our class. Not that it was love at first sight; quite the opposite. In fact, my first impression was that he seemed aloof. He was five feet eleven-and-a-half, slim, handsome, a Stephanian, a good cricketer to boot, and immensely popular. Fate intervened to bring us together when we were chosen by two of our respective friends to resolve their lovers' tiff.[1]

Vinod proposed to her while both of them were travelling in a DTC (Delhi Transport Corporation) bus in 1958. She accepted the proposal, but it took them till July 1962 to get married. In the interim, Vinod was selected for the Indian Administrative Service in 1959.

A couple of years later, they got married and had two children, Sandeep and Latika. She assisted her father-in-law when Indira Gandhi had entrusted him with the task of getting V.V. Giri elected as the president of India.[2] She also helped her father-in-law manage his schedule and public engagements when he was the governor of West Bengal and Karnataka. Much later, it was Mrs Gandhi who first nominated Sheila Dikshit to the Indian delegation on the status of women to the United Nations Commission.

Full-fledged politics was not something Sheila Dikshit had envisioned for herself. Things changed drastically in 1984 when Mrs Gandhi was assassinated. The nation had lost a sitting prime minister. She writes in her autobiography, 'One day I received a phone call that had the power to change my life's trajectory completely. The call was from Rajiv Gandhi telling me that he wanted me to contest from Uttar Pradesh in the coming elections.'[3]

In an interview to *The Quint*, she said, 'I didn't want to get into politics, I didn't have the desire. When the opportunity came after Indira Gandhi died and Rajiv Gandhi wanted me to contest, I was still very hesitant. I was very scared and didn't know what it was all about. But my father-in-law and my husband encouraged me.'[4]

She was assigned the constituency of Kannauj (Uttar Pradesh) just ahead of the 1984 general elections. It was a constituency she knew nothing about. She was the first female candidate to contest from that constituency. Her daughter and her sister accompanied her on the campaign trail. She was firm about two things when she started her campaign: she would not cover her head with a pallu (veil) or travel with a security escort even in dacoit-infested areas. Her opponent in the fray, Chhote Singh Yadav, is reported to have said that she was a novice who spoke English, went ballroom dancing and would not make Unnao her home. He was proven wrong in his assessment of the public mood; she went on to defeat him by a resounding margin of over 50,000 votes.[5] The huge emotional outpouring in support of Rajiv Gandhi in the wake of the assassination of his mother, Indira Gandhi, helped her win.

Between 1984 and 1989, she was the Member of Parliament from the Kannauj constituency. During her stint in Parliament, she served on the Estimates Committee of the Lok Sabha and represented India at the United Nations Commission on the Status of Women for five years (1984–89). She was a Union minister from 1986 to 1989, first as the minister of state for Parliamentary Affairs and then as the minister of state in the Prime Minister's Office (PMO).

Tragedy struck in 1987, when her husband passed away from a heart attack while travelling in a train. She was away, in New York, at the time on official engagements. He was barely 48 then and she submerged herself in her work to deal with her grief. When Rajiv Gandhi lost the general elections in 1989, she, too, decided to put politics away to look after her father-in-law, who at the time was seriously unwell.

In 1991, Rajiv Gandhi was assassinated. Unable to bear the shock, her father-in-law passed away in the next few weeks. With his death, Sheila Dikshit decided to step back from active politics. Through her long exile, she did stay in touch with Sonia

Gandhi on a personal level. She writes about it saying, 'Perhaps it had to do with my own experience, not so long ago, of the loss of a husband and companion in mid-life, I felt a need to be in touch with Mrs Sonia Gandhi in one of the most difficult phases of her life.'[6] In 1998, Mrs Gandhi called her, asking her to contest from the East Delhi Lok Sabha seat. She could not refuse Mrs Gandhi. She would lose this election to the Bharatiya Janata Party's (BJP) Lal Bihari Tiwari, but this was her first step into what would eventually become a much larger role in Delhi politics. She had never been to East Delhi; it was a constituency she was unfamiliar with, always having lived in South Delhi. East Delhi had been a Congress stronghold held by veteran Hari Kishan Lal Bhagat until 1991, when he lost the elections. The BJP had held it since. In her comeback campaign, she managed to garner the highest number of votes achieved by any Congress candidate in Delhi on any seat. Sadly, though, this wasn't enough for her to win.

Later in 1998 itself, she was elected the chief minister of Delhi, a position she would hold for three terms, making her the longest-serving chief minister of Delhi, as well as the longest-serving female chief minister of any Indian state.

During her term, the 2010 Commonwealth Games, held in New Delhi, was mired in controversy. Her greatest remorse, she would say, was that the Games did not get the due recognition it deserved. It helped bolster the infrastructure of the city substantially, but the slur campaign against her overshadowed the positives. She came under the scanner for allegedly misusing government funds but no charges were brought against her. She would eventually come out clean of all the accusations, but the damage had been done.[7] This, as well as the anti-incumbency wave of 2013, the soaring prices of vegetables and the Nirbhaya case affected her tenure. The perception about her now changed from that of a kindly matriarch to an arrogant one, who was disconnected with the issues of the citizenry. Even the members from within the party felt that her 'golden touch' was now fading. It was in 2013 that her era as the chief minister of Delhi came to an end with her defeat in the Delhi Legislative Assembly Elections to the newly formed AAP's Arvind Kejriwal, a debutante politician who won with a resounding margin.

Political observers would say her Waterloo was the way the authorities handled the Nirbhaya protests in December 2012. Spraying protestors with water cannons in peak Delhi winter made Mrs Dikshit come across as uncaring about the concerns of the citizenry. Her remark at the time, 'These things happen,' seemed insensitive.[8] She deflected blame later, but the damage had been done. To quote her, 'The central government, the home ministry, and the Police were really directly responsible for it. But sometimes you have to keep quiet because it is not wise, it is not courteous to blame somebody else for something that has happened in your city.'[9] In 2015, the elections called after the short-lived Kejriwal government fell in Delhi saw the Congress fail to win a single seat. She was then appointed the governor of Kerala, but resigned a few months later when the BJP came to power at the Centre, and contested the 2019 elections only to lose to BJP's Manoj Tiwari. In 2019, when the Congress received overtures from Kejriwal's AAP to form a joint alliance to take on the BJP, she refused to do so, despite other members of the party feeling that they should. Her stand was vindicated when the AAP lost, coming third in the five of the seven Lok Sabha seats in Delhi.

Sheila Dikshit was prescient for her time and understood the challenges the city would face due to its growth. Back in 1998, the Supreme Court had ordered that all the buses in the city should shift to compressed natural gas (CNG) by March 2001 and that no buses older than 80 years must be allowed on the roads if they weren't running on CNG.[10] In her autobiography, she spoke about how she approached the then Union Minister for Petroleum and Natural Gas, Ram Naik for assistance, and he kindly offered to create a 2,100-km pipeline from Gujarat to Delhi, enabling the latter to meet the March 2001 deadline. She would say, 'Despite all the hiccups, by the end of 2002, we could claim that we had made a beginning in providing the cleanest public transportation system in the world.'[11] In another first, she inaugurated the Delhi Metro Rail system in 2002, which eased the traffic congestion in the city.

Her health had been shaky for some years. In 2012, she underwent an angioplasty, and in 2018, she had to undergo further heart surgery in France. Her ill health continued even after her surgery in France. She was admitted to the Fortis Escorts Heart Institute on 19 July 2019 for cardiac arrhythmia. She was put on the ventilator, but suffered multiple cardiac arrests and died the next day. She was 81 years old.

Hers was a life filled with achievements, power, tragedy and loss in equal measure. For someone who made her foray into politics late in life through chance and circumstance, what better testimony to the mark she had left on the city of Delhi than the collective mourning that spread through the city upon her passing?

NOTES

1. Sheila Dikshit, *Citizen Delhi: My Times, My Life*, Bloomsbury, New Delhi, 2018.
2. Soni Mishra, 'Sheila Dikshit: Delhi's tallest leader who transformed the city', *The Week*, 20 July 2019, https://www.theweek.in/news/india/2019/07/20/sheila-dixit-delhi-tallest-leader-who-transformed-city.html. Accessed on 14 January 2022.
3. Sheila Dikshit, *Citizen Delhi: My Times, My Life*, Bloomsbury, New Delhi, 2018.
4. Nishtha Gautum, 'How Sheila Dikshit Joined Politics When Her IAS Husband Couldn't', *The Quint*, 20 July 2019, https://

5. Sheila Dikshit, '"I refused to cover my head with the pallu of my sari": How Sheila Dikshit began in politics', *Scroll.in*, 22 July 2019, https://scroll.in/article/931300/i-refused-to-cover-my-head-with-the-pallu-of-my-sari-how-sheila-dikshit-began-in-politics. Accessed on 14 January 2022.
6. Shivam Vij, 'The life and times of Sheila Dikshit, in her own words', *ThePrint*, 21 July 2019, https://theprint.in/opinion/the-life-and-times-of-sheila-dikshit-in-her-own-words/265618/. Accessed on 14 January 2022.
7. 'Sheila Dikshit under scanner for Commonwealth Games spend', *The Hindu BusinessLine*, 6 February 2014, https://www.thehindubusinessline.com/news/national/sheila-dikshit-under-scanner-for-commonwealth-games-spend/article20722938.ece1. Accessed on 14 January 2022.
8. Puneet Nicholas Yadav, 'In Cut-throat Delhi, Sheila Dikshit Steered Congress with Poise and Dignity', *Outlook*, 20 July 2019, https://www.outlookindia.com/website/story/india-news-sheila-dikshit-the-grand-matriarch-of-delhi-politics-passes-away/334570. Accessed on 14 January 2022.
9. Nishtha Gautum, 'How Sheila Dikshit Joined Politics When Her IAS Husband Couldn't', *The Quint*, 20 July 2019, https://www.thequint.com/news/politics/sheila-dikshit-former-cm-reluctant-politician-citizen-delhi. Accessed on 14 January 2022.
10. Dipankar De Sarkar, 'How Sheila Dikshit rolled out the world's biggest clean air project' *Mint*, 25 July 2019, https://www.livemint.com/opinion/columns/opinion-how-sheila-dikshit-rolled-out-the-world-s-biggest-clean-air-project-1564063648636.html. Accessed on 14 January 2022.
11. Ibid.

3

M. FATHIMA BEEVI

LADY JUSTICE

Even before the phrase 'glass ceiling' entered common parlance, we had a female judge in the Supreme Court already smash it. With a quiet efficiency that defined her career, on 6 October 1989, M. Fathima Beevi became the first female judge in the Supreme Court, a position she held till her retirement on 29 April 1992.

For all her achievements, she remains an enigma, shunning the spotlight and living a quiet life in her hometown post her retirement. Her photographs show a determined expression: her head firmly covered with her saree's pallu, spectacles lodged on the bridge of her nose and her matter-of-fact demeanour.

Justice M. Fathima Beevi began her journey to the Supreme Court from a small village in Kerala. She was born on 30 April 1927, in Pathanamthitta town in the erstwhile princely state of Travancore in Kerala in pre-Independence India. Born to Annaveetil Meera Sahib and Khadeeja Beevi, she was the eldest of eight siblings. As a young girl, Fathima was an earnest student, and her father, a government servant, encouraged both his sons and daughters equally to study well. She did her early schooling in the Catholicate High School in Pathanamthitta and passed her matriculation in 1943, going on to study Science for six years in Trivandrum (now Thiruvananthapuram), where she graduated.

At the time, for a young girl to live apart from her family and go to the city was a bold move, and her father backed her decision wholeheartedly. She wanted to pursue her MSc in Chemistry but her father dissuaded her. He felt that if she did her MSc, she would end up as a college teacher or a professor in Trivandrum. He was ambitious for her and wanted her to study law. In keeping with his wishes, she joined the Government Law College, Trivandrum. At the time, Anna Chandy was the first woman judicial officer working near Travancore. Her father was very impressed by Chandy's achievements and perhaps, she motivated him to dream of his own daughter making her mark in the judiciary.

An earnest and hard-working student, Fathima Beevi was but one of the five girl students in her class to enrol. After that, she did an internship under a senior lawyer for a year. In 1950, she would make the first of the many firsts her career was dotted with. She became the first woman to top the Bar Council of India's exams and was awarded the Bar Council gold medal for 1949–50.[1]

Her formal career in law began on 14 November 1950 when she was enrolled as an advocate in the lower judiciary in Kollam, Kerala. She was an outlier in the courts of the time. Men dominated the premises and women were barely seen, especially in positions of authority. That said, she faced many a raised eyebrow, questioning glances and even censure, being the only woman and that too one wearing a headscarf, in the court. She went on to practise for nearly eight years in Kollam. To quote her, 'Judicial service was more attractive than the practice at that time. Women were not very much encouraged by the general public, very few succeeded as lawyers.'[2]

In 1958, she was appointed as a munsiff in the Kerala Subordinate Judicial Services, and a decade later, promoted to subordinate judge in 1968. She rose swiftly in the ranks then on; she was made chief judicial magistrate in 1972, and district and sessions judge in 1974. In January 1980, she was appointed the judicial member of the Income Tax Appellate Tribunal and three years later, on 4 August 1983, to the Kerala High Court as a judge. It was a meteoric rise by any standards, given the times and lack of diversity in the judiciary back then. She was now the first Muslim woman to be appointed to the higher judiciary. A year later, she was made a permanent judge of the Kerala High Court from which she retired in April 1989. However, barely a few months later, she was appointed to the Supreme Court as judge in October 1989, making her the first female judge of the Court. This was indeed a watershed moment in the history of the Indian judiciary. In an interview with *Scroll.in*, she would say of this historic moment, 'I opened a closed door.'[3]

Some would say that her appointment to the Supreme Court over other senior judges was a political decision by the then Prime Minister Rajiv Gandhi in the wake of the controversy over the Muslim Women (Protection of Rights on Divorce) Act of 1986. Whether or not it's true, it was indeed a momentous appointment. It had taken the Supreme Court of India almost four decades after Independence to appoint a woman as a judge. Even today, decades later, the representation of women in the judiciary is far from equal to that of men.

In a 2016 interview with *The Week*, she was asked if she felt the Indian judiciary was patriarchal. Her response was unequivocal. 'Absolutely. No doubt about that.' To quote her further,

> There are many women in the field now, both at the bar and in the bench. However, their participation is meagre. Their representation is not equal to men. There is a historical reason also for that... Women took to the field late. It will take time for women to get equal representation in the judiciary. When I went to Law College, there were only five girls in my class in the first year. The number went down to two or three in the second year. Today, in law colleges, we are seeing that a good percentage of the students are women.[4]

With this appointment she would also become the first woman judge of a Supreme Court in Asia. She would also be the first female Muslim judge of a Supreme Court in India and Asia. She is reported to always have been courteous and balanced in court, and made it a point to be well prepared with the case history whenever she heard a case. She was reportedly in favour of reservations for women which could possibly increase the number of women judges at the higher judiciary. To quote her on this, 'However, there should not be any discrimination between candidates on [gender basis]. A woman should get equal treatment and equal consideration.'[5]

After she retired from the Supreme Court in 1992, she was appointed as the governor of Tamil Nadu five years later on 25 January 1997 on the recommendation of Dravida Munnetra Kazhagam (DMK) chief M. Karunanidhi. On her appointment, the then President of India, Shankar Dayal Sharma, said, '[her] experience of and insights into the working of the Constitution and the laws comprise valuable assets.'[6] She was an unassuming governor, unswayed by the pomp and pageantry that came with the office. In fact, so simple was she that it was said she lived like a recluse in Raj Bhavan.[7]

Her term as the governor of Tamil Nadu was rocked by a major controversy over the appointment of Jayalalithaa as the chief minister of Tamil Nadu. As the governor, she had accepted Jayalalithaa's contention of majority after the assembly elections, although Jayalalithaa had been convicted under charges of corruption and barred from contesting elections for six years thereafter. Fathima Beevi had invoked Article 164 of the Constitution, which allows a non-member of the state legislature to become the chief minister, accepting Jayalalithaa's claim that she had 'the will of the people.'[8]

Of the decision to swear Jayalalithaa in as the chief minister of Tamil Nadu and the ensuing controversy, M. Fathima Beevi said in a later interview to *Scroll.in*,

She was acquitted and had no charges of corruption at the time I appointed her. I had even consulted Supreme Court judges before considering it. And they all agreed with me. I talked to Fali Nariman. I talked to Chief Justice Ahmadi. All of them agreed. I had legal opinion also for doing these things; I did not do anything spontaneously or randomly. I thought about it, I have worked on it and then only I have taken the decision. But views differ. I didn't want to continue there when some conflict arises, so I just resigned and came back.[9]

This was in July 2001.

This was then an ignominious close to a glorious career that had made her the first female judge and the first Muslim woman at the Supreme Court.

She had been a quiet governor during her ill-fated term, little seen, little heard. She kept to herself, performing her constitutional duties without any of the pomp or pageantry normally associated with the office of governor. She vacated the Raj Bhavan in a similar manner too, without any fuss. Once the unpleasantness had set in, she felt, it was impossible to continue in the position. In retrospect, she is reported to have said that she enjoyed the position of the judge better than that of the governor, because she felt she had more freedom as a judge to perform her duties.[10]

After resigning from her position as governor of Tamil Nadu, she returned to her ancestral home at Pathanamthitta in Kerala, to live out her years in relative seclusion. She resigned at the age of 73. She lives out her retirement as quietly and unobtrusively as she lived while in the eminent positions she held.

NOTES

1. Khushi Agarwal, 'Justice Fathima Beevi: The First Indian Woman to Become a Supreme Court Justice', *Feminism in India*, 13 September 2019, https://feminisminindia.com/2019/09/13/justice-fathima-beevi-first-indian-woman-supreme-court-justice. Accessed on 14 January 2022.
2. https://www.facebook.com/watch/?v=1956006401148897. Accessed on 22 January 2022.
3. Smitha Nair, 'Justice Fathima Beevi', *Scroll.in*, 27 April 2018, https://scroll.in/tag/Justice%20Fathima%20Beevi. Accessed on 14 January 2022.
4. Soni Mishra, 'Reservation will help women', *The Week*, 13 November 2016, https://www.theweek.in/theweek/cover/reservation-will-help-women.html. Accessed on 14 January 2022.
5. Ibid.
6. The SSC Online Blog, https://www.scconline.com/blog/post/tag/women-in-law/. Accessed on 14 January 2022.
7. 'A quiet governor leaves a storm behind', Rediff.com, 3 July 2001, https://www.rediff.com/news/2001/jul/03tn1.htm. Accessed on 14 January 2022.
8. Ragamalika Karthikeyan, 'Governor Vidyasagar Rao will remember what Fatima Beevi did in 2001: Here's why', The News Minute, 7 February 2017, https://www.thenewsminute.com/article/governor-vidyasagar-rao-will-remember-what-fatima-beevi-did-2001-here-s-why-56897. Accessed on 14 January 2022.
9. Smitha Nair, 'Video: "I opened a closed door," India's first woman SC judge on breaking the glass ceiling', 27 April 2018, https://scroll.in/video/877110/video-i-opened-a-closed-door-india-s-first-woman-sc-judge-on-breaking-the-glass-ceiling. Accessed on 14 January 2022.
10. 'Justice Fathima Beevi hits a glorious 90', *Mathrubhumi*, 3 May 2017.

4

MAHASWETA DEVI

MOTHER OF THE DISPOSSESSED

It was winter in Jaipur at the 2013 edition of the Jaipur Literary Festival. The feeble winter sun glowed on a packed venue, with the crowd jostling to listen to a slight, elderly lady speak. The elderly lady was unperturbed about being the focus of everyone's attention. 'I am tapping my 90th year and look at how much damage I have done by being around,' she said, tongue in cheek. The speaker was Mahasweta Devi—author, iconoclast, social activist; the labels didn't really matter.[1]

This ability to take a sharp dig at herself was characteristic of Mahasweta Devi. She had an incisive sense of humour, was scathing, irreverent, spoke her mind and did not suffer fools gladly. Of this, G.N. Devy, an activist who had worked closely with her, wrote, 'It was impossible to predict when, in the middle of the most polite conversation with persons she had not previously met, she would curtly dismiss civility and tell the person that he was a fraud.'[2]

Having been conferred with the Sahitya Akademi Award, the Jnanpith Award, the Ramon Magsaysay Award and India's highest civilian awards, the Padma Shri and the Padma Vibhushan, Mahasweta Devi bore her distinctions with the ease that came from being unconcerned about laurels.

Born on 14 January 1926 in Dacca (now Dhaka) in East Bengal (modern-day Bangladesh), her maternal grandfather was an acclaimed and successful lawyer of the time. She was one of nine children. Her father, Manish Ghatak, was a well-known poet and novelist who wrote under the nom de plume of Jabanshwa and his brother was the renowned filmmaker Ritwik Ghatak. Her mother, Dharitri Devi, was herself a noted writer and a social worker. As a child, Mahasweta Devi saw her mother and aunt take on the cause of educating illiterate girls in Dacca. On visits to her grandparents' ancestral village, she was encouraged to dress simply so as not to alienate the children from the village. 'Everyone [in the family] read and read and read' as she said in her later years.[3]

She did her early schooling in Dacca's Eden Montessori School and continued her education at the Midnapore Mission Girls High School in West Bengal after her family moved to Midnapore. Having completed her intermediate studies, she joined Rabindranath Tagore's Visva-Bharati University. Her years at Shantiniketan, between 1936 to 1938, were seminal to her creativity.

'Don't write any more,' she is reported to have said to Tagore while at Shantiniketan, 'I can't read so much.' The impertinence apart, Tagore was a profound influence on her.

Her social activism would begin early, during the horrific Bengal Famine of 1942-44 when she worked actively in relief work, distributing food and going through the bodies on the streets to check for survivors. These traumatic times were also intensified by the Quit India movement of 1942 and then the Calcutta Killings of 1946, followed by the Hindu-Muslim riots of Partition.

Despite pursuing her education in English and majoring in the language, she would go on to write her books and short stories primarily in Bengali, her mother tongue. Although she had been writing since the age of 13, she was first published much later, in 1956. Her folks did not understand what she got from writing so much. A friend of her father's once said,

'Mahasweta...what could she possibly be writing?' What does she write? She just does reportage.' She vowed to make writing her profession, her means of sustenance.

Her first novel, *Jhansir Rani* (The Queen of Jhansi), written when she was around 30, was based on the epochal story of the valiant Rani Lakshmi Bai of Jhansi, the iconic warrior queen who rode into battle against the British, her young son strapped onto her back. To write this book she did not depend on existing reference materials on the Queen. She visited Jhansi, travelling through villages, a lone woman, sitting around open fires with the villagers, listening to the stories they had heard about the Queen passed down over the generations. The book, a fictionalized account of the Queen's life, reconstructed the life of Rani Lakshmi Bai from this extensive field research including folk tales, oral tradition as well as historical documents sourced from G.C. Tambe, the grandson of the fabled queen. In an interview with the journal *Revolutionary Democracy* in 1999, she said, 'Since then, I have a firm opinion that the most precious historical material is what is preserved in the memory of the common people.'[4]

It was a tradition that continued to inform her writing, the first-hand experience of living with and interacting with the people she wrote about. She would, in the course of her extensive career, write over 120 novels and short stories, focusing on India's tribal communities and Maoist rebels, prostitutes and nomads, beggars and labourers. While she would write primarily in her mother tongue, with tribal dialects included, her work has been translated into many Indian and international languages. Her stories were never written from the perspective of a detached observer, but rather as one from amongst the people.

Among her most famous novels, *Hajar Churashir Maa* (Mother of 1084), published in 1974, stands out for her sensitive tackling of the Naxalite insurgency. The book was later adapted into a critically acclaimed movie. By writing about the insurgency from the gaze of a bereaved mother, she made it a story that every person could empathize with. To quote her, 'One day, two or three Naxalite boys came to me and said, "How come you are writing about the Naxalites in the rural context? What about us who are butchered daily in the streets of Calcutta?" I said, I have heard, I will try. And out of that came the Mother of 1084.'[5]

Apart from this, four of her other works have been made into films: *Sunghursh* (1968), *Rudaali* (1993), *Maati Maay* (2006) and *Gangor* (2010).

From her cross-country travels, meeting people from different walks of life, sprang forth her writing about them. To quote her, 'I constantly come across the reappearance, in various forms—of folklore, ballads, myths and legends—carried by ordinary people across generations. For me, the endless source of ingredients for writing is in these amazingly noble, suffering human beings. Why should I look for my raw material elsewhere, once I have started knowing them? Sometimes it seems to me that my writing is really their doing.'[6]

Her work with the Sabar tribal community in Purulia, West Bengal, earned her the moniker, 'The Mother of the Sabars'. She was also the founder of India's first organization for bonded labourers in 1980.

Her novel *Aranyer Adhikar* (Right to the Forest; published in 1977) was based on the tribal activist Birsa Munda, who agitated against British rule, and as a consequence of her consistent activism, the state government of Jharkhand finally removed the manacles from the commemorative sculpture of the young tribal icon. She was awarded the Sahitya Akademi Award for this novel in 1979. Her writing has been critiqued as simplistic. 'Her tribal characters are too much the noble savage,' said Gayatri Chakravorty Spivak, who herself translated a collection of Devi's short stories into English.[7] Her writing was far removed from the genteel themes that informed much of the Bengali writing of the time. She had, through her involvement with the lives of the tribals, become one of them: the Kherias called her Ma and the Santhals called her Marang dai (sister). 'The tribals are more civilised than us,' she had said.[8]

Through all the acclaim her writing and activism received, she lived a difficult personal life. A little before India attained Independence, in February 1947, she got married to the playwright Bijon Bhattacharya, one of the founders of the Indian People's Theatre Association. He had also acted in her uncle, Ritwik Ghatak's movies and was a member of the Communist Party of India. It wasn't going to be an easy marriage. The year after they were married, they had a child, Nabarun. Communists and their sympathizers were shunned at the time, and her husband could not find a job. Mahasweta did what she could to put food on the table and a roof over their heads. She sold dye products and dabbled in a failed scheme to supply thousands of research monkeys to laboratories in the United States with a friend. She got a job as an upper-division clerk in the regional office of the Deputy Accountant General of Post and Telegraph but was dismissed when books of Karl Marx, Friedrich Engels and Lenin were allegedly planted in her office drawer and she was accused of being a communist. She wrote stories for *Sachitra Bharat*, a Bengali weekly, to bring in the money to keep the family afloat. Using the pen name Sumitra Devi, she wrote romantic short stories, as well as family and horror stories. While these writings earned her an income, they did not satisfy her creatively. Her first major breakthrough would come with the writing of *Jhansir Rani*, a work of literature that firmly deposited her amongst the firmament of literary giants in Indian writing. The book received critical acclaim and she followed it up with *Nati* (1957), *Madhrey Madhur* (1958), *Yamuna ke Teer* (1958), *Etotuku Asha* (1959) and *Premtara* (1959).

All through the writing of these books, she was going through a difficult time in her marriage. She walked out of the marriage in 1962, leaving behind her son, then 14, with his father. To quote her, 'I don't know what created this barrier, this void inside me. Something I was not getting. Love, attention, physical satisfaction—I don't know what.'[9] She reportedly even attempted to kill herself by overdosing on sleeping pills. When she emerged, she says she felt a tremendous urge to live. She began writing about this traumatic phase of her life and had almost finished half of it, but sadly this manuscript was lost and never recovered. 'All through my life, I've done whatever I felt like doing,' she would say in retrospect. She moved into a rented house after her divorce. She was told by people, that the rented house she had moved into had a 'horrid' bathroom. She would reply, 'All my life I have lived in so many houses. This is my house, my room, this is my bathroom. In this place I can be myself. That was a very great release.' She would remarry, but sadly, the second marriage would end too, in 1975.

Personal tragedy continued to pepper her life. She would lose the ones she loved. Her son, Nabarun, passed away in 2014. They hadn't been on the best of terms and the estrangement was the cause of much sadness for her.

Her social activism and her work in championing the cause of the tribals, the marginalized and the dispossessed won her the Padma Shri in 1986, the Jnanpith Award in 1996 and the Ramon Magsaysay Award in 1997. In 2003, she was awarded the Officier de l'Ordre des Arts et des Lettres from France. In 2006, the Indian government awarded her the Padma Vibhushan. The year 2007 saw her receiving the SAARC Literary Award, and in 2009, she was shortlisted for the Man Booker Prize. In 2012, she was nominated for the Nobel Prize in Literature. Sadly, she wouldn't win it.

On 28 July 2016, she passed away after a major heart attack and multiple organ failure. She was 90. The house in which she spent her final days has been converted to The Mahasweta Devi Shangraha Shala, a museum dedicated to her life and work. It is said that in the untouched, unrenovated corners of the home, sometimes you can hear whispers, voices.[10] Perhaps, she still has more to say, more to write.

One must remember her by these words, in which she encapsulates the agony of women and tribals, that of being doubly condemned. She wrote, 'I am going to write this—I am a witch, I am going to be killed.'[11]

NOTES

1. Resham Sengar, 'Jaipur Literature Festival 2013: Mahashweta Devi urges people to "swim against the tide"', Zee News, 24 January 2014, https://zeenews.india.com/entertainment/bookworm/jaipur-literature-festival/jaipur-literature-festival-2013-mahashweta-devi-urges-people-to-swim-against-the-tide_2700.htm. Accessed on 15 January 2022.
2. G.N. Devy, 'Mahasweta Devi: Writer, Activist, Conscience-Keeper of Our Times', *The Wire*, 29 July 2016, https://thewire.in/books/mahasweta-devi-writer-activist-conscience-keeper-times. Accessed on 15 January 2022.
3. Prof. Shubha Tiwari, 'Writing as Social Service: The Literary Compass of Mahashweta Devi', Boloji.com, https://www.boloji.com/articles/11565/writing-as-social-service. Accessed on 15 January 2022.
4. Kaushik Swaminath, 'Mahasweta Devi, Bengali Writer and Activist Who Fought Injustice, Dies at 90', *The New York Times*, 2 August 2016, https://www.nytimes.com/2016/08/03/books/mahasweta-devi-bengali-writer-and-activist-who-fought-injustice-dies-at-90.html. Accessed on 14 January 2022.
5. Debojit Dutta, 'I am a Witch, I am Going to be Killed: Watch Mahasweta Devi on Writing, Naxalites and Men in Her Life', *Anti-serious.com*, 28 July 2016, https://antiserious.com/i-am-a-witch-i-am-going-to-be-killed-watch-mahasweta-devi-on-writing-naxalites-and-men-in-her-cf14c135bbdc. Accessed on 15 January 2022.

6. Ranabir Samaddar, 'Mahasweta Devi, Champion of the Underdog Who Took on the Left Front in Bengal', *The Wire*, 3 August 2016, https://thewire.in/books/through-her-life-mahasweta-devi-remained-the-champion-of-the-underdog. Accessed on 15 January 2022.
7. Gayatri Chakravorty Spivak, 'Mahasweta Devi: The Life Immortal', *The Indian Express*, 30 July 2016, https://indianexpress.com/article/lifestyle/books/mahasweta-devi-the-life-immortal-gayatri-chakravorty-spivak-2943277/. Accessed on 15 January 2022.
8. Sirshendu Panth, 'Mahasweta Devi lived like she wrote: Fearlessly and without restraint', *Hindustan Times*, 28 July 2016, https://www.hindustantimes.com/books/mahasweta-devi-lived-like-she-wrote-fearlessly-and-without-restraint/story-ypNPCoE1gX1D0VDKjjaueO.html. Accessed on 15 January 2022.
9. Debojit Dutta, 'I am a Witch, I am Going to be Killed: Watch Mahashweta Devi on Writing, Naxalites and Men in Her Life', *Anti-serious.com*, 28 July 2016, https://antiserious.com/i-am-a-witch-i-am-going-to-be-killed-watch-mahashweta-devi-on-writing-naxalites-and-men-in-her-cf14c135bbdc. Accessed on 15 January 2022.
10. Prof. Shubha Tiwari, 'Writing as Social Service: The Literary Compass of Mahashweta Devi', Boloji.com, https://www.boloji.com/articles/11565/writing-as-social-service. Accessed on 15 January 2022.
11. Debojit Dutta, 'I am a Witch, I am Going to be Killed: Watch Mahashweta Devi on Writing, Naxalites and Men in Her Life', *Anti-serious.com*, 28 July 2016, https://antiserious.com/i-am-a-witch-i-am-going-to-be-killed-watch-mahashweta-devi-on-writing-naxalites-and-men-in-her-cf14c135bbdc. Accessed on 15 January 2022.

5

AMRITA SHER-GIL

ON HER OWN TERMS

All the photographs of Amrita Sher-Gil have one thing in common—the confidence of her gaze and the unabashed narcissism of her presence. She stares into the camera, challenging it to capture her essence. But then, perhaps it was impossible to capture the essence of a life so meteoric that it lives on even today, decades later—a subject of much fascination and discussion.

Regarded as one of the greatest avant-garde artists of the early twentieth century and a pioneer in modern art, Amrita Sher-Gil was born of a unique cross-continental and cross-cultural love story that came about through serendipity. Her parents, Umrao Singh Sher-Gil and Marie Antoinette Gottesmann might have never met had the latter not made a trip to India in 1912, as the companion of Maharaja Ranjit Singh's granddaughter. Umrao Singh Sher-Gil, a descendant of Sikh aristocracy himself, was a scholar of both Sanskrit and Persian. Her mother, Marie Antoinette Gottesmann, was a Hungarian opera singer, and came from a fairly affluent family herself. On her trip to India, she was introduced to Umrao Singh Sher-Gil. They fell deeply in love and were soon married. A year later, on 30 January 1913, Amrita was born in Budapest. A couple of years later, her sister, Indira, was born. Both girls spent their early childhood in Budapest, but strained circumstances made them move back to India in 1921 and take up residence in the family home in Shimla (formerly known as Simla).

The move was a blessing of sorts, for it was here that Amrita began discovering her creative talents. She and her younger sister began taking lessons in piano and violin and were soon giving concerts and acting in plays in the famed Gaiety Theatre on Shimla's Mall Road.[1]

Both sisters had quite an unusual upbringing, making them question societal norms. At school, young Amrita scandalized the nuns with her declaration of being an atheist and got herself expelled. As a young girl, she would get the house staff in their Shimla residence to pose for her. In 1923, an Italian sculptor had come to stay in Shimla. Amrita's mother convinced him to take Amrita under his wing and give her lessons in art. When he returned home to Italy in 1924, Marie moved there with Amrita, and enrolled her at the Santa Annunziata art school in Florence. They would return to India soon, but this brief exposure to the works of the Italian masters would be a revelation for the young Amrita. Her maternal uncle from Hungary visited them in Shimla in 1926. He was the renowned Indologist, Ervin Baktay. He saw potential in the young girl and advocated that her parents enrol her in a renowned art school abroad. This led to a stint in Paris, first at the Académie de La Grande Chaumière, where she learnt under Pierre Henri Vaillant and Lucien Simon, and then at the famed École des Beaux-Arts.

Amrita was now a self-assured young woman, exotic and very beautiful. She was heavily influenced by the works of noted European painters such Paul Cézanne and Paul Gauguin. Her teacher there, Lucien, and then Boris Taslitzky, a French painter renowned for the social realism in his work, were a huge influence on her work. It is said that her phase in Paris saw experts talk highly of her conviction and the maturity of her work, which were rare for a girl her age.

In 1931, she was briefly engaged to Yusuf Ali Khan, the

son of a landowning nawab from India. At the same time, she was rumoured to be having an affair with her first cousin on her maternal side, Dr Victor Egan. The engagement with Yusuf Ali Khan would later break up.[2] Her early works were strongly influenced by the post impressionist style, attributable to the influence of the Bohemian circles she was part of. 'I painted a few very good paintings,' she would write to her mother in October 1931, when she was 18. 'Everybody says that I have improved immensely; even that person whose criticism in my view is most important to me—myself.'[3]

Her breakthrough work that catapulted her to the limelight was an oil painting titled 'Young Girls' (done in 1932), which was awarded a gold medal in 1933 at the Grand Salon in Paris, the renowned art show, where artists from all over Europe competed. With this gold medal, she was elected as an associate of the Grand Salon in 1933, making her the youngest member and the only Asian to receive this honour at the time. 'Young Girls' showed her sister, Indira, dressed in a contemporary European attire, seated across a French friend, Denise Proutaux, who is partially undressed, with her face and by extension her identity obscured by her long hair. This painting has been interpreted as being indicative of the duality of Sher-Gil's personality, the bon vivant, the social butterfly versus the cloistered artist. It has also been an expression of the duality of the fractured identity she experienced with her parentage.[4]

Some art critics felt that her work 'Two Women' was a manifestation of her desire for the painter Marie Louise Chassany. However in the book *Same-Sex Love in India*, authors Ruth Vanita and Saleem Kidwai state that she had denied being in a relationship with Chassany in a letter to her mother written in 1934. She wrote, 'We never had anything to do with each other in sexual terms.'[5]

The self portraits she made during this phase have been described by the National Gallery of Modern Art in New Delhi as, '[capturing] the artist in her many moods—somber, pensive, and joyous—while revealing a narcissistic streak in her personality.'[6] This narcissistic streak, or perhaps, the urge to examine herself dispassionately as a subject, was something that the Mexican artist Frida Kahlo had as well. Perhaps it was a sign of the times, when female artists were rejecting what was prescribed as canonical themes and stunning the world with their unwavering focus on themselves. She studied painting, she says, but would not be taught. She would write in *The Hindu* much later, in 1936, 'Although I studied, I have never been taught painting...because I possess in my psychological makeup a peculiarity that resents any outside interference...'[7]

By the time 1933 rolled around, Amrita became nostalgic about India to the point of it becoming an obsession. She wrote that she 'began to be haunted by an intense longing to return to India [...] feeling in some strange way that there lay my destiny as a painter.'[8] It would take her till the end of 1934 to make up her mind and finally take the plunge to move back to India, to their family home in Shimla. On her return, she had an intense but short-lived affair with the journalist Malcolm Muggeridge, then the assistant editor at *The Calcutta Statesman*. While the relationship wasn't destined to last, it did result in a casual portrait of Muggeridge, now on display at the National Gallery of Modern Art in New Delhi. In September 1935, Amrita saw Muggeridge off, him travelling to England for a new professional position. She stayed back in Shimla.

Her restlessness to learn more about the country she came from would have her eventually leave the comforts of Shimla and the confines of the familiar to travel across the country in 1936. She was spurred on in this journey of exploration by the renowned critic and art collector, Karl Khandalavala. It would be a seminal journey, in terms of how it influenced her art, exposing her to the two great schools of painting in India—the Mughal and the Pahari schools—as well as the cave paintings at Ajanta.

She would tour South India extensively in 1937, and from this tour would come her trilogy: 'Bride's Toilet', 'Brahmacharis' and 'South Indian Villagers Going to Market'. In these works, Sher-Gil, despite her early art education in the western tradition, shows a distinct Indian influence, tempered by an empathetic gaze towards her subjects.[9] Of this phase she said, she had now found her artistic mission. She wrote to a friend, 'Europe belongs to Picasso, Matisse, Braque and many others. India belongs only to me.'[10]

In an essay published in 1937, she wrote, 'Good Art never appeals at first sight. In fact, I will go so far as to say that more often than not it repels. Bad Art, on the other hand, based as it is on cheap effect, appeals immediately to the artistically underdeveloped mind and therein lies its danger.'[11]

At 25, she would get married to her first cousin, Dr Egan. They moved to Saraya, near Chauri Chaura in Uttar Pradesh. This triggered her next phase of work which was strongly influenced by the Bengal School of Art and its pioneers such as Rabindranath Tagore and Jamini Roy. The Bengal School was a precursor to the Calcutta Group of artists which would fall into place in 1943, followed by the Progressive Artists Group which would eventually be founded by F.N. Souza, K.H. Ara, M.F. Husain, S.H. Raza and others only in 1948. She would describe her style at this point as becoming 'fundamentally Indian'.

'I realized my artistic mission then: to interpret the life of Indians and particularly of the poor Indians pictorially, to paint those silent images of infinite submission and patience, to depict their angular brown bodies,' she wrote.[12]

While she stayed at Saraya, she would paint her works, 'The Village Scene', 'In the Ladies' Enclosure' and 'Siesta', which were all based on the life she observed around her in rural India. In these works, she would also draw upon the miniature tradition of painting as well as the Pahari tradition. To quote author

Yashodhara Dalmia from her biography of Sher-Gil, *Amrita Sher-Gil: A Life*, 'In addition to paintings of relatives, lovers and friends, she created self-portraits that showed her grappling with her own identity.'[13]

While critics like Karl Khandalavala and Charles Fabri called her the greatest painter of the century, she was not commercially successful. During this phase of her life, Sher-Gil steered away politically from her family which was strongly loyal to the British Raj. She had an interesting friendship with Pandit Jawaharlal Nehru, but strangely never painted a portrait of him, telling a close friend that she would never paint Nehru because 'he is too good looking'. To quote her biographer Dalmia, 'The exact nature of their relationship is difficult to gauge, because many of Nehru's letters were later burnt by Amrita's parents, much to her chagrin, while she was away in Budapest getting married.'[14]

She would write to her father, 'I suppose I have to resign myself to a bleak old age unrelieved by the entertainment that the perusal of old love letters would have afforded it.'[15]

The marriage to Dr Egan too was an interesting life decision and has been seen as an attempt to get away from the overwhelming domination of her parents over her life choices. She fell into a depression during their stay in Saraya. She and her husband then relocated to Lahore in 1941. Her last work was left incomplete on her sudden shocking death, barely days before the opening of her first major solo show in Lahore. She was only 28 at the time and had just about begun taking on commissioned works. She slipped into a coma after falling seriously ill and died at around midnight on 5 December 1941. While the reason for her death has never been ascertained, it was allegedly the result of a botched abortion.

Her works are national treasures, there is a road named after her in the prestigious Lutyens Delhi. She has a postage stamp to her credit, released by India Post, featuring her painting 'Hill Women', in 1978. Her work, when auctioned, must remain within the country as mandated by the Government of India and the Indian cultural centre in Budapest is called the Amrita Sher-Gil Cultural Centre. As recently as 2018, at a Sotheby's auction in Mumbai, a painting by her titled 'The Little Girl in Blue' fetched a whopping ₹18.69 crore.

She was called India's Frida Kahlo. But by calling her so, we do her a disservice. We would do well to insist that she is the world's Amrita Sher-Gil and in that, recognize the genius of her work and her mindset, both of which were iconoclastic.

NOTES

1. Nandita Singh, 'Remembering Amrita Sher-Gil, one who loved sex, art and India, and never said sorry for it', ThePrint, 5 December 2018, https://theprint.in/features/remembering-amrita-sher-gil-one-who-loved-sex-art-and-india-and-never-said-sorry-for-it/158839/. Accessed on 14 January 2022.
2. Ibid.
3. Tariro Mzezewa, 'Overlooked No More: Amrita Sher-Gil, a Pioneer of Indian Art', The New York Times, 20 June 2018, https://www.nytimes.com/2018/06/20/obituaries/amrita-shergil-dead.html. Accessed on 15 January 2022.
4. Ibid.
5. Ibid.
6. Virtual Galleries: Amrita Sher-Gil, http://ngmaindia.gov.in/sh-amrita.asp. Accessed on 15 January 2022.
7. Nandita Singh, 'Remembering Amrita Sher-Gil, one who loved sex, art and India, and never said sorry for it', ThePrint, 5 December 2018, https://theprint.in/features/remembering-amrita-sher-gil-one-who-loved-sex-art-and-india-and-never-said-sorry-for-it/158839/. Accessed on 14 January 2022.
8. Making Queer History, https://www.makingqueerhistory.com/articles/2018/10/22/amrita-sher-gil. Accessed on 15 January 2022.

9. *Culture Trip*, https://theculturetrip.com/asia/india/articles/india-s-frida-kahlo-amrita-sher-gil-s-contribution-to-indian-modern-art/. Accessed on 15 January 2022.
10. 'Rediscovered: Amrita Sher-Gil's lost masterpiece', Christie's, 12 March 2021, https://www.christies.com/features/Amrita-Sher-Gil-lost-masterpiece-11539-1.aspx?sc_lang=en. Accessed on 15 January 2022.
11. 'Amrita, in her own words', *Live Mint*, 19 March 2010, https://www.livemint.com/Leisure/ZFztgbfWuk5StdcAQkVrhM/Amrita-in-her-own-words.html. Accessed on 15 January 2022.
12. Tariro Mzezewa, 'Overlooked No More: Amrita Sher-Gil, a Pioneer of Indian Art', *The New York Times*, 20 June 2018, https://www.nytimes.com/2018/06/20/obituaries/amrita-shergil-dead.html. Accessed on 15 January 2022.
13. Yashodhara Dalmia, *Amrita Sher-Gil: A Life*, Penguin India; Illustrated edition (2006).
14. 'Why Amrita Sher-Gil refused to draw Nehru's portrait', *India Today*, 30 January 2017, https://www.indiatoday.in/education-today/gk-current-affairs/story/amrita-sher-gil-957961-2017-01-30. Accessed on 15 January 2022.
15. Ibid.

6

AMRITA PRITAM

I WILL MEET YOU AGAIN

The most iconic photograph of Amrita Pritam, perhaps, is the one of her sprawled across a divan, a pen in her hand, staring thoughtfully into the distance. Even within the constraints of that single photographic frame, she conveys the restlessness of her mind that no photograph can ever capture.

Considered the first prominent female Punjabi poet of the twentieth century, she wrote for over six decades, leaving behind a vast legacy of work that encompasses over 100 books of poetry, fiction, biographies, essays, a collection of Punjabi folk songs and an autobiography—all searing tales of love, loss, redemption, angst and more. She is considered one of the most important female voices in Punjabi literature, and was awarded the Sahitya Akademi Award for her long poem 'Sunehade' in 1956. In 1969, she was awarded the Padma Shri, in 2004 the Padma Vibhushan, and the Sahitya Akademi Award and the Sahitya Akademi Fellowship in the same year. She was awarded the Bharatiya Jnanpith in 1982 for *Kagaz te Canvas*.[1]

They say the best thing to happen to a writer is an unhappy life. For Amrita, unhappiness and tragedy began when she was a very young girl. Born on 31 August 1919 in pre-Partition India, in Punjab, she was the only child of Raj Bibi, a school teacher, and Kartar Singh Hitkari, a poet, a Braj Bhasha scholar, a preacher of Sikhism and the editor of a literary journal.[2] The first great tragedy struck her when she was barely 11. Her mother fell very ill and succumbed to her illness soon after. The death of her mother was the moment, she writes in her autobiography, when she lost faith in God and became an atheist. She would remain an atheist all her life.[3]

They moved to Lahore after this tragedy, and she would live there until 1947 when she migrated to India during Partition. Being uprooted from her childhood home, and growing up in a strange city without a mother and with a busy father made her self-reliant. She took refuge in the collection of books in her father's library. This early withdrawal into the world of words saw her write and publish her first anthology of poems, *Amrit Lehran* when she was barely 16. Her father would have preferred her to write religious poetry, but Amrita was fiercely individualistic and she wrote what she pleased and in a language she was comfortable in, namely Punjabi. She had grown now, from the young girl of 11 who'd been bereft when her mother passed away, to a self-contained young woman of 16. This was the year she got married to Pritam Singh, a boy she had been engaged to since she was barely four, as was the custom of the day. While she was not happy about getting married, she did not resist it either.[4] She had now, as Emily Dickinson famously wrote, laid down the playthings of childhood and stepped into the role of wife and mother. She would follow her first book of poems with over six collections of poems published between 1936 and 1943. She would read out her poems on the radio, something her husband wasn't too happy about. He told her he would pay her the money she earned as a radio announcer in Lahore, an offer she turned down. She wasn't doing it for the money. What was important to her was the adulation and direct connect with her listeners. While she began as a romantic poet, she would shift her ideologies to socialism and become part of the Progressive Writers' Movement. The result of this shift in affiliation would reflect in her collection, *Lok Peed,* in 1944, which took a hard look at the misery of the poor post Second World War and the horrors of the Bengal famine of 1943.

A turning point in her writing came with Partition. The horrors she witnessed and heard of, and her fleeing Lahore for Delhi with her family through the tumultuous violence that Partition unfolded had a profound impact on her. What emerged from the crucible of this terrifying experience was the elegiac Punjabi poem, 'Ajj Aakhaan Waris Shah Nu', which would not only immortalize her as a poet but also serve as a poetic documentation of the horrors of Partition for generations to come.

Written on a train journey from Dehradun to Delhi, the poem was addressed to the Sufi poet Waris Shah, who had given the world the classic love story of Heer Ranjha. He also hailed from the same place in Punjab where Amrita came from, and she felt a kinship with him.

She wrote:

> Today, I call Waris Shah, 'Speak from your grave,'
> And turn to the next page in your book of love,
> Once, a daughter of Punjab cried and you wrote an entire saga,
> Today, a million daughters cry out to you, Waris Shah,
> Rise! O' narrator of the grieving! Look at your Punjab,
> Today, fields are lined with corpses, and blood fills the Chenab.[5]

She would often revisit Partition through her writing. Her novel *Pinjar*—the story of how Partition affected the women who went through it, told through the experience of the central character, Puro—was a poignant, deeply felt account of the times. This book was made into a film of the same title in 2003 and would go on to be critically acclaimed and win the National Award that year.

Some of her other books would also be made into movies. The first was *Dharti Sagar Te Sippiyan*, which was made as *Kadambari* and then *Unah Di Kahani* as *Daaku*. She was the editor of a monthly literary magazine in Punjabi for years, though post Partition a major portion of her writings was in Hindi. Amongst her works are her autobiographies *Kala Gulab* (1968), *Raseedi Ticket* (1976) and *Aksharon Kay Saayee* (1977).

Amrita Pritam was also the first recipient of the Punjab Rattan Award, the international Vaptsarov Award from the Republic of Bulgaria in 1979 and the Degree of Officer dens, Ordre des Arts et des Lettres from the French government in 1987. She was also nominated to the Rajya Sabha in 1986, a term she served till 1992.

For all the acclaim her work received, her personal life was conflicted. After moving to Delhi post Partition, she gradually rebuilt her life, working with the All India Radio in their Punjabi service. By 1960, her marriage was beyond the point of repair and Amrita left her husband. Among the many reasons for the failure of her marriage, perhaps the most prominent was her unrequited love for the famous poet and lyricist Sahir Ludhianvi. Her obsession with him can be gauged by a diary entry she made decades later, in 1986, when she wrote, '*Aaj mera Khuda mar gaya* (Today my God died)'. It was the day Sahir passed away.

Theirs was a love story that was not a love story. She first met Sahir at a mushaira in another town when she had been married for a few years. She writes about how she walked that day to the bus waiting to ferry them back home, mindful of the fact that she was walking in his shadow, engulfed in his presence. She wrote unreservedly about her love for Sahir in her autobiography, *Raseedi Ticket*. In fact, in an interview to the Hindi magazine *Kadambini*, Amrita would say, '*Sahir mere Sartre aur main unki Simone thi* (Sahir was my Sartre and I was his Simone).'[6] She wrote this for him in the initial days of their relationship, '*Tumhare darakht ki tahani ka jo aasra mila/Mere toote hue dil ka parinda wahin ruk gaya* (When I found the branch of your tree/The bird of my broken heart perched there permanently).'[7]

She was quoted saying, 'In our relationship, I was the more passionate one, my book of poems, titled *Sunehade*, was full of messages for him. But they did not melt him. However, my love was not wasted. I got the Sahitya Akademi Award for the book.'[8]

She wrote that she went to call Sahir to tell him about the Sahitya Akademi Award, but as she was dialling, she noticed an article in the *Blitz* magazine on sale at the phone booth. The headline said, 'Sahir has found his new love'. The article was about Sahir's new love interest, the singer Sudha Malhotra. She put the phone down and returned home. She would later write *Saat Baras* on the silence between her and Sahir that stretched for years.[9]

A broken Amrita would then find companionship and love in the artist and writer Inderjeet, who went by the nom de plume Imroz. They moved in together, a radical decision for the time. They were partners for over four decades, he designed all her book covers, and painted her over and over in several paintings. Their life has been documented in the book *Amrita Imroz: A Love Story by Uma Trilok*.[10] Sahir was the unattainable, the love she yearned for but never received, while Imroz was an equal partner. Her biographer Uma Trilok wrote that this relationship with Imroz would melt 'the cold frost of long lonely years'. Imroz was almost a decade younger than her and became everything to her: her lover, her companion, her homemaker, her driver, her advisor. Although aware of her obsession with Sahir, Imroz knew the depth of his own love for her and never felt threatened. In fact, Sahir and Imroz would go on to become good friends, and Imroz would design the cover for one of Sahir's books.[11]

Although she would spend over four decades with Imroz, it

was her relationship with Sahir that would define her writing. From the lack of fulfilment and closure arose writing that shook the literary landscape. It was uncertain whether they were in a relationship at all. She wrote, 'The beginning of this tale was silence, and the intensity of it too was carried out in silence.'[12]

In an interview, she would say, 'Man has not yet tasted the friendship and company of a liberated woman as an equal partner. Men and women have not yet met as two independent human beings.'[13]

She made no bones about her fondness for smoking, a habit she picked up when she was obsessed with Sahir. He would visit her in Lahore and smoke for hours in silence. She would pick up his half-smoked, discarded cigarette stubs when he left, and smoke them. 'Our smoke mingled in the air as did our breath, the words of our poems too,' she wrote.[14] She said by smoking the cigarette stubs he had left behind, she felt like she was touching him. She would write about smoking in *Raseedi Ticket*, uncaring of the scandal her writing so honestly about it would cause. In one of her poems, she writes, 'Pain, I inhale silently like a cigarette, and a few sons, I flick off like ashes from the cigarette.'[15] The years would mellow the rancour between her and her ex-husband, Pritam Singh. In his final days, Amrita would visit him twice a day, and spend a couple of hours with him every day until the day he died.

She herself passed away peacefully in her sleep on 31 October 2005, at the age of 86. Perhaps the most touching poem by her, is a poem to Imroz, 'Main Tenun Phir Milangi' (I Will Meet You Again). Her funeral was held according to her wishes, with no speeches, no huge gathering and only her children and her partner Imroz taking her body for the last rites.

She was commemorated by Google on 31 August 2019, her centenary birth anniversary, with a doodle. They wrote, 'Today's Doodle celebrates Amrita Pritam, one of history's foremost female Punjabi writers, who dared to live the life she imagines.'[16] In her writings and her life, she leaves behind a legacy for women writers in India which urges them to defy social constructs and constraints, challenge them, and to live and write as she did—unfettered.

NOTES

1. Simrin Sirur, 'A hundred years of Amrita Pritam, who wrote passionately about love, Partition & sexuality', *ThePrint*, 31 August 2019, https://theprint.in/theprint-profile/a-hundred-years-of-amrita-pritam-who-wrote-passionately-about-love-partition-sexuality/284629/. Accessed on 15 January 2022.
2. Amjad Parvez, 'Amrita Pritam had a hint of Punjabi in her poetry', *Daily Times*, 7 January 2020, https://dailytimes.com.pk/534750/amrita-pritam-had-a-hint-of-punjabi-in-her-poetry-daily-times/. Accessed on 15 January 2022.
3. Amrita Pritam, *Raseedi Ticket*, 1976.
4. '10 facts about Amrita Pritam her fans would want to know', *The Times of India*, 31 August 2020, https://timesofindia.indiatimes.com/life-style/books/features/10-facts-about-amrita-pritam-her-fans-would-want-to-know/photostory/70911761.cms. Accessed on 15 January 2022.
5. Amjad Parvez, 'Amrita Pritam had a hint of Punjabi in her poetry', *Daily Times*, 7 January 2020, https://dailytimes.com.pk/534750/amrita-pritam-had-a-hint-of-punjabi-in-her-poetry-daily-times/. Accessed on 15 January 2022.
6. Sumit Paul, 'The intriguing love story of Amrita Pritam and Sahir Ludhianvi', *The Indian Express*, 1 September 2019, https://indianexpress.com/article/lifestyle/feelings/the-intriguing-love-story-of-amrita-pritam-and-sahir-ludhianvi-5917330/. Accessed on 21 January 2022.
7. Ibid.
8. Vijaya Pushkarna, 'A life well lived: Imroze and Amrita Pritam', *The Week*, 31 August 2019, https://www.theweek.in/leisure/

society/2019/08/31/a-life-well-lived-imroze-and-amrita-pritam.html. Accessed on 21 January 2022.
9. K.K. Kohli, 'The sublime love story of Amrita Pritam', *National Herald*, 8 September 2019, https://www.nationalheraldindia.com/cafe/the-sublime-love-story-of-amrita-pritam. Accessed on 15 January 2022.
10. Amjad Parvez, 'Amrita Pritam had a hint of Punjabi in her poetry', *Daily Times*, 7 January 2020, https://dailytimes.com.pk/534750/amrita-pritam-had-a-hint-of-punjabi-in-her-poetry-daily-times/. Accessed on 15 January 2022.
11. K.K. Kohli, 'The sublime love story of Amrita Pritam', *National Herald*, 8 September 2019, https://www.nationalheraldindia.com/cafe/the-sublime-love-story-of-amrita-pritam. Accessed on 15 January 2022.
12. Gayathri Prabhu, 'When Amrita Pritam wove her autobiography around love, she also demonstrated the many ways to love', *Scroll.in*, 13 October 2019, https://scroll.in/article/940264/when-amrita-pritam-wove-her-autobiography-around-love-she-also-demonstrated-the-many-ways-to-love. Accessed on 16 January 2022.
13. Simrin Sirur, A hundred years of Amrita Pritam, who wrote passionately about love, Partition & sexuality', *ThePrint*, 31 August 2019, https://theprint.in/theprint-profile/a-hundred-years-of-amrita-pritam-who-wrote-passionately-about-love-partition-sexuality/284629/. Accessed on 15 January 2022.
14. Gayathri Prabhu, 'When Amrita Pritam wove her autobiography around love, she also demonstrated the many ways to love', *Scroll.in*, 13 October 2019, https://scroll.in/article/940264/when-amrita-pritam-wove-her-autobiography-around-love-she-also-demonstrated-the-many-ways-to-love. Accessed on 15 January 2022.
15. Ibid.
16. https://www.google.com/doodles/amrita-pritams-100th-birthday. Accessed on 15 Janury 2022.

7

SONAL MANSINGH

AGAINST ALL ODDS

It was in 1974 that the acclaimed dancer Sonal Mansingh was reborn. That year, she met with a fatal car accident while travelling abroad. It was terrible and she almost lost her life. While she survived the accident, the injuries were so serious that the doctors told her that she needed months of physiotherapy before she could even think of walking again. Dance was out of the question—dance, which was her life. She had defied family diktats, chosen dance over everything else in her life, given up a marriage in pursuit of her métier, mastered multiple dance forms and received critical acclaim for her art not just in India but also abroad.

For her, it was unthinkable to be alive without the ability to dance. At that point, she didn't want to live on. Letters, phone calls and telegrams poured in from around the world, wishing her a speedy recovery and lamenting the end of her career as a dancer. She was determined to change her destiny. She would dance again, she told herself. She would prove the doctors wrong. She not only got back on her feet, but started dancing as well.

This has been Sonal Mansingh's story, over and over again, where she has consistently defied all odds in pursuit of her passion, where dance has been the only raison d'être of her life and where she has subsumed all of herself to the study and practice of the art form.

Born into a highly cultured and socially aware family, Sonal Mansingh was the second of three children. Her parents were Arvind Pakvasa, the son of Mangaldas Pakvasa, a freedom fighter and a close associate of Mahatma Gandhi and Poornima Pakvasa, a noted social worker from Gujarat who was awarded the Padma Bhushan in 2004. Mansingh's paternal side of the family was very illustrious. Her paternal grandfather, Mangaldas Pakvasa, was appointed the governor of the Central Provinces and Berar (Nagpur) post Independence and this was followed by terms as the governor of Bombay and Mysore. Her childhood was spent growing up in the splendour of the various Raj Bhavans where her grandfather was posted. It was a childhood suffused with an early exposure to renowned vocalists, musicians, dancers and artists. There were baithaks by maestros and legends such as Siddheshwari Devi, Pandit Omkarnath Thakur, Bade Ghulam Ali Khan, Ustad Faiyaz Husain Khan, Ustad Hafiz Ali Khan, Ustad Vilayat Khan, Rukmini Devi Arundale, M.S. Subbulakshmi and the senior Dagar brothers, Moinuddin and Aminuddin, in her home as she grew up. Pandit Jasraj even gave a special recital on her twenty-first birthday. The Darbar Hall in the Raj Bhavan was always echoing with a performance through her formative years. In such a fecund atmosphere that venerated the performing arts and Indian culture, is it any wonder that the young Sonal, or Sonya as her doting grandfather fondly called her, would make performing arts her life's passion?

Dance came into her life early on, at the age of four. She along with her elder sister began learning Manipuri dance from Rabin Roy, a teacher from Shantiniketan, when they were living in Nagpur. She however considers her true initiation into classical dance at the age of seven, when she began learning Bharatanatyam from famous gurus, and had her arangetram (debut on-stage performance) in 1961, a lavish affair which saw the who's who of the time in attendance, along with the most feared critics of the era.

Although, academically, she has Praveen and Kovid degrees in Sanskrit from the Bharatiya Vidya Bhavan and a BA (Hons.) degree in German from Elphinstone College in Mumbai, she was clear from an early age that dance is where her heart and soul lay. The family was supportive of her passion for dance, but was insistent it had to be in consonance with another professional pursuit or she was to get married. Her sister opted to get married. The young Sonal was determined though that she would only dance. She decided to rebel against her family and went to Bangalore in the face of their opposition.

When she returned to Bombay to complete her graduation in German literature from Elphinstone, she began learning dance under Guru Jayalakshmi Alva. She then got married to the former Indian diplomat Lalit Mansingh, whom she had met at an art festival. Moving to Delhi after her wedding saw her learn dance under the last devdasi Swarna Saraswati. Her husband was posted to Geneva and Sonal had to relocate with him. However, being in Geneva proved to be an impediment in pursuing dance and she ended up returning to Delhi to continue her passion. This was when long-distance marriages were unheard of, so the duo mutually decided to end their marriage. Sonal did not ask for alimony and decided to bravely rebuild her life, with absolutely no financial support.

What did come out of this brief marriage was her taking on the Mansingh surname and retaining it, and learning Odissi, at the behest of her illustrious Odiya father-in-law, under the tutelage of the very acclaimed Odissi exponent Guru Kelucharan Mohapatra in 1965.

Rebuilding her life after the separation was difficult. Having decided to not accept alimony, she went through very tough times. She confesses that she has never been financially savvy, whatever money came in went out, but she made sure her musicians were paid well. She lived in rented homes and even sold her mother's jewellery to stay afloat. She wrote letters to everyone, she says, even to the then Prime Minister Dr Manmohan Singh but didn't get any help.[1] It was a rough phase of her life. She would stay with friends or camp with whoever was kind enough to accommodate her. From the grandeur of the Raj Bhavans she grew up in, this was a change of circumstance that would have broken a lesser person. But she was made of sterner stuff and was driven by her passion.

Returning to India and pursuing dance also brought her in contact with Kamaladevi Chattopadhyay, the social reformer and textile revivalist, who was a major influence in her life. It was the fertile intellectual atmosphere at Kamaladevi's home that reinstated Mansingh's equilibrium and her bearings after the separation.

It was at this point that she met Dr Georg Lechner, a German photographer and director of Max Mueller Bhavan in Delhi. They first met when she had been called by Max Mueller Bhavan for a photo shoot meant to showcase the non-German cultural shows to be presented at the 1972 Olympics in Munich. She was a little late for the shoot. Dr Lechner, who was to shoot her, was absolutely irate at being delayed but by the end of the shoot, he was smitten and wanted to see her again.[2]

In 1973, she filed for divorce by mutual consent from Lalit Mansingh, and the parting was amicable. In fact, the day the divorce came through in 1974 from the Tis Hazari court in Delhi, she and Mansingh went to Standard Hotel for lunch to celebrate the fact that they wouldn't 'be at loggerheads anymore'.

Georg was transferred to Goethe-Institut, Montreal. This turned out to be a blessing in disguise. She had accompanied him and it was here that she met with the car accident that had her bedridden for nine months. She thought she would never dance again, but the efforts of a determined chiropractor and her own willpower got her back on her feet. She began walking again, and from there, got back to dance. It was, she says, a rebirth of sorts. She eventually decided to return to India and so she did. It was also when she began teaching, first with a single student in her garage, and slowly expanding into a full-fledged dance institute.

In 1977, she formally found her dance institute in New Delhi. Her best choreographic works include Devi Durga, Mera Bharat, Indradhanush, Manavtta, Sabras Aatmayan and Draupadi.

Interestingly, Sonal Mansingh had a socialist phase and was known for dissent during the Emergency. In the 1990s, she was part of a group of performing artists, writers and poets called 'Artists against Communalism'.

She has received many national and international awards for her devotion and contribution to dance. The Government of India awarded her the Padma Bhushan in 1992, making her the youngest recipient of this award, the Sangeet Natak Akademi Award in 1987 and the Padma Vibhushan in 2003. She is the second female danseuse in India to be awarded the Padma Vibhushan after Balasaraswati. The Madhya Pradesh government conferred the Kalidas Samman on her in 2006. She was also selected by Prime Minister Narendra Modi as a Navaratna for her work on Swachh Bharat Abhiyaan (Clean India Mission). In 2003, she was appointed the chairperson of the prestigious Sangeet Natak Akademi. She is presently a member of the Rajya Sabha.

She's always been a distinctive personality, with her imposing persona, impeccable posture and carriage honed from years and years of rigorous dance training. To quote her biographer, Sujata Prasad, from an interview, 'Sonal has a very real and distinctive aura—sharp, outspoken, irreverent, and acerbically witty, without any prima donna hang-ups. She is stripped of any artifice with an incredible almost brutal candidness.'[3]

Sonal Mansingh is indeed outspoken, candid and irreverent. It comes from living life on her own terms, to the exclusion of everything but her pursuit of dance. She refuses most interviews, preferring to be away from the spotlight, and is uncaring of the labels people put on her. In commemoration of her 40 years as a danseuse, the noted film director, Prakash Jha made a documentary on her which won the National Film Award for Best Non-Feature Film in 2002.

A danseuse from an era when powerful performers ruled the proscenium, Mansingh continues to be a mentor, an innovator and an entertainer who embodies the spirit of dance through all she does. Through her life and her art, she has proved that a woman who follows her dreams and her passion to the exclusion of all else, uncaring of the boxes that limit her, is a force unto herself.

Excerpts from a conversation with her:

You were born into a very illustrious family, your grandfather was a freedom fighter and a governor. How did your early childhood shape and influence the eventual path your life took?

I think the answer to your question lies in the question itself. When one grows up in a certain atmosphere and ambience, with the sense of aesthetics and pride in one's culture and heritage instilled by one's family and the Gujarati-medium school that I went to in Bombay, all that does leave a mark on one's thinking, one's character. I would call it a character-building phase. This was back at Fellowship High School steered by its principal, Mr Vyas. This was founded in 1933 and was perhaps one of the earliest co-educational and non-convent schools. Great artists and leaders such as Rabindranath Tagore and Gandhiji had visited the school. It had a strong leaning towards the Theosophical Society. All these influences, along with the atmosphere of the Raj Bhavan in the various places I lived—Nagpur, Mysore and Bombay—had a cumulative impact on me.

You began learning dance very young, at the age of four. What made you decide that dance was going to be your calling?

It was that one was learning and enjoying the dance lessons. While I was learning dance at that young age, I was also learning music, learning to play the sitar and teachers were coming home to teach us. It was just whatever my mother could manage to find in Nagpur, where we were posted then, which was the capital of Central Provinces and Berar, where my grandfather was governor in 1947. It became Madhya Pradesh much later. My mother found a dance teacher then, Rabin Roy, if I remember right, who had come from Shantiniketan. I wouldn't call that the start in my journey of dance, the real start was at the age of seven or eight when we came back to Bombay, with me beginning to learn Bharatanatyam.

When you were 18, you decided to defy the wishes of your family and run away to learn Bharatanatyam. It was a very courageous decision. How difficult was it to defy the pressure you faced, given you were so young at the time?

My grandfather was the governor of Mysore at the time. My parents began looking for an appropriate teacher for me when we were there and everyone pointed out to the very respected Professor U.S. Krishna Rao and his wife Chandrabhaga Devi as gurus for me, and so I was going to them to learn further. In fact, my arangetram was also held at the Bangalore Raj Bhavan in 1961. In the audience were the Maharaja of Mysore, the great actress Devika Rani and her husband, the painter Nicholas Roerich, and great gurus, dancers and critics such as Venkatachalam, E. Krishna Iyer and P.V.K. Shastri. Back then, we did our matriculation plus four years of college to complete our bachelor's degree in Arts. In 1963, I finished my BA in German. My family sat me down and asked me what is it that I wanted to do now. My elder sister had opted to get married after her graduation and that was just not what I wanted to do. 'What do you want to do?' they asked me, and I replied I want to dance. Yes, yes, you can also dance, they said, but you must also do something. And I replied, it is not 'also' but it is 'only'. I want to *only* dance. This was not acceptable to them, and at that point, a lot of gadbad (chaos) happened.

After two or three days of all this, I think, I just left for Bangalore. I took my scholarship money, packed my little bag and holdall, went to Teenbatti, caught a bus to Victoria Terminus, took the train to Poona and changed to meter gauge at midnight for Bangalore, and then took a rickshaw to their home at night, and that was that. And now when everyone asks about it, I say there was nothing to think about, it had to be done. I wanted to dance, I will dance, I don't want to do anything else, I will not do anything else.

There's always words like 'brave' that we can now use in retrospect, but what I can say is that if there is a flame within you, a passion, it does not allow you to do anything else.

Having studied under the guru-shishya parampara, do you feel we are losing that ethos of total submission and devotion to the guru in the modern day? What have we lost when we lost this tradition and how do we revive or adapt to the changing times?

That's a huge issue, and one that we need to consider. I've had my early students come and stay with me for a day, a week, a month, children who came from outside Delhi, or even children who came from Delhi itself when their parents were going off on summer vacations; sometimes they would opt to come and stay with me. I took them with me on my tours, sometimes to temples, at others to dance with me at my performances, despite the fact that I am a solo dancer; I don't need anyone to dance with me. But when I began the school, much later, 1978-79 onwards, they began to ask if they can come with me.

I would say, the guru-shishya parampara is an entirely different concept from, say, boarding schools. Because they say boarding schools are also where you are with the teachers constantly, in the atmosphere, on the campus, but it is not the same. Guru-shishya parampara only has connotations of vidya in its purest form and vidya is not information downloaded from Google. It is vidya, deeply lived and experienced with the guru, 24/7, 365 days a year. It includes aesthetics, ethics, dance, culture, philosophy, music, values and so many other things. The Indian classical performing arts are not understood in all its dimensions even today, particularly today. It was understood earlier, but with the kind of 'education' today, we're all wearing specs, we are all staring at computers, now everything is on the laptop and computer. It is the virtual world as against the real world, where there is so much beauty. I used to take my students to gardens to observe the trees: what about the abhanga, samabhanga, tribhanga and atibhanga that you can observe in trees? What about the hand movements that you can find in the swaying of the leaves? It is such a complete art that only after spending years with a guru can you hope to get all the dimensions right.

Now you can only get one or two dimensions. You wear a nice costume and look pretty, you book a hall and fill it with your friends and relatives, you give a performance, you post pictures and videos on Facebook and YouTube, and that's it. The guru-shishya parampara is something totally different, it is a lived experience, it is a lifestyle.

The guru-shishya parampara is all about etiquette. Ten or 12 years ago, I had to teach children how to fall at the feet of their guru, to put their heads at the feet of the guru and to do the same to their mothers. They'd never done that, and when I asked why, they replied that they had never been taught to do so.

The Parampara is not just about teaching dance, it is about teaching the entire Bharatiyata, what is our Pranali, our sanskar. I am very kattar (rigid) about it, and that's why people find me difficult and so be it. I am difficult, I will be difficult. I am what I am, I am not about to give up my values and my sanskars. Things that matter to us spiritually and emotionally, we have sadly given them up.

You learnt Odissi at a much later stage in life, when it is assumed that one's body is already trained in one art form and would be resistant to learn another. What was the impetus for you to begin learning Odissi, and how difficult was it to have the body learn a different form of dance?

I met an Oriya gentleman and we were to get married. His father invited me and my family to Cuttack in 1965. This was a very educated, cultured and highly respected family in Orissa and my father-in-law said to me, 'You are a star in Bharatanatyam and as an Oriya bahu, I want you to learn Odissi' and it was as simple as that.

So, it was my father-in-law who introduced me to Odissi. He was Dr Mayadhar Mansingh, a greatly respected gentleman whom I will always remember with a great deal of affection and respect, and he put me on the path to learning Odissi. And things unfolded as they did. Dr Mansingh took me to the institute Kala Vikas Kendra, where Guruji Kelucharan Mohapatraji was also teaching, and requested Guruji to teach me Odissi. That was it.

Among the many struggles you've faced in your life, perhaps your accident in 1974 and the impact it had on your dance career, and your subsequent comeback through sheer grit is very inspirational. What did it take in terms of mental strength and courage to overcome such a setback and return to dance?

After my accident, I was told by the doctors and the surgeons that I would never dance again, perhaps walk again normally in two years. I was brought to Montreal, where my German fiancé was then the director of the Goethe-Institut.

I couldn't talk clearly, with all the medications and painkillers, but I'm told I was mumbling that I wanted to be given poison. I wanted to die. I had given up and so my systems began folding up. I was told I'd gone white as a corpse. The Canadian chiropractor got new X-rays made and took on my case as a challenge. After three weeks, he told me, 'I'm afraid...' and I started crying, and he continued, 'I'm afraid you will be able to dance again.' He wanted to kick-start my system, so first the disappointment and then the catalytic moment. Then he took me through the whole journey, bit by bit, and he put me back on my feet. It took nine months, it was truly a rebirth of sorts. The entire process to get back to walking took me about a year.

In your personal life, you've been strong and feisty and faced a high-profile divorce, when the word was looked down upon. You also faced adversity and tough times after it. What are the lessons you learnt from that phase that you think every woman should know and keep in mind?

I don't believe in giving advice because everyone's life is different, every need and desire is different and what is good for me may not be good for another. The only thing I would say is follow your passion and you need guts for that.

Self-respect above all, that has been my motto and that was given to me by my grandfather, Dadaji, who was the governor, when I was 17, and that has been my guiding line throughout my life. So, I don't advise anyone. I would say why compromise on small things, even that compromise is difficult for me to swallow, but then that is me. It is different for every woman. The women who carry bricks and do labour, they have such huge stories and I'm very happy that these stories are coming out. I'm very happy that the Padma awards are going to women with these stories that we didn't hear about earlier. What they've done is amazing, I salute these women.

You began your dance academy in a garage, and today it is one of the best institutions in the country. What was the vision behind beginning it and where do you see it going?

I had absolutely no interest in teaching. But a girl called Swati Gupte, now Bhise, came and stood outside my home, sometimes with her mother, sometimes with her maasi, wanting me to teach her dance.

They stood there for all of two and a half or three months, and I would tell them I don't teach, and finally I relented and said, 'Okay, but you have to be willing to meet my many conditions—you will come for practice when I call you, no complaints, no questions.' She agreed to all my very difficult conditions and became my first student.

After a couple of months, she asked about the fees and I told her to get out (*laughs*). Then her friends came with her, and asked if they could watch me teaching her, and promised that they would be very quiet, sit outside the door and not make any noise. And slowly they slipped into the corner of the room, and then they asked if they too could learn. At this point, a South Indian gentleman who was taking care of my kitchen finally felt compelled to tell me, '*Thoda fees toh lena chahiye* (You should take some fees).' So that's how it all began, in my garage.

My academy truly began in my garage. I've always lived in rented apartments and rented homes, I don't own any property at all, that's one thing I emphasize all the time. I don't have any property of my own. Where I live right now is a government property and when my tenure is over, I will have to look for accommodation. But the house where I began my academy became quite famous. I was there for 37 years, and then finally I had to move out. So that little garage and the driveway was my institution and that is where I taught. Well, from there it grew and we got a plot of land for the institution and for a long time the plot of land remained just a plot of land, because I had no money to build it up. I did plant many neem trees though. Then we had to make a pact with a builder that they would have one part and we would have the other, because I am not good with finances, I have no practical sense at all. I'd like to say, one detail that most people seem to miss out about my life and growth is that I have lived alone. For 99 per cent of the dancers, they either have their husband, father, son, brother or the whole family backing them, I don't have anyone and never had. I could have possibly done much more, people would have looked after my archives, they could have put it up on YouTube, etc. I've lived alone, I've helped so many, I've brought up so many musicians and dancers. And also, my finances, I don't know where the money went. At one point I was even selling the jewellery my mother had left me. In the late '70s and '80s, I got loans from banks and friends, which I returned. Financially, I was very impractical. I went to a builder for the centre, and I have one portion, and the Shri Kamakhya Kalapeeth is the goddess's property and it belongs to her.

As a performer you have always been someone who does not believe art exists in a vacuum, but has to be contextualized in the backdrop of the sociopolitical atmosphere. Do you feel artists have a responsibility to society to be expressions of the zeitgeist?

We live in a society, whatever happens does have an impact on an artist. When that impact is internalized, it comes out in your work; if it doesn't, then no problem. It depends on one's awareness, alertness, one's involvement with issues, basically if one is a thinking artist. One learns and one goes on creating new varnams, new padams, new pallavis and whatever. It should not be too overt, that you lecture about it. It should reflect in your work, but each one has their own way of doing things. You have to be an involved person in society.

And as you look back, do you have any regrets, anything you think you could have done differently in your inspiring journey?

It is all as it is meant to be, that is how I live. Mine is a lived experience.

NOTES

1. Suanshu Khurana, 'Colours of Her Life: Bharatanatyam and Odissi exponent Sonal Mansingh on her dance, being branded saffron', *The Indian Express*, 3 December 2017.
2. Sujata Prasad, *Sonal Mansingh: A Life Like No Other*, Penguin Random House India, 2017.
3. Kunal Ray, 'Sonal's art is driven by her mind', *The Hindu*, 27 April 2017, https://www.thehindu.com/entertainment/dance/sonal-mansingh-gets-candid-in-her-biography/article18253637.ece. Accessed on 16 January 2022.

8

LATA MANGESHKAR

NIGHTINGALE OF INDIA

On 6 February 2022, the news trickled in over the news wires. Lata Mangeshkar had passed away at Breach Candy Hospital. She had been admitted in early January when she had tested positive for COVID-19 and also had pneumonia. She'd been in the ICU, on the ventilator; the nation held its breath. She recovered, and was taken off the ventilator on 28 January, but her health deteriorated again on 5 February, only to pass away the next day. She was 92.

A collective outpouring of grief and mourning swamped the nation. We had lost our nightingale. It was truly the end of an era.

Her voice was one that most Indians have grown up listening to, across generations. Music came into her life when she was very young; she was born into a household steeped in music. The oldest of five siblings, her father, Pandit Deenanath Mangeshkar was a Marathi theatre actor, a Natya Sangeet musician and a Hindustani classical vocalist of Maharashtrian ancestry. Her paternal grandfather, Ganesh Bhatt Navathe Hardikar was a priest attached to the famous Mangeshi temple in Goa.

When she was very young, the family went by the surname Hardikar. Later, her father would have it changed to Mangeshkar, to denote the family ancestry from the town of Mangeshi in Goa. The name Lata, too, wasn't her original name. She was named

Hema when she was born, and renamed Lata after a character in one of Deenanath's plays.

Lata Mangeshkar was the name that she would ultimately earn global fame with. Her first public performance came about through happenstance when she was all of nine. She wrote about it in the foreword to the book, *On Stage with Lata*.[1] Some concert organizers had come to meet her father and asked him if he would like to perform at the event. The young Lata overheard them and told her father that she too would like to sing. Her father agreed. On the day of the programme, she sang Raga Khambavati; he performed after her and his performance went on till late into the night. The young Lata eventually rested her head on her father's lap while he was singing and fell asleep. She recalled that everyone was very happy with her first performance.

A few years after her first stage performance as a singer, tragedy struck. Her father suddenly passed away and the responsibility of providing for the family fell on young Lata's tender shoulders. A close family friend, Master Vinayak, the owner of the Navyug Chitrapat movie company, stepped in to help the desolate family. He encouraged Lata to start off her career as a singer and actor in movies. Her first song was for a Marathi movie made by Vasant Joglekar titled *Kiti Hasaal* in 1942. She sang a song composed by Sadashivrao Nevrekar, but unfortunately it was dropped in the final cut on the edit table. She then got a small acting role, given to her by Master Vinayak in Navyug Chitrapat's Marathi movie *Pahili Mangalagaur*. This was in 1942. She went on to sing her first Hindi song 'Mata ek sapoot ki duniya badal de tu' for the film *Gajabhau* a couple of years later in 1943.[2] In 1945, when Master Vinayak's company moved to Bombay, she decided to relocate too. She began training in Hindustani classical singing and started formal lessons with Ustad Aman Ali Khan from the Bhendi Bazaar gharana. Along with her sister, Asha, she played a minor role in Master Vinayak's first Hindi movie, *Badi Maa*, released in 1945. During the second Hindi movie that Master Vinayak had produced, titled *Subhadra*, she met music director Vasant Desai, who would support her career. In 1948, Master Vinayak, who had been a strong support all these years, passed away.

It was then that music director Ghulam Haider spotted the potential in young Lata and took her under his wing. She got her first major break in the movie *Majboor*, in 1948. In an interview, decades later, Lata would say, 'Ghulam Haider is truly my godfather. He was the first music director who showed complete faith in my talent.'[3]

At the time, the lyrics of songs in the Hindi movies were written by famous poets with Urdu as the primary language. Reportedly, when the then reigning film hero Dilip Kumar was introduced to the aspiring young singer, he stated that her diction was strongly *'daal bhaat,'* by which he meant she had a very strong Marathi accent. Lata met the criticism head-on. She decided to work on her Urdu diction and took Urdu lessons for a while.[4] In fact, in Nasreen Munni Kabir's book, *Lata Mangeshkar: In Her Own Voice*, Mangeshkar said, 'When I speak, my Urdu isn't good, but when I sing I make sure there are no flaws in my diction.'[5]

She was also made of steel in a way few young women of the time were. When she was just a newcomer in the Hindi film industry, the young Lata created a furore by refusing to sing with the then reigning king of male playback singing, G.M. Durrani after he reportedly misbehaved with her during a recording in 1949.[6] Her big break came with the song 'Aayega aanewaala', for the superhit film *Mahal* (1949), composed by music director Khemchand Prakash and picturized on the beauteous, young Madhubala. The song became a rage, and Lata would go on to be in great demand as a playback singer for the leading ladies through the 1950s. She won her first Filmfare award for Best Female Playback Singer for the popular song 'Aaja re pardesi' from the movie, *Madhumati* (1958), composed by Salil Chowdhury. If the 1950s were a good decade for her, the 1960s were destined to be even better. The song 'Jab pyar kiya toh darna kya' from *Mughal-e-Azam* (1960) set to music by Naushad and picturized on Madhubala in K. Asif's magnum opus became a rage across the country.

After the Indo-China War of 1962, she would become the voice of patriotism and mourning to a country battered by war. Her rendition of 'Aye mere watan ke logo' on 27 January 1963 at the National Stadium, New Delhi, in the presence of Pandit Jawaharlal Nehru, is said to have brought tears to his eyes.[7]

At around this time in her career, she had a falling out with the legendary singer Mohammed Rafi. Lata was adamant in her demand that singers should get half of the five per cent song royalty that producers gave composers, and had hoped that Rafi Saab would back her. They reportedly got into a major argument during the recording of the song 'Tasveer teri dil mein' (1961, *Maya*) and refused all songs with each other in the near future. A rapprochement between the two was said to have been initiated by the music director Jaikishan and the actress Nargis according to varying reports.[8]

The 1970s was momentous for Lata Mangeshkar with the release of *Pakeezah* (1972), Kamal Amrohi's magnum opus that took over 10 years to complete and would be the swan song of the famous actress Meena Kumari, who would pass away shortly after. Two songs from the film, 'Chalte chalte' and 'Inhi logon ne', catapulted Lata firmly into becoming the darling of the nation once again. She was also S.D. Burman's singer of choice for many of his later films before he passed away. She also sang for Madan Mohan's compositions for *Hanste Zakhm* (1973), *Mausam* (1975) and more. The 1970s saw Lata sing primarily for Laxmikant-Pyarelal and R.D. Burman.

Of her singing, the venerated singer Ustad Bade Ghulam Ali Khan had once said, '*Kambakht, kabhi besuri na hoti* ([She] is never off-key).' Actor Dilip Kumar, who had inadvertently put her onto the path of polishing her Urdu diction with his offhand comment when he was first introduced to her all those years ago, would say of her voice years later, 'Lata Mangeshkar's voice is a miracle from God.'

She also performed in many concerts abroad and was the first Indian to sing at the Royal Albert Hall, London, in 1974. She recalled in the preface to the book, *On Stage with Lata*,

> My first concert outside India was in 1974 at the Royal Albert Hall in London. It was a wonderful show. A close friend, S.N. Gourisaria, and the celebrated diplomat and statesman, V.K. Krishna Menon, who had launched the India League in London, organized the show beautifully. Dilip Kumar introduced me in glowing words, but when I stepped onto the stage and faced the audience, I felt a trembling sensation in my throat. I could not utter a sound. I did not know what to do. I knew it was the daunting pressure of getting it right. I somehow sang the opening shloka and by the time I had finished singing, I had become a tigress![9]

There's an interesting anecdote about this concert at Albert Hall about how she never wore shoes when she sings. Even during this performance, she removed her shoes and sang on stage wearing only socks. Dilip Kumar, who introduced her at the concert, told her she would die of cold, but she just giggled, went on to the stage and then sang for hours. To quote her,

> Two hours before the show, I'd choose the sari I was going to wear; sometimes I got ready in the hotel and sometimes I would change at the venue itself. Then I'd sit in the green room thinking that I had to sing well, people should not say that Lata was nervous or scared. I didn't want to hear people say, 'This went wrong, that went wrong.' What I wanted to hear was, 'Lata sang well.'[10]

Her story would be incomplete without the mention of the imposing Raj Singh Dungarpur, who passed away in 2009. He was an integral part of her life for years and theirs was an unconventional relationship for its times. The imposing six-footer, much respected in the cricket world, had sworn to his father that he would never bring a 'commoner' into the family through marriage.[11]

In an interview, he spoke of how they first met.

> In 1959, could be August, I came to Bombay to do law. I told Dilip Sardesai's first cousin Sopan Sardesai that I can't exist without playing cricket. He told me that the only place that you get cricket was at a Walkeshwar house where Lata Mangeshkar's brother and his friends played tennis ball cricket. I said I'm not bothered by who plays, but I have to be there. They used to stay in a two-bedroom flat in a building behind the Walkeshwar house. She was in those days, I suppose, recording all day; nor was I hung up on seeing her. I just played and went back to my sister's house in Napeansea Road.
>
> But her family must have discussed that I had come, so she said, 'We must offer him a cup of tea.' I was invited to come up. I can't remember if it was raining. She was utterly charming; she came to see me off and gave me her car. They were celebrating nariyal poornima shortly and she invited my brother and me for dinner.[12]

To quote him on their relationship from an interview,

> We came from different backgrounds. The '60s was very different. Perhaps, both were very attached to their respective families. It was one of those things that just didn't happen. But that has neither enhanced the relationship, nor has it reduced. She is the treasure house of my admiration and affection and I continue to be in touch with her.[13]

Another often discussed facet about her life was her supposed rivalry with her sister Asha Bhosle, also a renowned singer. Both sisters have denied these rumours. Lata said in an interview, 'We are sisters first and foremost, and forever. We were never rivals as singers. What Asha can do before the mike I can never do. I can never sing "Piya tu ab to aaja" or "Chura liya hai tumne jo dil ko" the way she can.'[14]

In 1999, she was nominated as a member of the Rajya Sabha, but could not attend the sessions due to ill health. She has been honoured by honorary doctorates from the Sangeet Natak Akademi, the Indira Kala Sangeet Vishwavidyalaya and Shivaji University. She was awarded the Padma Bhushan in 1969, the Dadasaheb Phalke Award in 1989, the Padma Vibhushan in 1999 and the Bharat Ratna in 2001.

Her commitment to perfection remained undiminished. In his book, *The Stranger in the Mirror*, Rakeysh Omprakash Mehra speaks about how Lata Mangeshkar came to Chennai three days in advance just to rehearse the song 'Lukka chuppi' to be recorded in A.R. Rahman's studio for the movie *Rang De Basanti* (2006).[15] She recorded it over five hours standing in front of the mike at the age of 70 plus. She didn't believe in revisiting the songs she had sung. 'Once I record my songs, I don't go back to them. I spend my time doing riyaz, puja, and watching TV.'[16]

With her passing, we lost not just a legend, but a voice that was an intrinsic part of every Indian's memories, one that had enthralled music lovers for generations, a voice that will stay evergreen for generations to come.

NOTES

1. Mohan Deora and Rachana Shah (ed. N.M. Kabir), *On Stage with Lata*, HarperCollins, 2017.
2. 'Happy Birthday, Lata "Didi": 10 interesting facts about the Nightingale of India', *India Today*, 28 September 2018, https://

www.indiatoday.in/education-today/gk-current-affairs/story/lata-mangeshkar-338407-2016-09-28. Accessed on 16 January 2022.

3. Lata Mangeshkar, *MusicBio*, https://musicianbio.org/lata-mangeshkar/. Accessed on 15 January 2022.
4. PTI, 'Lata Mangeshkar has to thank Dilip Kumar for her Urdu skills!' *Deccan Herald*, 25 June 2009, https://www.deccanherald.com/content/10118/lata-mangeshkar-has-thank-dilip.html. Accessed on 15 January 2022.
5. Nasreen Munni Kabir, *Lata Mangeshkar: In Her Own Voice*, Niyogi Books, 2009.
6. Subhash K. Jha/IANS, 'When Lata Mangeshkar took on GM Durrani', *National Herald*, 29 March 2020, https://www.nationalheraldindia.com/entertainment/when-lata-mangeshkar-took-on-gm-durrani. Accessed on 15 January 2022.
7. Ajay Mankotia, 'Ai mere watan ke logon: Story behind the song that moved a nation to tears', *DailyO*, 26 January 2016, https://www.dailyo.in/arts/republic-day-lata-mangeshkar-asha-bhonsle-patriotism-india-china-war-jawaharlal-nehru/story/1/8670.html. Accessed on 15 January 2022.
8. 'Unboxing Lata Mangeshkar's life: Five lesser-known stories about "Daughter of the Nation"', IndiaTvNews, 28 September 2019, https://www.indiatvnews.com/entertainment/celebrities/lata-mangeshkar-birthday-love-story-temper-asha-bhosle-552908. Accessed on 15 January 2022.
9. Mohan Deora and Rachana Shah (ed. N.M. Kabir), *On Stage with Lata*, HarperCollins, 2017.
10. Lata Mangeshkar's Introduction to *On Stage with Lata*, written by Mohan Deora and Rachana Shah, and edited by Nasreen Munni Kabir, HarperCollins, 2017.
11. 'Raj Singh Dungarpur obituary', *The Guardian*, https://www.theguardian.com/sport/2009/sep/21/raj-singh-dungarput-obituary. Accessed on 15 January 2022.

12. Shradha Sukumaran, 'Revisited: Dungarpur on special friend Lata', *Mid-Day*, 13 September 2009, https://www.mid-day.com/mumbai/mumbai-news/article/revisited--dungarpur-on-special-friend-lata-57332. Accessed on 15 January 2022.
13. Ibid.
14. 'Unboxing Lata Mangeshkar's life: Five lesser-known stories about "Daughter of the Nation"', IndiaTvNews, 28 September 2019, https://www.indiatvnews.com/entertainment/celebrities/lata-mangeshkar-birthday-love-story-temper-asha-bhosle-552908. Accessed on 15 January 2022.
15. Rakeysh Omprakash Mehra and Reeta Ramamurthy Gupta, *The Stranger in the Mirror*, Rupa Publications, 2021.
16. Subhas K. Jha, 'Blindly following doctor's advice: Lata Mangeshkar', *Deccan Chronicle*, 23 March 2020, https://www.deccanchronicle.com/entertainment/music/300320/blindly-following-doctors-advice-lata-mangeshkar.html. Accessed on 15 January 2022.

9

ANITA DESAI

THE WRITER IN THE FAMILY

The starting point of when a person becomes a writer is always unknown. For a young girl in Delhi decades ago, this starting point came perhaps when she sat on a cane stool in her home at a round, green table, writing out her stories, illustrating them, stitching them into little books with spines and putting them on the shelves alongside the books of the great authors she venerated. But perhaps her story begins before that, in the languid hill town of Mussoorie in pre-Independence India, when she was born on 24 June 1937 to a German mother and a Bengali father.

This little girl would grow up to become Anita Desai, the name etched on the many books she's authored, books that have gone on to claim shelf space across the world. An acclaimed Indian novelist, Emerita John E. Burchard Professor of Humanities at the Massachusetts Institute of Technology, thrice shortlisted for the Booker Prize, Sahitya Akademi awardee and winner of the Guardian Prize UK, her books are today the subject of much academic research and have even been made into award-winning movies. However to start, we need to go back, right to when a young Bengali lad, D.N. Mazumdar, from Dacca, went to pre-war Berlin as an engineering student to pursue higher studies. There, he fell in love with Toni Nime, a teacher by profession. They got married and moved to New Delhi. Soon they had children.

As a child, Anita grew up speaking German at home. The other language she learnt to speak at a young age was Hindi, which she used to communicate with her neighbours. She would eventually also learn to speak Bengali, her father's mother tongue, and Urdu. English was a language she would learn when she entered school, but she learnt it quickly and by the time she was just nine years old, she had already published her first story.

Given that she didn't speak the language as a young child but learnt it later, she has often been asked why she chose to write in English. To quote her,

> According to the rules laid down by critics I ought to be writing half my work in Bengali, the other half in German. As it happens, I've never written a word in either language. Possibly I found English to be a suitable link language, a compromise. But I can state definitely that I did not choose English in a deliberate and conscious act. If it did not sound like a piece of arrogance, I'd say perhaps it was the language that chose me.[1]

Her writing continues to be dominated by the influence of European writers she began reading in her childhood and through her early adulthood. She recognizes this dissonance between the life she led and the reading that influenced her own writing. To quote her, 'My reading was so European: Woolf, D.H. Lawrence, Proust, Camus, Dostoyevsky, Chekhov, it had so little to do with the life I led, so I worked hard to bend the English language to bring in the sounds and tempo and rhythms of spoken languages around me, which are part of my world too.'[2]

She recalls filling up notebooks with her writings, sitting on a cane stool at a round, green table in her childhood home and being labelled 'the writer in the family'. It was a prescient label. Her ambition was to see books with her name on the spines on the shelves at home, nestled next to the books by authors she loved.³

Theirs was a close and intense family. She would recall later, 'My family was an oddity; it didn't belong where it was. Going to school, I became aware of its difference, of things that set us apart.'⁴ Her home was very Indian, but her mother brought Europe and more specifically Germany into the children's lives, narrating German fairy tales, playing *'O Tannenbaum'* on the piano, making them listen to recordings of Beethoven and Mozart on the gramophone, and introducing them to books by German authors such as Goethe, Schiller and Heine along with other authors of the time.⁵

'I remember being very lost at school, not being popular or successful. It was always a great struggle to belong. It was an immense relief to come home to books, to be alone.'⁶ Being left alone led her to take refuge in words. She writes about her early years, 'I was always a scribbler. As soon as I was taught the alphabet I scribbled—even before I could spell so that I was always harassing everyone in the household (including the cook who knew no English) "How do you spell 'house'?" "How do you spell tree, fire, bird, fish...?"'⁷

Her earliest stories were written when she was barely seven and she remembers years later that she illustrated them diligently and sewed them into covers so as to make them look as proper books. She remembers reading *Wuthering Heights* when she was barely 10. To quote her, 'It struck me with force of a gale and I still vibrate to it. Ever since, literature has seemed to me more interesting, more significant and overwhelming than the real world.'⁸ As she, and her reading repertoire, grew, she was deeply influenced by the novels of Japanese writers such as Yasunari Kawabata and modern poetry, particularly that of Rimbaud, Hopkins and Lawrence. Her reading influences included the likes of the post-colonial Indian writers in English like R.K. Narayan, Raja Rao and Mulk Raj Anand, as well as women writers such as Attia Hosain, Kamala Markandaya and Nayantara Sahgal, but she found herself totally isolated as a woman who wrote, until she met the noted writer Ruth Prawer Jhabvala.

The young Anita and her mother would often go down a wide avenue lined with banyan trees to the Maiden's Hotel to visit the library in it or further down to the Qudsia Bagh. They often passed a young European woman with a baby in a pram, accompanied by another young girl, obviously her daughter. The lady was Ruth, who was married to the architect Cyrus Jhabvala and lived in a bungalow just off Alipur Road. The two were formally introduced when Ruth's mother, a German Jewish lady, was visiting India. An Indologist, Dr Charles Fabri, who knew both families, suggested that Ruth's mother might find it interesting to chat with Anita's mother, who was also German. The two met and what emerged from this meeting was a longstanding friendship between Anita and Ruth, both at very different stages of their lives, a friendship built firmly over a shared love for books and a passion for writing. Desai would say about her visits to Jhabvala's home, 'Whenever I came away with an armful of books on loan, with her talk still in my ears, I felt elated, a visitor to another world, the writers' world I had only imagined and now proved real.'[9]

In Ruth, of German-Polish descent and married to an Indian architect, the young Anita found a role model. In her own words, 'When I started, I suffered from a great sense of being utterly alone. I would have loved the society of other writers, or even readers. I was working in a vacuum, turning out words with no echo. I saw you could live in Old Delhi and write books. She was very encouraging—a woman with two small children—while I was a schoolgirl.'[10] Jhabvala would recall the young Anita as a beautiful, well-read, sensitive and self-contained young girl. Her writing, she would say, was 'exquisite and beautiful, as a reflection of her.'[11]

When Anita was in college, she had her short stories published in the college magazine. She also wrote for an English magazine called *Envoy*, until she had her first book published in 1963. She was then barely in her twenties. Growing up in Delhi played an instrumental role in the waiting necessary to be a creator. Her writing is predominantly scenes and impressions, moods and emotions. She says, 'It is like chain smoking: I chain smoke with words, with books.' She lived for a bit in Calcutta in the late 1950s, and worked at the Max Mueller Bhavan there, looking after the library. Her brother got her to rethink what she was doing with her life. She reminisces in an interview, 'Then my brother said, why are you doing these things? Don't forget you are supposed to be writing.'[12]

She studied at Queen Mary's in Delhi and graduated in English literature from Miranda House in 1957. When she was 19, she met Ashvin Desai and the next year, in 1958, they were married and she moved to Bombay. She says, 'My writing career was entirely subservient to being a wife and a mother. I lived the life of the typical Indian housewife; wrote in the gaps and hid it away, kept it secret.'[13]

Interestingly, her children didn't even realize for the longest time that she was a writer. She would write in term time, when the children were at school, putting away the manuscripts during vacations and waiting for school to reopen so that she could get back to her writing. It was only when she reached her fifties that she would consider herself a full-time writer. Anita Desai would say about these years, 'Because the time was limited and I knew I couldn't overstep that, I think I made good use of those hours. People often ask, how could you write when you had small children at home? The fact is I wrote much more in those years than in the years when I had far more time to myself.'[14]

While in Bombay, the family spent their weekends at Alibaug, in a seaside resort close to the city, which would eventually result in Desai's novel *The Village by the Sea* that would win the

Guardian Children's Fiction Prize in 1983. She had already been writing for 20 years by then. She had published her first novel, *Cry, the Peacock* in 1963. Her most autobiographical work, she says, is her book *Clear Light of Day*, published in 1980, which is set around the time of her coming of age and is located in the neighbourhood she grew up in. She would however find international acclaim with her book *In Custody*, published in 1984, a delicately sensitive novel about an Urdu poet in his declining years. The book would be shortlisted for the Booker Prize. Merchant Ivory Productions, helmed by the fabulous director producer duo James Ivory and Ismail Merchant, adapted her novel into a movie with the same name, starring Shashi Kapoor, Shabana Azmi and Om Puri. It won the President's Gold Medal for Best Picture in 1993.

In 1993, she moved to the Massachusetts Institute of Technology to teach creative writing. Her book *Fasting, Feasting*, published in 1999, would also be shortlisted for the Booker. This was followed by *The Zigzag Way*, which was set in twentieth-century Mexico and was published in 2004, and the collection of short stories, *The Artist of Disappearance* was published seven years later. While her career as an author is distinguished, her career as a professor has been no less so. She's been on the faculty of Mount Holyoke College, Baruch College and Smith College. She has also been a Fellow of The Royal Society of Literature, the American Academy of Arts and Letters, and Girton College (Cambridge). She dedicated her work *Baumgartner's Bombay* to Girton.

Her writing comprised three to four hours of dedicated work, every day without fail. She prefers to write in the mornings, and does not believe in counting output whether in terms of words or pages. She must work in solitude, in a quiet room to herself. To quote her, 'the creative art is a secret one'.

With her immense body of work, she remains firmly one of the most powerful female voices in post-colonial Indian writing in English. She has received countless awards too, those too she wears lightly. In her own words, 'Awards are certainly incidental. They are unexpected; they are not something you work towards, no.'[15]

After all, all she really wanted to do was to tell her stories, and tell them well, right from the days she sat on that cane stool at her small, round, green table, in her Delhi home.

NOTES

1. 'Introduction: Making of Anita Desai as a Writer', https://shodhganga.inflibnet.ac.in/bitstream/10603/22060/3/ch-1.pdf. Accessed on 16 January 2022.
2. 'A passage from India', *The Guardian*, https://www.theguardian.com/books/1999/jun/19/books.guardianreview11. Accessed on 15 January 2022.
3. https://www.encyclopedia.com/people/history/historians-miscellaneous-biographies/anita-desai. Accessed on 15 January 2022.
4. 'A passage from India', *The Guardian*, https://www.theguardian.com/books/1999/jun/19/books.guardianreview11. Accessed on 15 January 2022.
5. https://www.encyclopedia.com/people/history/historians-miscellaneous-biographies/anita-desai. Accessed on 15 January 2022.
6. 'A passage from India', *The Guardian*, https://www.theguardian.com/books/1999/jun/19/books.guardianreview11. Accessed on 15 January 2022.
7. 'Anita Desai: "Every once in a while, a short story pursues you"', *The Guardian*, https://www.theguardian.com/books/2017/jul/08/anita-desai-short-story-writers-novelist-80-tales. Accessed on 15 January 2022.
8. 'Introduction: Making of Anita Desai as a psychological realism in this genre with her debut novel', https://

vdocuments.mx/introduction-making-of-anita-desai-as-a-psychological-realism-in-this-genre.html. Accessed on 16 January 2022.
9. Azra Raza, 'My Literary Apprenticeship With Ruth Prawer Jhabvala', *3 Quarks Daily*, 17 November 2017, https://3quarksdaily.com/3quarksdaily/2017/11/my-literary-apprenticeship-with-ruth-prawer-jhabvala.html. Accessed on 16 January 2022.
10. 'A passage from India', *The Guardian*, https://www.theguardian.com/books/1999/jun/19/books.guardianreview11. Accessed on 15 January 2022.
11. Anita Inder Singh, *Existential Dimensions in the Novels of Anita Desai*, Sarup & Son (2008).
12. Sandip Roy, 'Half-Outsiders', *Live Mint*, 12 February 2017, https://www.livemint.com/Leisure/rHMSio1phIgILaoR3cwGCI/Halfoutsiders.html. Accessed on 15 January 2022.
13. 'A passage from India', *The Guardian*, https://www.theguardian.com/books/1999/jun/19/books.guardianreview11. Accessed on 15 January 2022.
14. Ibid.
15. Veena Gokhale, 'Writers Should Maintain a Certain Distance with the World: Anita Desai', *The Wire*, 9 May 2017, https://thewire.in/culture/anita-desai-interview. Accessed on 15 January 2022.

10

M.S. SUBBULAKSHMI

THE VEENA IN HER THROAT

Pandit Jawaharlal Nehru had famously said of her, 'Who am I, a mere Prime Minister before a Queen, a Queen of Music.'[1] Sarojini Naidu called her the Nightingale of India, and Kishori Amonkar would famously say of her that she was the *aathavaa sur*, or the eighth note—a note beyond the seven notes of music. Mahatma Gandhi is said to have requested her to sing his favourite bhajans including '*Vaishnava Janato*' and '*Raghupati Raghav Raja Ram*'. Madurai Shanmukhavadivu Subbulakshmi, or M.S. Subbulakshmi as we know her, or even M.S. Amma as those who revered her called her, rose magnificently from the humble circumstances she was born into, to make herself respected, loved and adored the world over.

She was awarded the Bharat Ratna, India's highest civilian honour, becoming the first musician in the country to receive it. She was also the first Indian musician to receive the Ramon Magsaysay Award in 1974, for her charitable work.

M.S. Subbulakshmi was born on 16 September 1916 in the town of Madurai, into a family steeped in music but which was humble in circumstance. Her mother, Shanmukavadiver Ammal, was a Devdasi and a veena player of some repute who had also recorded a few albums at the time, as both a veena player and a singer. Her grandmother, Akkamal, was a violinist. They lived in the vicinity of the famous Meenakshi temple in Madurai.[2]

She would accompany her mother to concerts, listen to her and sometimes be part of the chorus. As a child, she took a liking to the tanpura and would practise for hours plucking at the string of the instrument until her voice matched the pitch of the string. It was this that led to her developing her pitch to an incredible level of perfection. Her first teacher was her mother. Nonetheless, she soon started learning Carnatic music formally under Semmangudi Srinivasa Iyer and Mayavaram Krishna Iyer, who visited her home, and followed that with Hindustani music under Pandit Narayanrao Vyas.

Her initiation into public performances came rather early. She had accompanied her mother to one of her veena performances, and her mother suddenly announced that her daughter would sing a bhajan. She was barely 10 at the time, and was playing outside the venue in the sand. Someone picked her up, dusted her off and took her to the stage. She should have had stage fright seeing the number of people in the audience, but it was an ambience she was familiar with. She was keener to be allowed to get back to play.[3]

In 1926, when she was barely 10, she recorded a song in a recording studio for the very first time. The next year, in 1927, she gave her first public performance. On 1 January 1932, she performed to an audience comprising renowned names in the world of Carnatic music such as T.N. Rajarathinam Pillai, Chembai Vaidyanatha Bhagavathar, Mysore T. Chowdiah and Tiger Varadachariar, as well as music critics, it was a performance that was truly path-breaking.[4] With this performance she had 'arrived' on the Carnatic music scene. *Ananda Vikatan*, the leading Tamil weekly of the time, carried an article on her. Overseeing the article was Thiagaraja Sadasivam, the advertising manager of the weekly, who would go on to play a major role in both her personal life and her career.

Subbulakshmi's mother was keen to get her settled, and turned to their traditional arrangement with men from the wealthy

Chettiar or landlord community who were often patrons of the Devdasi community, and settled on an alliance with a wealthy Chettiar man. Subbulakshmi would have none of this. One night while her family was fast asleep, she left home and boarded a train to Madras. She knew no one in Madras, except for two people. One was a prominent citizen who had helped arrange a few concerts for her. The second was Sadasivam of *Ananda Vikatan*. From the railway station, she took a horse carriage to the official's house. She explained her predicament. He could not obviously keep her in his home. It would be the cause of much scandal. He took her to Sadasivam's house in Triplicane, explaining the situation to him. Sadasivam took Subbulakshmi in, although his house was temporarily empty at the time with his wife having gone to her maternal home for her second delivery. This decision would lead to a lot of controversy.[5]

Back in Madurai, her mother asked her son and Subbulakshmi's brother, Shaktivel, to go to Madras and find her. Her brother tracked her down to Sadasivam's home, and tried his utmost to convince her to return home. M.S. Subbulakshmi was adamant, she did not want to go back to the life that had been laid out for her by her mother. When Shanmukavadiver heard that her daughter was to act in movies, she was terrified. Becoming an actress would end Subbulakshmi's ascending star as a classical singer of serious repute. It was a time of much controversy and gossip, but all of it stayed behind the scenes. In public, Subbulakshmi continued to be serene and unperturbed as she entranced audiences with her mellifluous voice and expressive face. Sadasivam was a social activist and a freedom fighter who was well connected politically and socially. He was very ambitious too. He was convinced that Subbulakshmi was a star in the making and became her manager, getting her lead roles in Tamil cinema. He got the well-known filmmaker, K. Subrahmanyam, who had the rights to the Premchand novel *Seva Sadan*, to sign Subbulakshmi on as the heroine of the Tamil film based on it. The film was released in 1938 and with it, Subbulakshmi became a star. Her next hit movie was *Sakuntalai* (1940), based on the epic play by Kalidas, where she played the title role and starring opposite her as the king, Dushyant, was the famous Carnatic vocalist, G.N. Balasubramaniam. Reportedly, the two came close during the filming, and there are even reports of love letters being exchanged between them.[6]

Sadasivam's wife passed away in 1940. After her demise, Sadasivam and Subbulakshmi tied the knot. She was now the wife of a respectable Brahmin. It gave her the societal acceptance and respectability she had sought. He was 14 years senior to her, and had already taken on the role of her mentor, guide and manager. She would raise his daughters with his first wife as her own. She also went through an image makeover of sorts at the time. No longer was she in crumpled cotton sarees, a young girl nonchalant about her appearance. She looked resplendent in luxurious Kanjeevaram sarees, impeccably and modestly draped, her hair tied back, diamonds flashing in her ears and nose and a demure jasmine mala around her bun.

What shot her to the limelight across the country was her role as Meera, in the 1945 film of the same name, which was remade in Hindi a couple of years later. It was a strategic decision by Sadasivam to have Subbulakshmi play Meerabai, the Princess Saint, given how popular her bhajans were. She was now no longer the romantic interest as in Shakuntala, but the Princess Saint in the eyes of her adoring public. The film was directed by Ellis R. Dungan and ran in cinema halls for over 25 weeks.

On 5 December 1947, the Hindi version of the movie was released at the Plaza theatre in Delhi. It was a high-profile premiere graced by the prime minister of the newly independent India, Pandit Nehru along with the last Viceroy of India, Lord Mountbatten and his wife Edwina Mountbatten, and Sarojini Naidu. It would be the last movie she would act in. In her entire acting career, she only acted in four Tamil movies: *Seva Sadanam* (1938), *Sakuntalai* (1940), *Savithri* (1941) and *Meera* (1945). Of these, *Meera* was remade in Hindi in 1947.[7]

Musicians who had trained with her speak of how she would wake up early in the morning, at around 6 a.m., and have an idli or a dosa along with a cup of filter coffee. She would only then begin practising, matching her pitch to the tanpura she played. She would wander around her house, continuing to sing and return to ensure her pitch remained constant. She would begin practising for a concert at least 10 days in advance. Before every concert, she would perfect her pitch with the tanpura for at least half an hour until she was satisfied enough to begin her performance.

Sadasivam was the star maker behind the icon that Subbulakshmi became. He negotiated and signed deals for her, micromanaged her public appearances completely, sat in the front row of every concert she performed at and approved the requests from the audiences beforehand, to the extent of even deciding what she would sing at concerts and who would accompany her, according to some reports. Although those around felt that Sadasivam was too controlling of her, it was an arrangement she was comfortable with. His taking charge of every decision regarding her career allowed her to pursue her craft with no worries. The couple were also great philanthropists, doing concerts for charity, having her royalties from albums go to charity. Back in the 1940s, she is said to have raised over a crore through benefit concerts, a mind-boggling sum at the time.

In 1966, she was invited to perform at the United Nations (UN) General Assembly. This invite resulted in a seven-week concert tour across Europe and the United States. At the UN, as she took the stage in her customary Kanjeevaram silk from Chettiar, jasmine in her hair and the diamonds twinkling in her ears, the then Under Secretary-General of the UN, C.V.

Narasimhan introduced her to the distinguished audience as the 'First Lady of Carnatic Music'.

In 1997, her husband passed away and she completely withdrew from the public gaze. Steeped in depression, she stopped eating properly, confined herself to her home and made no public appearances. A few months later, on 14 January 1998, she was conferred with the Bharat Ratna by President K.R. Narayanan.

Through her career she received several accolades and honours. The Padma Bhushan in 1954, the Sangeet Natak Akademi Award in 1956, the Sangeetha Kalanidhi in 1968, the Ramon Magsaysay Award in 1974, the Padma Vibhushan in 1975, the Sangeetha Kalasikhamani in 1975, the Kalidas Samman in 1988, the Indira Gandhi Award for National Integration in 1990 and the Bharat Ratna in 1998. In 2005, she had a commemorative postage stamp issued on her by the Government of India, the UN issued a stamp commemorating her in 2016, her birth centenary year as well as the fiftieth anniversary of her performance at the UN General Assembly in 1966.[8] Most interestingly though, there is even a special shade of blue Kanjeevaram saree that is named after her as M.S. Blue, a shade darker than sapphire and yet not a royal blue.

On 11 December 2004, she passed away in Chennai as gently and graciously as she had lived, at the age of 88. With her passing ended a life that was replete with achievement, grace and humility that touched the lives of all those who knew her, personally or through the magic of her voice.

NOTES

1 A. Seshan, 'When M.S. Subbulakshmi brought Meera to life', *Business Standard*, 11 September 2015, https://www.business-standard.com/article/beyond-business/when-m-s-subbulakshmi-brought-meera-to-life-115090900800_1.html. Accessed on 17 January 2022.

2. 'Bharat Ratna Smt. M.S. Subbulakshmi', https://www.maduraidirectory.com/madurai/legends.php. Accessed on 15 January 2022.
3. 'A tribute to M.S. Subbulakshmi; 1916 – 2004', *A Tribute to MSS*, http://newlook.msstribute.org/?page_id=120. Accessed on 15 January 2022.
4. Vikram Sampath, 'From Mahatma Gandhi to Nehru, everyone was an MS Subbulakshmi fan', *ThePrint*, 7 July 2019, https://theprint.in/opinion/treasured-tunes/from-mahatma-gandhi-to-nehru-everyone-was-an-ms-subbulakshmi-fan/259757/. Accessed on 17 January 2022.
5. T.J.S. George, 'Why did MS Subbulakshmi run away from her mother's attempt to find a man for her?' *Scroll.in*, 16 September 2016, https://scroll.in/article/816591/how-ms-subbulakshmi-ran-away-from-her-mothers-attempt-to-find-a-man-for-her. Accessed on 15 January 2022.
6. Mohan V. Raman, 'In Only Five Films, M.S. Subbulakshmi Made Her Way to the Stars', *The Wire*, 16 September 2016, https://thewire.in/film/ms-subbulakshmi-films. Accessed on 15 January 2022.
7. Vikram Sampath, 'From Mahatma Gandhi to Nehru, everyone was an MS Subbulakshmi fan', *ThePrint*, 7 July 2019, https://theprint.in/opinion/treasured-tunes/from-mahatma-gandhi-to-nehru-everyone-was-an-ms-subbulakshmi-fan/259757/. Accessed on 17 January 2022.
8. Ruchira Ghosh, 'M.S. Subbulakshmi: The Voice That Mesmerized Millions | #IndianWomenInHistory', *Feminism in India*, 18 June 2018, https://feminisminindia.com/2018/06/18/ms-subbulakshmi-essay/. Accessed on 15 January 2022.

11

HARITA KAUR DEOL

FLYING HIGH

In 1992, the Indian Air Force first advertised vacancies for women pilots. Hitherto, the Indian Air Force had been an exclusively male bastion in the skies; women could only dream of being in command of aircraft. Among the thousands who had applied for the positions was a young girl from Chandigarh, Harita Kaur Deol. Slim, with wide eyes and a ready smile, she came from a Sikh family that had its roots in the Indian military. Her father was Colonel Deol, an army veteran. She had always dreamt of being part of the Indian Armed Forces, but her sights were not set on the Army or on following in her father's footsteps. She instead dreamt of flying high in the skies, guarding the borders of the country in a fighter plane. While growing up, this might have seemed like a pipe dream. Women weren't commissioned as pilots in the Indian Air Force, but this innocuous advertisement would change it all.

There is little about her in the public domain, her achievement as an Indian Air Force pilot is the primary thing that one reads about in whatever is written about her. The details are sketchy, a life that was lived away from the spotlight. We know the essentials that she was born on 10 November 1971 and grew up in Chandigarh. As such, her childhood seemed like a regular one. She studied and graduated from Punjab. All one knows is that she was a child of the Armed Forces, she grew up with the valour of our servicemen all around. From the snippets of information available about her, snippets that are few and far between, we learn that as a child, she was passionate about flying.

Back then, women were not part of the Indian Air Force, not as pilots and it would seem that young Harita's dream would never see fruition. However, the Indian Air Force announced a recruitment drive to induct women pilots in 1992, making Harita overjoyed; it was a dream come true for her. She now had a fighting chance to become an Indian Air Force pilot. While these were not positions advertising recruitments for fighter pilots (those would come much later), these were recruitments for women as transport pilots. This did not dishearten her; it was the first step towards being a pilot in the Air Force. She applied for the position despite the stiff competition. In fact, it would take India until 2016 to have three women pilots commissioned into the Indian Air Force's fighter stream, with Flight Lieutenant Bhawana Kanth qualifying as the first woman combat pilot in 2019.

There were just eight vacancies for women pilots that had been advertised by the Indian Air Force. In response to this advertisement, they were flooded with over 20,000 applications from across the length and breadth of the country. Like the other applicants, Harita, too, had applied for the position of Short Service Commission Officer. What were the odds of her making it? The competition was intense. Of the 20,000 who had applied, only 500 applicants qualified for the first written examination which was held at three centres: Mysore, Dehradun and Varanasi. From each centre, only around 10 to 12 candidates cleared the written tests, and these were further sent for a week's physical training followed by a medical check-up. Of these, only 13 candidates finally made it through this rigorous process and were selected to be trained for the Indian Air Force's transport fleet in October 1993. By the time the shortlisted candidates went through the entire training, only seven of them would make it to the end of the tough grind. Harita would be part of this team of seven women who would go on to make history and break the glass ceiling in the Indian Air Force, literally touching the skies.

However, individually, she would go on to do more; she would go down in the annals of Indian aviation history, becoming an inspiration for young women pilots years down the line.

This commissioning of women as Short Service Commission Officers was an important step forward in gender equality within the Armed Forces, which had so far been a traditionally male bastion. This recruitment was specific to training women as transport pilots, an initial step perhaps to bringing in more women into the Air Force. Upon selection, Harita and the 12 other women officers would receive their initial training at the Air Force Academy, Dundigul, near Hyderabad.[1]

At the Academy, the selected candidates underwent three months of pre-flying training. This was followed by Stage I flying training on HPT-32 aircraft for a period of two months, followed by Stage II flying training for five months on Kiran aircraft. The training was exacting and demanding. They would garner an average of 120 hours of total flying. After the training at Hyderabad, they would go on to receive further training at the Air Lift Forces Training Establishment (ALFTE) at the Yelahanka Air Force Station in Bangalore. When they had successfully completed their Stage III training on Avro and AN-32, they would get their 'Wings' and be commissioned, prior to being posted out.

Perhaps she had no idea that of the 12 selected as her batchmates, she was the one destined to make history. And that happened on the unremarkable morning of 2 September 1994. A clear sky dawned, the weather was pleasant, suitable for the first solo flights awaiting the pilots in training. The young girls about to take their first solo flights must have been nervous, but didn't show it. They were resolute and firm, this had to be done, they had trained hard for it. They assembled on the airfield. Harita was the first to give her test. She was tiny, 5 ft 2 inches, zipped up into the regulation navy blue overalls and strapped into the pilot's seat in an Avro HS-748. Composed and calm, at the controls, she awaited the commands from the control. The media invited to the Yelahanka Air Force Station at Bangalore to report on this historic event watched as she took off. She was piloting this aircraft solo and went right up to a height of 10,000 feet. With this, she became the very first Indian woman to fly solo in the Indian Air Force without a co-pilot, shattering a glass barrier and how. She was up for around half an hour in the clouds, manoeuvring the aircraft at that height while being monitored by her seniors and training officers from the ground. When she landed, she emerged from the aircraft smiling with joy. There was a resounding applause from the crowd awaiting her on the ground. Her instructors and colleagues shook her hand, patted her back and hugged her. Everyone was overjoyed. She was barely 22, when she became the first Indian woman to fly solo above 10,000 sq. ft in the Indian Air Force. It was one for the records.

To quote Wing Commander I.K. Khanna (Retd), who had trained this batch of cadets, about his memories of this day, 'During the training of the first batch of women pilots at Yelahanka, not a day would pass when the media would not visit to interview the women and see them in action. On one of those days, we had someone from the media coming onboard Harita's training flight. As Harita and I walked to the aircraft, I told her to ignore the journalist and focus on the flight for the day. On that day, she was scheduled to learn shutting down an engine and restarting it in air. As she went through the paces with a demonstration of the exercise by the instructor followed by practice by her, I could see the journalist sweating more than Harita.'[2]

He writes about her success, 'One of my trainees, cadet Harita Kaur Deol (later Fg Offr Harita Deol) was the first to go solo. I still recall the day. In response to my inquisitive look about her performance in her solo check, the examiner just smiled and gave me a big thumbs up.'[3]

When asked if she was overwhelmed by the achievement, her measured response to the media was: 'No, not at all. I am happy I was the first to do a solo and that I lived up to the expectations of my instructor.'[4] She added that she had always been confident about her abilities, and this solo sortie had only strengthened it further. She faced the barrage of cameras clicking her with composure and confidence. When asked about her future plans, she said that she would speak to my parents first and perhaps celebrate the success with her friends over the weekend.

At the time, Air Commodore P.R. Kumar, Air-Officer-in Command at the ALFTE, Yelahanka Air Force Station, Bangalore, who was in charge of checking the solo flight, had said about her achievement, 'She was confident and in full control of the aircraft. Her take-off and landing were excellent. The standard she demonstrated was much more than my expectation. Girls are much clearer in their expression.'

On that day, two more women from the batch—Flight Cadet Archana Kapoor and Flight Cadet Bindu Sebastian—completed their solos on the Avro. Four women pilots from this batch—Priya Nalgundwar, Pamela Rodrigues, Priya Paul and Anisha Shinh—were scheduled to do their solos in the forthcoming week, two on the Russian AN-32 aircraft and the other two on the Avro. The luck of the draw was with Harita, though, she had been the first to go up into the sky solo, create a record and with this make her place in the history books. It was an achievement she wore lightly. She was commissioned into the Indian Air Force on 17 December 1994 as a flying officer, having successfully completed her training.

After the highs of being the first woman to make a solo flight in the Indian Air Force, little did she know that tragedy awaited her, barely a couple of years later. On 24 December 1996, she was assigned a regular operational flight as a co-pilot. She took off from Chennai in an HS-748 Avro aircraft along with her co-pilot. The sortie was to fly from Chennai to Hyderabad. Unfortunately, the aircraft reportedly had technical glitches compounded with wing fatigue and crashed near the Bukkapuram village in Prakasam district of Andhra Pradesh. It would be a fatal crash, taking all the 24 lives onboard the aircraft. Fg Offr Harita Kaur Deol, barely 25 then, would lose her life on duty. With her death, she would tragically have another first to her credit—becoming the first woman Indian Air Force pilot to lose her life in the line of duty.[5]

Harita was awarded with the Pride of MCM (Mehr Chand Mahajan) Award posthumously which was received by her mother. With Indian women conquering the skies, flying fighter planes and going into the line of combat, Harita's legacy is one that has sadly been clouded over with the passage of time, but it remains a legacy for all those who come after her, to dare reach out and touch the sky.

NOTES

1. 'Inspiring Story of Harita Kaur Deol: The First Woman to Fly Solo in Indian Air Force', *Be an Inspirer*, 5 October 2018, https://www.beaninspirer.com/inspiring-story-harita-kaur-deol-first-woman-fly-solo-indian-air-force/. Accessed on 17 January 2022.
2. WG CDR I.K. Khanna (Retd), 'I trained IAF's 1st batch of women pilots. "Gunjan Saxena" gets a lot wrong', *ThePrint*, 12 August 2020, https://theprint.in/opinion/i-trained-iaf-1st-batch-women-pilots-gunjan-saxena-gets-a-lot-wrong/486378/. Accessed on 17 January 2022.
3. Ibid.
4. https://www.facebook.com/OurGurdwara/photos/incredible-story-of-the-first-indian-female-pilot-a-sikh-

named-harita-kaur3-june/937965502900776/. Accessed on 17 January 2022.
5   Lekshmi Priya S., 'Famous Indian women who died in line of duty', *The Week*, 23 March 2017, https://www.theweek.in/webworld/features/society/famous-indian-women-who-died-in-line-of-duty.html. Accessed on 17 January 2022.

12

MADHURI DIXIT

THE 'DHAK DHAK' GIRL

Her hit dance numbers define her: 'Ek do teen', the dance number that made her an overnight hit, 'Dhak Dhak' that cemented her as the nation's darling and 'Choli ke peechey', which was on the lips of every movie-goer, despite its rather risqué lyrics. Madhuri Dixit is an unlikely film heroine, so removed was her family from Bollywood.

Born on 15 May 1967 to a middle-class home in Mumbai, she was one of four children, born to Shankar and Snehlata Dixit from the tight-knit Kokanastha Hindu Brahmin community, a cultured and refined community that set a great deal by education as well as the performing arts and literature.[1] She began training in Kathak when she was three years old and would get a scholarship in the dance form when she was not even 10. To quote her, 'It was due to a dance performance that the first time my name had appeared in the paper. I was seven or eight years old at that time and had performed at the Guru Purnima festival. And there was a journalist who was there and he had written this article saying that "this little girl stole the show"—something like that.'[2]

In an interview to *Savvy* magazine, she said,

> I am the youngest in the family and have three older siblings, and the age difference between me and my oldest

sibling is 10 years. So I was literally the baby of the family. My sisters and I started learning kathak from a very young age. My mom's artistic interests were passed down to us. She was interested in art, used to learn singing and wanted to learn dancing when she was growing up, but her times were very different. It was not considered good to learn dance, especially for a girl from a Maharashtrian family.[3]

After her tenth board exams, she joined Sathaye College in Mumbai, but a few months into her first year at junior college, she dropped out to make her debut in Bollywood with the movie *Abodh* (produced by Rajshri Productions) in 1984. *Abodh* was followed by a slew of nondescript movies that went unnoticed. The turnaround would begin in 1988, which would be *her* year. She had four releases that year, three of which were box-office duds: *Mohre*, *Khatron ke Khiladi* and *Dayavan*. However, *Dayavan*, with Vinod Khanna as the protagonist and Madhuri as the female lead, was critically acclaimed and her performance was much appreciated by both critics and movie watchers. But it was N. Chandra's *Tezaab* (1988), starring Anil Kapoor, that catapulted her to the limelight. She played the role of Mohini in *Tezaab*, a young girl pushed into becoming a commercial dancer by an alcoholic gambler father. The movie went on to become a runaway commercial success. It was the highest grossing film that year, running in theatres for over 50 weeks. The film won Madhuri her first Best Actress nomination from Filmfare. What really made *Tezaab* a turning point in her career was the song 'Ek do teen', choreographed by Saroj Khan, which became a rage across the nation.

With deceptively simple lyrics, the catchy tune would win Saroj Khan a Filmfare award for best choreography in 1989. The rehearsals for the song took 16 days and the shooting itself took a week. On the last day, they shot the entire day and night.[4]

To quote Madhuri about this iconic song, 'Saroj Khan always considered me to be a classical dancer. When 'Ek do teen' was to be shot, she told me to rehearse, because it is a very Bollywood number. The camera, the angles are very important. And I wanted to learn about the Bollywood style of dancing so I rehearsed thoroughly.'[5] Saroj Khan would go on to choreograph some of Madhuri's most iconic songs, and Madhuri and she would share a guru-shishya relationship, with Madhuri considering Khan her mother on the set. In fact, she would say that Saroj Khan taught her how to romance the camera. On her part, Saroj Khan considered Madhuri her favourite student.

Pairing up again with Anil Kapoor for *Ram Lakhan* (1989), Madhuri delivered yet another megahit. In her next release, *Prem Pratigyaa* (1989), she starred opposite veteran actor Mithun Chakraborty, and got her second Filmfare Best Actress Award nomination. She was also part of *Tridev*, a multistarrer ensemble blockbuster which was one of the biggest hits of 1989. Her next notable role was in Vidhu Vinod Chopra's *Parinda* (1989), where she had a small role, but managed to create an impact nonetheless, and her work was critically acclaimed. In 1990, she starred in another blockbuster, *Dil*, opposite Aamir Khan. She totally stole the show in the movie *Beta* (1992) directed by Indra Kumar, dominating even the hero Anil Kapoor. The song 'Dhak Dhak' in the movie became one of the landmark songs of her career after 'Ek do teen' and Madhuri became, with this movie, the 'Dhak Dhak' girl.[6]

In 1993, the crime thriller *Khalnayak*, with Sanjay Dutt and Jackie Shroff, gave her the next box-office hit. This movie would give her the other song that would become a landmark in her career, 'Choli ke peechey kya hai'. In the 1994 revenge thriller *Anjaam*, she played a wronged woman who seeks to get revenge from a pathological stalker played by Shah Rukh Khan. This role got her the seventh nomination for the Best Actress at the Filmfare Awards, and it would also be the first of a series of movies in which she would be cast as the female lead opposite Shah Rukh. But it was her next movie, *Hum Aapke Hain Koun...!*, with Salman Khan that would go on to break box-office records and become a mega hit, breaking the record set by *Sholay* (1975), a record that would go unchallenged for seven years. In 1997, her role in Prakash Jha's *Mrityudand*, as part of an ensemble cast with Shabana Azmi and Shilpa Shirodkar, was much lauded and critically acclaimed. Her next notable film was Yash Chopra's musical *Dil To Pagal Hai* (1997) with Karisma Kapoor and Shah Rukh Khan. The movie set the box office on fire, and got Madhuri her fourth Best Actress Award from Filmfare.

In 1998, she did the forgettable *Wajood*, in a lacklustre role, and in 1999, *Aarzoo* which came and went without ruffling the box office. She came back into the limelight in 2000 with her role in *Pukar*, opposite Anil Kapoor. She took a major career risk by playing a negative character but her superlative performance got her the twelfth nomination for the Filmfare Best Actress Award. In fact, in this movie she had a song with noted choreographer and dancer Prabhu Deva, 'Kay sera sera'. Later, Prabhu Deva would say about Madhuri, 'When she dances, it's like fire and lightning together. When we started rehearsing for the song in *Pukar*, I realized everything I had heard about her was true. She was so driven. A lot of heroines ask me to make the dance steps easier. But not Madhuri. She not only matched me but even outdid me in the number.'[7]

In 2000, she was featured in the *Guinness World Records* as the highest-paid Indian actress. Of her career, *Reuters* had said, 'In her prime, Dixit was the undisputed queen of Bollywood, the world's largest film industry by audience size, and her popularity and fees rivaled even the biggest male stars.'[8]

Her role in *Yeh Raaste Hain Pyaar Ke* (2001) went as unnoticed as the film itself. It was the fiery *Lajja* (2001) by Rajkumar Santoshi that brought her critical acclaim again. While the film failed to make waves at the box office, it cemented Madhuri's reputation as a stellar actress and got her a nomination at the Filmfare Award for Best Supporting Actress.

Her next big release was *Devdas* (2002) by Sanjay Leela Bhansali, with her playing the courtesan Chandramukhi, and Shah Rukh Khan and Aishwarya Rai playing Devdas and Paro, respectively—the star-crossed lovers of the classic love story. In this film, Madhuri rendered perhaps one of her most nuanced performances.

Her personal life has largely been off limits to the tabloids except for a reported relationship with Sanjay Dutt. The duo apparently got close during the filming of the hit movie *Saajan* in 1990. However, Dutt was arrested in 1993 under the Terrorist and Disruptive Activities (Prevention) Act or TADA and Madhuri ended the relationship. Both Dutt and Madhuri however, have consistently denied that they were ever in a relationship.

In 1999, she got married to Dr Shriram Nene, a cardiovascular surgeon and a second-generation immigrant from India. Interestingly, her husband, who had grown up in the United States, had absolutely no idea of what a phenomenon she was. They have two sons, Arin and Ryan. She lived in Denver for over a decade, living the quintessential soccer mom life, bringing up her boys and living away from the spotlight. It was a life she loved, being just a regular suburban mom. In an interview with *Rediff*, she said, 'When I was with my family in Denver I was happy being unknown. I enjoyed being on my own and taking my car out for grocery shopping—I loved doing that—taking my kids to school, dropping them off, picking them up...'[9]

She's received six Filmfare Awards, and in 2008, the Government of India awarded her the Padma Shri. In 2011, she received special jury recognition from Filmfare for completing 25 years in the film industry. In October 2011, she decided to move back to Mumbai with her husband and family. The move back was not easy for her sons and her supportive husband. When she returned to India with her family, the paparazzi culture had grown so much that her kids and she were chased everywhere.

For her comeback, she chose the dark comedy *Dedh Ishqiya,* which was released in 2014. She chose this role, she says, because of how fierce and unapologetic Vidya Balan's character was in *Ishqiya* (prequel to *Dedh Ishqiya*), thanks to director Abhishek Chaubey. She followed it up with *Gulaab Gang* (2014), playing the leader of a women's group, inspired by the real-life leader of the women's collective, Sampat Pal Devi, who founded the Gulabi Gang, a group of women who take on the patriarchy.

In 2018, she acted in the Marathi comedy *Bucket List.* The year 2019 saw her reuniting with her most popular on-screen pairing with Anil Kapoor in *Total Dhamaal.* She produced *15 August,* a Marathi movie, for Netflix, under her production company RnM Motion Pictures. A small film, set in a Mumbai chawl, it examines what freedom means to different people.[10]

She keeps a low profile, away from work, using Instagram to keep in touch with her fans. She has judged multiple seasons of dance reality shows. And through her entire journey as an actress nonpareil, Madhuri has retained the discipline to stay focused on her dance, on her acting, and to remain first and foremost, an entertainer. Like the superstar she is.

NOTES

1. 'Madhuri Dixit: Lesser known facts', https://timesofindia.indiatimes.com/entertainment/hindi/bollywood/photo-features/madhuri-dixit-lesser-known-facts/after-her-marathi-stint-madhuri-dixit-nene-to-also-produce-a-hindi-film/photostory/64379432.cms. Accessed on 15 January 2022.
2. '"I Danced My Way Through My Childhood..." – Madhuri Dixit Nene', *The Humming Notes,* 15 November 2017, https://thehummingnotes.com/i-danced-way-childhood-madhuri-dixit-nene/. Accessed on 15 January 2022.
3. Ekta Chanana, 'Madhuri Dixit Shares a Rare Childhood Picture with Sister that Shows off Their Uncanny

Resemblance', bollywoodshaadis.com/articles/madhuri-dixit-shares-a-rare-childhood-picture-with-sister-17933. Accessed on 17 January 2022.

4. Scroll stuff, 'The story behind Madhuri Dixit's "Ek Do Teen", the most famous counting exercise in Hindi film music', *Scroll.in*, 22 March 2018, https://scroll.in/reel/872889/the-story-behind-madhuri-dixits-ek-do-teen-the-most-famous-countdown-in-hindi-film-music. Accessed on 17 January 2022.

5. 'Madhuri Dixit: After Ek Do Teen, Saroj Khan and I made a pact to never repeat steps', *India Today*, 29 May 2020, https://www.indiatoday.in/movies/celebrities/story/madhuri-dixit-after-ek-do-teen-saroj-khan-and-i-made-a-pact-to-never-repeat-steps-1683429-2020-05-29. Accessed on 17 January 2022.

6. 'Madhuri Dixit Birthday: 7 times when Dhak Dhak girl made 90s kids go head over heels', *Catch News*, 15 May 2020, https://www.catchnews.com/bollywood-news/madhuri-dixit-birthday-7-times-actress-made-every-90s-kids-heart-go-dhak-dhak-191129.html. Accessed on 16 January 2022.

7. 'Madhuri Dixit wishes Prabhudheva on his birthday: Que Sera Sera will always be close to my heart', *India Today*, 3 April 2020, https://www.indiatoday.in/movies/celebrities/story/madhuri-dixit-wishes-prabhudheva-on-his-birthday-que-sera-sera-will-always-be-close-to-my-heart-1662807-2020-04-03. Accessed on 17 January 2022.

8. Krittivas Mukherjee, 'Bollywood diva shines in insipid comeback film', *Reuters*, 3 December 2007, reuters.com/article/us-india-film-dixit-idUSDEL474620071203. Accessed on 17 January 2022.

9. 'Madhuri Dixit: I was happy being unknown in Denver', *Rediff.com*, 11 March 2014, https://www.rediff.com/movies/report/slide-show-1-madhuri-dixit-i-was-happy-being-unknown-in-denver/20140311.htm. Accessed on 15 January 2022.

10. Priyanka Bhadani, 'In conversation with Madhuri Dixit, Dr Shriram Nene', *The Week*, 6 April 2019, https://www.theweek.in/theweek/leisure/2019/04/05/in-conversation-with-madhuri-dixit-dr-shriram-nene.html. Accessed on 17 January 2022.

13

BACHENDRI PAL

CLIMBING MORE THAN MOUNTAINS

It wasn't something you'd expect a girl from a remote village in Uttarkashi to do, to climb the highest mountain in the world. Girls from villages in Uttarkashi, at the time, would complete their basic education, get married and perhaps become teachers. However, there were also outliers like Bachendri Pal, who would fight to climb the highest peak in the world.

It wasn't ambition that made her the first Indian woman to climb the Mount Everest in 1984; it was simply her fascination with mountains. She was born on 24 May 1954 to a Bhotiya family settled in Nakuri, Uttarkashi. She was the third of five children in the family. Her mother, Hansa Devi, was a homemaker, and her father, Kishan Singh Pal, was a trader who traded between India and Tibet.

Circumstances were difficult as their home got washed away in flash floods. All the children pitched in in the carpet-weaving and belt-making work to support the family. In fact, back then, girls from little villages high up in the mountains of Garhwal didn't even study beyond Class 10, but Bachendri was different. To quote her, 'In my village, if girls studied till Std 10, people would say "she is mad". Who cared for girls or their education? I did an MA and a BEd. No one—not even my parents—approved of my becoming a mountaineer.'[1]

The mountains called out to her when she was still in school. During a school picnic, she, with some of her friends, scaled a peak and crossed the snow line. She was bitten by the mountaineering bug since.

Bachendri was academically very sound. A clever and sincere student, she had to give up her studies in Class 8 due to financial constraints. She was heartbroken, but continued reading her brother's books at home. Seeing her determination, her mother and sister pleaded with her father to allow her to study further. He relented. When she passed her Class 10 boards, her father refused to send her to college due to lack of funds, but her principal intervened. She went on to do her BA. Once she graduated, her father was keen she become the first MA from her village, and to fulfil his ambition, she went on to do her master's from Dehradun, and then her BEd.

Despite her qualifications, she wasn't able to land a job. She applied to a number of places, but only found low-paying, primary-level teacher positions. She revisited her passion for mountaineering and joined the National Institute of Mountaineering (NIM) for their basic course. Col. Premchand, who was the vice principal of the Nehru Institute of Mountaineering, was the one who saw potential in her, and even wrote on her certificate 'Everest material'. She paid no heed, but when the planning for the mixed expedition to Everest began in 1984, she was surprised to find herself receiving a letter inviting her to the screening camp. She did not reply to the letter. When she went for her next-level certification, her instructors learnt that she had ignored the screening letter and told her she was throwing away a golden opportunity. The villagers found it amusing that after her BEd degree, she chose to climb mountains, instead of teaching in a school.

Her parents believed in her though, and supported her, as

did Col. Premchand, who had faith in her potential to make it to the Everest Summit's final team. In her own words, 'My first guru Colonel Premchand was one of those leaders who himself took to adventure to teach students like us lessons of leadership, teamwork and discipline in life.'[2] While doing her course at NIM, in 1982, she would scale Mt Gangotri 1 (21,889.77 feet) and Mt Rudragaria (19,091 feet). This, however, didn't solve the financial problems her family was facing, and there was an added pressure on her at the time as her family wanted her to get married. It was around this time that Brig. Gyan Singh, director of the National Adventure Foundation (NAF), visited Uttarkashi to set in place an adventure course for teachers at the NIM. She confided in him about the pressure she was facing financially at home as well as the pressure to get married. He offered her a job as one of the 'Seven Sisters' to run the adventure course they were starting at the time.

She began her training at home much before the formal training began. She had to climb 600 metres every day carrying 15 kilograms on her back and jog 10 kilometres with the same weight. Her diet comprised protein-rich foods, milk, greens and sugar, all in all, an intake of around 4,000 calories to give her the energy she required. The villagers in Nakuri found it amusing to see her climbing from the bottom of the hill to the top, carrying a rucksack filled with the heaviest stones she could find. Her father would joke that her degrees were of no use and that she was now training to be a construction worker. She says, 'I would carry stones in my rucksack from my house in the mountains to higher reaches and return with firewood and fodder. A few in the village were convinced that I was building a house on top.'[3]

She conquered a number of small peaks and was chosen to be part of the first-ever mixed gender team to attempt conquering Mount Everest in 1984. She says, 'I was the least experienced in terms of mountaineering, so I did not carry any baggage, as was the case with the other women, who knew how big the expedition was. If at all, I was simply competing with myself to better my performance.'[4]

The group selected to ascend to the summit comprised six women and 11 men from India. Her training began in December 1983 at the Indian Mountaineering Foundation in Delhi. In January 1984, their instructor took them to Gulmarg in Jammu and Kashmir to practise climbing the steep, snow-laden slopes. At this time, Brig. Gyan Singh did another remarkable act of kindness towards Bachendri, he contacted Tata Steel and persuaded them to employ Bachendri to promote adventure sports.

On 7 March 1984, the selected members were flown out to Kathmandu and the journey to the summit of Everest began from there. An advance party had already gone to do the opening of the route through the ice for them. Thinking back to her first glimpse of the formidable and imposing Mount Everest, with the almost 10-km-long snow plume flying off its peak, thanks to the terrifying winds whipping around its summit, Bachendri would write, years later, 'We the hill people have always worshipped the mountains...my overpowering emotion at this awe-inspiring spectacle was, therefore, devotional.'[5]

Two months later, after their arrival in March, it was time for the team to begin its ambitious ascent. Their first trial came when an avalanche buried their camp on the night of 16 May. They had settled down for the night at an altitude of 24,000 feet. She recalls it was a full moon night, and the moonlight shone off the icy slopes of the Lhotse: 'I was sleeping in one of the tents with my teammates at Camp III at an altitude of 24,000 feet (7,315.2 metres). On the night of 15-16 May 1984, at around 00:30 hours IST, I was jolted awake; something had hit me hard; I also heard a deafening sound and soon after I found myself being enveloped within a very cold mass of material.'[6] Luckily, her climbing partner managed to emerge from the debris and pulled her out. She says in the book, *The Call of Everest: First*

Ascent by an Indian Woman: 'I found myself under some heavy load. I shouted for my companion Lopsang. He was awake, but trapped in the tent. He cut it open with his swiss knife and tried to pull me out with one arm…I had too much load over me. He then frantically removed the ice slabs from over my body. He tugged me again and I came out with some difficulty.'[7] Many members were injured and some opted to return to base camp. She writes, 'When the male members decided to return to base camp due to injury or shock, the leader asked me, being the only female member on the summit team, whether I would like to give it another try. I did not tell him about the head injury I had suffered. I simply said, "Yes sir, I will".'[8]

On 22 May 1984, the team decided they would attempt the summit. Bachendri was the only woman left on the final team of the total of six women who had joined the expedition. The team reached the South Col and would spend the night there at Camp IV. This was at an altitude of 26,000 feet above sea level. On the morning of the 23rd, she awoke at 4 a.m., before the break of dawn. It was a calm morning. She made some tea with snow that she had melted, ate half a slab of chocolate and put on her climbing gear. The thin air at that elevation made coordination difficult, the incessant wind wasn't making things easier either. It whipped around them, increasing in ferocity as they resumed their ascent to the summit at the crack of dawn, 6.20 a.m. It was a tough climb. They were literally climbing vertical sheets of frozen ice, with chilly winds whipping around them at 100 kilometres per hour in temperatures that were well below freezing point, at minus 30 to 40 degrees Celsius. It wasn't just about climbing at that point, it was about surviving. At 1.07 p.m., she had finally reached the summit of Mount Everest, all of 8,848 metres, 29,030 feet above sea level. She was on top of the world. For the young girl who had first climbed a mountain when she was barely 12, this was a dream come true. She had truly touched the sky. Overwhelmed, she knelt down and kissed the Summit, where they haulted for around 45 minutes. She placed a small statue of Durga and a copy of the Hanuman Chalisa, wrapped in red cloth there, burying it in the powdered snow at the top.

Pal did not rest on her laurels. She went on to lead an Indo-Nepalese Women's Mount Everest Expedition team in 1993, which had 18 people conquer the Summit, with seven women amongst them. She was part of an all-woman team of rafters in The Great Indian Women's Rafting Voyage in 1994. This maiden attempt saw the women completing the entire stretch of the mighty Ganga via raft from Haridwar in Uttarakhand to Calcutta, a distance of 2,155 kilometres. Another first was the First Indian Women's Trans Himalayan expedition in 1997, which saw eight women trek from the Himalayas in the east in Arunachal Pradesh, right to the extreme western end of the Himalayas at the Siachen Glacier, reaching Indira Col, which is the northernmost tip of India at an altitude of 20,100 feet, thus covering more than 4,500 kilometres in 225 days, and crossing over 40 high mountain passes. She was also part of an all-women team on a desert safari covering the complete Indo-Pak border in 2015. She led the Mission Namami Gange in 2018 where she and her team of 40 went from Haridwar to Patna on rafts on the Ganga.

In 1984, she was awarded the Gold Medal for Excellence in Mountaineering by the Indian Mountaineering Foundation. In the same year, she was awarded the Padma Shri, followed by the Arjuna Award in 1986 and the Padma Bhushan in 2019.

Bachendri Pal had long been associated with the Tata Group of Industries as the chief of adventure programmes at Tata Steel Jamshedpur, and also as the director of the Tata Steel Adventure Foundation (TSAF). J.R.D. Tata of the Tata Group invited her to set up a mountaineering academy in Jamshedpur. She has retired from the Jamshedpur academy but continues to give back to society. She is passionate about working for a cause. To quote her, 'For me, my journey to Everest symbolized women's empowerment. It was an awakening of my abilities. In the end, the choice is yours: to stop or to keep pursuing.'[9]

NOTES

1. Bachendri Pal, *Everest: My Journey to the Top*, Nehru Bal Pustakalaya.
2. Parvinder Bhatia, 'Bachendri Pal: Queen of Adventure', *The Pioneer*, 27 March 2019, https://www.dailypioneer.com/2019/state-editions/bachendri-pal-queen-of-adventure.html. Accessed on 17 January 2022.
3. Shail Desai, 'Bachendri Pal's ascent of Mount Everest was just a stepping stone in her endeavour to touch people's lives positively', *FirstPost*, 9 February 2019, https://www.firstpost.com/sports/bachendri-pals-ascent-of-mount-everest-was-just-a-stepping-stone-in-her-endeavour-to-touch-peoples-lives-positively-6057101.html. Accessed on 17 January 2022.
4. Ibid.
5. Anupma Khanna, 'Bachendri Pal celebrates birthday camping in her native Uttarkashi', *The Pioneer*, 25 May 2013, https://www.dailypioneer.com/2013/state-editions/bachendri-pal-celebrates-birthday-camping-in-her-native-uttarkashi.html. Accessed on 17 January 2022.
6. 'On this day: India's first woman mountaineer conquered Mt Everest', AsisNet Newsable, 23 May 2021, https://newsable.asianetnews.com/positive-stories/bachendri-pal-india-first-woman-mountaineer-to-conquer-mt-everest-vpn-qtjp1n. Accessed on 17 January 2022.
7. Shail Desai, 'Bachendri Pal's ascent of Mount Everest was just a stepping stone in her endeavour to touch people's lives positively', *FirstPost*, 9 February 2019, https://www.firstpost.com/sports/bachendri-pals-ascent-of-mount-everest-was-just-a-stepping-stone-in-her-endeavour-to-touch-peoples-lives-positively-6057101.html. Accessed on 17 January 2022.

8   Ibid.
9   Harpreet Kaur Lamba,' No mountain too high for Bachendri Pal', *The Hindu BusinessLine*, 31 May 2019. https://www.thehindubusinessline.com/blink/explore/no-mountain-too-high-for-bachendri-pal/article27340225.ece. Accessed on 10 February 2022.

14

REKHA

A LIFE LIVED UNAPOLOGETICALLY

Hers has been a life that fairy tales are made of, of the ugly duckling morphing into a gorgeous swan. From her debut as a child actress to her current status as the mysterious, reclusive prima donna of the Hindi film world, Rekha has indeed come a long way.

She was named Bhanurekha Ganesan. When she entered the Hindi film industry, her name Bhanurekha got shortened to simply Rekha. She was born on 10 October 1954; she was the daughter of the Tamil superstar Gemini Ganesan and the noted actress Pushpavalli, born out of wedlock.[1]

Throughout her childhood, her father never acknowledged Rekha and her sister as his daughters. Years later, talk show host Simi Garewal would ask Rekha whether she had missed the presence of her father growing up. Rekha responded with grace, 'If you don't taste something, you don't know what it means. I didn't know what the word "father" meant.'[2]

Yasser Usman, the author of the biography *Rekha: The Untold Story*, talks about how Rekha's childhood shaped her. 'Rekha had a turbulent childhood. Her father Gemini Ganesan was a huge star but he was totally absent during Rekha's childhood. She said in an interview, "Though he never lived with us, we 'felt' his presence wherever we went or whatever we did. My mother constantly spoke about him." In the absence of her father, her mother Pushpavalli became the most important person in her life.'[3]

He adds that Rekha had to join the Bombay film industry against her wishes. She was pulled out of her school due to financial constraints. She was totally uninterested in acting, young as she was. In the interview with Simi Garewal, she says, 'When a 12-year-old or a 13-year-old wanted to have a chocolate or an ice cream and has been deprived of it for months together, somewhere you tend to snap. I mean I never used to run away, I would say "abhi aati hoon" and lose track of time.'[4]

She has vivid memories of those troubled early years as a child actor and then as a lead heroine when she was just a teenager. Years later she would say,

> Bombay was like a jungle, and I had walked in unarmed. It was one of the most frightening phases of my life... I was totally ignorant of the ways of this new world. Guys did try and take advantage of my vulnerability. I did feel, 'What am I doing? I should be in school, having ice-cream, fun with my friends, why am I even forced to work, deprived of normal things that a child should be doing at my age?'[5]

Her initial foray into the film industry was as a child actress, credited as Baby Bhanurekha, in her debut Telugu film *Inti Guttu* (1958), then as a heroine in the blockbuster Kannada film *Operation Jackpot Nalli C.I.D. 999* with the then superstar Rajkumar in 1969.[6]

She would go on to debut as a lead actress in the Hindi movie *Sawan Bhadon* (1970). It was a hit, and the teenaged Rekha was an unlikely star. While *Sawan Bhadon* was released as her first Hindi movie, it wasn't the first Hindi movie she had shot for. The first was *Anjana Safar* (1969) with the then 'chocolate' hero, Biswajeet. Later, Rekha would claim she was tricked into shooting a kissing scene with Biswajeet. The incident has found mention in Usman's biography of her. To quote from the book,

> Every last detail of the strategy had been decided before the shoot. As soon as the director Raj Nawathe said 'action', Biswajeet took Rekha in his arms and pressed his lips on hers. Rekha was stunned. This kiss had never been mentioned to her. The camera kept rolling; neither was the director ordering 'cut' nor was Biswajeet letting go of her. For all of five minutes, Biswajeet kept kissing Rekha. Unit members were whistling and cheering. Her eyes were tightly shut but they were full of tears.[7]

In the early '70s, she was part of several box-office hits such as *Raampur Ka Lakshman* (1972), *Kahani Kismat Ki* (1973) and *Pran Jaye Per Vachan Na Jaye* (1974), amongst others. She was still an outlier at the time, dark complexioned, plump and unable to speak Hindi. At a movie premiere, Shashi Kapoor is supposed to have said about her, 'How is this dark, plump and gauche actress ever going to make it?'[8]

She was called the 'ugly duckling' of Hindi films because of her dark complexion and South Indian features. She transformed herself completely. From a plump girl with over-plucked eyebrows and a dusky complexion, she became sleek, stylish and gorgeous. She would credit this transformation to yoga, diet and a mindful life. In 1983, she brought out a book titled *Rekha's Mind and Body Temple,* advocating a fit and healthy lifestyle. In the interview with Simi Garewal, she said, 'By the time *Ghar* was released, that's when it hit people that it's overnight. But it's not overnight, it took about two-and-a half years.'[9]

Interestingly, according to her biographer, Yasser Usman, it was Rekha's association with Amitabh Bachchan that transformed her on both the personal and the professional front. He says, 'Though the film media mainly talked about their personal association but in my opinion it was the powerful impact of

Mr Bachchan that completely transformed her professionally and also as a person. The manner in which she talks about this experience or her association with Amitabh Bachchan you can feel it is something sacrosanct and internal to her.'

He adds, 'Professionally, it was definitely *Do Anjaane* and the impact Mr Bachchan had on her. She became serious and soon stardom happened. Then came a very crucial film *Ghar*, where she got a chance to work with Gulzar. It was a bold film that dealt with the pain of a rape victim and the social stigma she faces. Rekha gave a memorable performance and everyone began to take her seriously as an actress of exceptional talent. This was a turning point and many films followed post *Ghar*, including *Khubsoorat, Silsila* and *Umrao Jaan* where she was in superb form.'

She also became more particular about the kind of roles she was accepting, her acting turnaround came with the movie *Do Anjaane* (1976), where she played a negative character, a scheming and ambitious wife to the then superstar, Amitabh Bachchan. It was the sensitively directed film *Ghar* (1978) that established her as an actress. This got her the very first nomination for Best Actress at the Filmfare awards. Interestingly, she also had one of her greatest hits that year, the commercial blockbuster *Muqaddar Ka Sikandar*, where she co-starred with Amitabh.

Her portrayal of Umrao Jaan, the nineteenth-century courtesan from the Urdu novel *Umrao Jaan Ada* by Mirza Hadi Ruswa and adapted by director Muzaffar Ali was much lauded. After reading the script, she had a strange feeling, that she had Umrao in her. She was awarded the National Film Award for Best Actress for *Umrao Jaan*. She also became more confident about her abilities as an actress, and began doing more experimental cinema. She worked in Shyam Benegal's contemporary retelling of the Mahabharata, *Kal Yug* (1981), Govind Nihalani's *Vijeta* (1982), Girish Karnad's classic *Utsav* (1984) and Gulzar's much-acclaimed *Ijaazat* (1987). In 1988, she played the lead in *Khoon Bhari Maang*, which won her a Filmfare Award.

In the 1990s, she did some interesting movies including Mira Nair's *Kamasutra*, playing a teacher of the erotic arts, and the action movie *Khiladiyon Ka Khiladi* (1996), which had her play a lady don. In another controversial movie, *Aastha* (1997), by Basu Bhattacharya, she played a housewife who takes to prostitution. In the 2000s, the roles she took on were few and far between, amongst the noteworthy ones being her role in Khalid Mohamed's *Zubeidaa* (2001).

She has three Filmfare awards for best actress and best supporting actress. Her performance as the noted courtesan Umrao Jaan in 1981 won her the National Film Award for Best Actress. She was awarded the Padma Shri in 2010 by the Government of India and she has also been a member of the Rajya Sabha.

While her professional life has been dotted with accolades, her personal life has been troubled. There were reports of relationships with actors Kiran Kumar, Vinod Mehra and Amitabh Bachchan. She was reported to have married Vinod Mehra in 1973, but later denied it.[10] She surprised everyone when she married Mukesh Agarwal, a Delhi-based entrepreneur and the owner of the Hotline brand of kitchen appliances. She had been introduced to him by her friend, the Delhi-based fashion designer and socialite, Bina Ramani. It was an impulsive decision; Agarwal was smitten by her and Rekha was looking for stability. They were married in a temple in Juhu, in March 1990.

Her husband hung himself to death with her dupatta, barely a year later, while she was away in London, leaving a note stating that no one be blamed for his decision. She consciously withdrew from public life, after the public witch-hunt that followed upon her husband's death. Says Yasser Usman, 'Rekha was known for her scandalous and bold interviews in the 1970s and 1980s. But surprisingly, this generation knows her as someone who doesn't talk to the media—a reclusive diva. When did this change happen? When I was writing the book, I realized that it all changed after her husband Mukesh Agarwal's death by suicide in 1990. That event changed her forever. There was a proper media trial and everyone blamed her for her husband's death. Her relationship with the media was broken.'

Since then, she has retained a Garboesque mystery around herself. In a rare interview, she said, 'I'm a loner. I don't network or meet people. It's tacky for a person to talk about herself.'[11]

What is glorious about Rekha's story is the triumph of a woman who lives her life on her terms, in an industry that is so fiercely male dominated. Says Yasser Usman, 'For me, it was always a story of an underdog, a complete outsider who came to the Hindi film industry without even knowing Hindi. She was ridiculed for not being "traditionally good looking" according to the crappy Bollywood standards. For years, she went through numerous episodes of humiliation. In her case, the humiliation continued even after she was famous. But she fought back. Like they say, the real glory is being knocked to your knees and then coming back. As a writer, I was really curious to know what transpired in her journey from being a 14-year-old Tamil-speaking girl from Chennai, who went on to win the National Award for playing Umrao Jaan, speaking impeccable Urdu and becoming the diva of the Hindi film industry...all in the course of a long journey of unbelievable tragedies and incredible triumphs. She ruled a male-dominated film industry for years. In fact, there was a time in the early 1980s when she was the bigger star than most of her male co-stars. Movie scripts were written keeping her in mind and despite all the turbulence in her personal life, she gave many blockbusters where *she* was the hero.'

She rarely gives interviews, lives alone in her magnificent sea-facing bungalow, a landmark in Bandra's Bandstand, and makes the occasional public appearance, dazzling in her trademark Kanjeevaram sarees and red lipstick. In her splendid isolation, she continues to be perhaps the most seductive woman contemporary Hindi cinema has seen, and perhaps the most misunderstood too.

NOTES

1. 'Gemini Ganesan Controversial Life', *India Times*, 16 November 2016, https://www.indiatimes.com/culture/who-we-are/gemini-ganesan-controversial-life-277414.html. Accessed on 17 January 2022.
2. 'What Rekha said about growing up without dad Gemini Ganesan: "My father never noticed me."' *The Indian Express*, 9 October 2021, https://indianexpress.com/article/entertainment/bollywood/when-rekha-talked-about-growing-up-without-dad-gemini-ganesan-my-father-never-noticed-me-7562576/. Accessed on 17 January 2022.
3. Yasser Usman, *Rekha: The Untold Story*, Juggernaut, 2016.
4. Geetanjali Taragi, 'From Being Sexualised at an Early Age to Tragic Relationships, Rekha Overcame the Worst & Triumphed', *ScoopWhoop*, 10 October 2017, https://www.scoopwhoop.com/rekha-timeless-actor/. Accessed on 17 January 2022.
5. '7 unseen pictures of Rekha sans makeup', News 24, 9 October 2018, https://news24online.com/news/entertainment/7-unseen-pictures-rekha-sans-makeup-d2a8ab58/. Accessed on 17 January 2022.
6. 'Rekha has acted with Rajkumar', *The Times of India*, https://timesofindia.indiatimes.com/entertainment/kannada/movies/did-you-know-rekha-has-acted-with-rajkumar/articleshow/39602409.cms. Accessed on 17 January 2022.
7. Yasser Usman, *Rekha: The Untold Story*, Juggernaut, 2016.
8. Rekha's Transformation Journey, from Being Bullied for Her Looks as Teenager to a Graceful Diva', https://www.

bollywoodshaadis.com/articles/transformation-of-rekha-9255. Accessed on 17 January 2022.
9. Ibid.
10. 'Kiran Mehra: Rekha Remained in My Husband Vinod Mehra's Life Till the End', *Outlook*, 27 December 2021, https://www.outlookindia.com/website/story/entertainment-news-kiran-mehra-rekha-remained-in-my-husband-vinod-mehras-life-till-the-end/407018. Accessed on 16 January 2022.
11. Mark Manuel, 'Rekha: The Story She Actually Told', *HuffPost*, 9 July 2016, https://www.huffingtonpost.in/mark-manuel/rekha-the-story-she-actually-told_a_21466967. Accessed on 16 January 2022.

15

CHHAVI RAJAWAT
THE VILLAGE SARPANCH

About an hour's drive time from Jaipur is a nondescript village called Soda, in the Tonk district of Rajasthan, which proudly bears the title of being a 'Sainik Gram,' with many gallantry medal awardees calling it their home. It is the ancestral village of Brigadier Raghubir Singh, who was awarded the Mahavir Chakra and given the title 'Saviour of Punjab', during the 1965 Khemkaran sector war. He had been the sarpanch of this village for three terms before he passed away.

Brigadier Singh was the grandfather of Chhavi Rajawat, who would follow in his footsteps, becoming the sarpanch of this village for two terms.

For a village in Rajasthan to be led by a young woman with a management degree and a corporate background was a revolution in itself. Chhavi was everything one did not expect a sarpanch of a village in the heart of Rajasthan to be. An alumna of Rishi Valley School, Mayo College Girls School and Lady Shri Ram College, she slipped right into her role as the sarpanch bringing to it the zeal and process-based thinking she would have brought to any corporate job.[1]

Tall and lithe, well spoken and 'modern', she might have seemed completely out of place in the village but for the fact that she knew the village and the villagers from the time she was a young girl, spending her vacations in the village with her grandfather, who was then the sarpanch. Her stint in village politics came about when the villagers of Soda approached her, requesting her to contest the village elections. They wanted a candidate who was unaffiliated with any political party. Besides, they had faith in the way her grandfather had run the village during his term. They approached her with the hope that his granddaughter would bring the same ethos to her term as sarpanch.[2]

'This wasn't my idea,' to quote her from an interview to *The Economic Times*, 'I had never dreamt of becoming a sarpanch. Fifty elders from the village who had pampered me as a child, approached me to contest the election. This is exactly what they had done with my grandfather, a brigadier, who had served as sarpanch after retiring from the army. But in the 20 years since he had been sarpanch, I had not seen any development in the village. Things were only getting worse. I chose to stand for elections, as I wanted to work for the betterment of the village, which for me is home.'[3]

With her election, she also became the first female sarpanch in India in 2010. When she was first elected to the position, she was also the youngest sarpanch to ever hold the position across India. These weren't records she set out to create. She wasn't the conventional sarpanch: an elderly man. For Chhavi, the decision to contest the panchayat elections for the post of the sarpanch was simple. She merely wanted to be hands-on in bringing about a change in her ancestral village, and she believed she could do it.

When they reached out to her, the village was in a state of crisis. For over a decade, it was bereft of a good rainfall. By 2009, they faced severe drought which had completely destabilized the precarious agrarian economy the villagers were dependent upon. The lack of rain had severely depleted the ground water table, making the situation dire. The salinity levels in the ground water was very high, causing birth defects in newborn babies, and children and adults were falling chronically ill. Forget irrigation and domestic chores, there was no safe potable water to drink even.

It was at this point, in 2010, that Soda needed to have a woman as the sarpanch under the Women's Reservation Bill. Instead of nominating a woman as a placeholder for her husband as was the common practice, the villagers decided they needed someone who could work towards the modernization of the village and redress the real issues the village was facing in terms of development and progress. They approached Chhavi to stand for the post of sarpanch in the panchayat elections. They told her that all she would have to do was attend two panchayat meetings in a month in the village and one at the district level, but she told them very clearly that if they wanted her to stand for elections, she would be fully involved and hands-on as the village sarpanch. They agreed and she won with a thumping majority. She was barely 30 at the time, and a woman at that. She wasn't even affiliated with any political party but was standing for elections as an independent candidate. This was something which definitely rubbed those in political parties the wrong way, and had them go out of their way to ensure that she would find things difficult.[4]

'I didn't have to think about it much because Soda is where I belong and it needs me. In fact, the villagers broke all barriers of caste, gender and religion to ensure my victory. In Soda, not even one per cent of the voters are from my own caste. They [the villagers] wanted to prove that development is the most important factor for which they can overlook all politically created differences.'[5]

On being elected sarpanch, she chose to live in Soda, giving up the luxuries of living in her family home in the city of Jaipur. The villagers called her Bai Sa, a term of respect and regard, normally given to an older woman, a matriarch of sorts. Her first task upon taking charge was to desilt the only source of water for the villagers, a 100-acre reservoir. To quote her,

I ran from pillar to post for months trying to gather funds from the Centre, the state and even the private sector, but to no avail. Government schemes prohibit the use of machinery but we needed to use earthmovers. Sensing that I was disheartened, my friends and family stepped in, organised a fundraiser and raised ₹20 lakh. JCB lent an earthmover to us with a driver for a whole month too. We managed to fix a tenth of the reservoir. In 2010, we saw a good monsoon—and the area we had desilted filled up.[6]

Her efforts included putting in solar energy projects to aid the electrification of the village, converting the dirt roads into pucca roads that could be driven on and introducing solid toilets for most of the houses in the village. She ensured that the girls of the village had a proper school to study in. In her own words, 'The girls were studying in the open, come hail or storm. We identified a defunct building and renovated it, complete with a playground. Bosch Power Tools donated 200 tables and benches.'[7]

There was no bank in the village. She ensured that a nationalized bank, State Bank of India, opened a branch in Soda. She got all the villagers to open a bank account in the branch and ensured that they took their first steps towards financial literacy and self-sufficiency. Drawing on her corporate expertise, she approached to initiate corporate social reponsibility (CSR) programmes for the upliftment of the village.

She did all this while living in the village, going around in a pair of jeans and a kurti. In fact, choosing to wear what she was comfortable in rather than deferring to tradition, and wearing clothes that the villagers wore, was a statement in itself. She knew the villagers would treat her with love and respect irrespective of her attire. She needed to dress comfortably given that she was on the go through the day, supervising construction sites and field work in the village.

She also ruffled quite a few feathers by doing away with closed-door panchayat meetings. While the villagers were totally supportive of her efforts, what she came up against was the wall of red tapism that the bureaucracy put up. To quote her, 'An officer sitting across the table is not used to an assertive and much younger woman, getting things done.'[8]

She stood again for the post of sarpanch for a second term and was voted in again by the villagers. To quote her on her second term in office,

> The first tenure was more about ensuring that the basic amenities and infrastructure are in place—water, electricity, road, drainage, waste management plant etc was worked on. I thought the next tenure would be reserved for the SC/ST or OBC community, but as luck would have it, they opened it up for women. I hadn't nominated my name, but the villagers insisted that I continue. One of the key things I always wanted to do was empower them to make them realise the power of the collective, so that no matter who was in power, they would continue the drive to change. In the second tenure, my focus is on four main agendas—education, skill development, evolving agricultural practices and bringing about an ecological balance.[9]

In 2011, she came into the spotlight when she spoke at the 11th Infopoverty World Conference held at the United Nations. She had said then at the Conference,

> I want people and organisations to adopt projects in my village as often projects fail owing to lack of a local connect and that is what I am here to provide by bridging that gap. I want the conference to help bring about faster change so that this generation can enjoy that kind of life that I—and you in this audience—take for granted.[10]

During her stint as sarpanch, she also faced immense personal risk. Those she was taking on didn't hesitate to physically attack her. According to news reports, in 2014, a group of men armed with sticks, stones and iron rods, attacked her, her father and the panchayat secretary over a land dispute.[11] She stated, 'Development plans were stalled and the then establishment turned a blind eye on our woes. When I was attacked twice by the unsocial elements that were unhappy by my kind of transparent governance, the police officials did not act on my complaints. As I suffered a fracture, doctors at the local government hospitals refused to issue a medico-legal report.'[12]

Chhavi has been a spokesperson for rural empowerment the world over. An Aspen Fellow, she was also part of the World Economic Forum India Summit 2012 as the co-chair. She was given the title of 'Young Global Leader' by the World Economic Forum in 2012, conferred with the Yuva award, been listed as amongst the Young Indian Leaders by the CNN and been honoured with the 'First Ladies' title by President Ram Nath Kovind in 2018.

In 2020, she decided to bow out of village politics. During the COVID-19 lockdown, she was instrumental in initiating online classes for girl students in Soda, creating online learning circles, and training first teachers and then students to use technology. During her stint as sarpanch of Soda, she not only proved that women can take charge in male-dominated and tradition-driven roles and places, but inspired other women to stand up for their electoral rights and be counted as change-makers.

NOTES

1 'Meet India's First Woman Sarpanch: Chhavi Rajawat, Who Quit Her Corporate Career to Uplift a Village in Rajasthan', Yahoo! https://www.yahoo.com/news/meet-indias-first-woman-sarpanch-chhavi-rajawat-who-quit-her-corporate-career-to-uplift-a-village-in-rajasthan-090434728.html. Accessed on 17 January 2022.

2. Binjal Shah, 'This "jeans-clad" city-girl used her MBA and corporate career to become the sarpanch of her village', *OutLook Business Wow*, https://wow.outlookbusiness.com/chhavi-rajawat/. Accessed on 16 January 2022.
3. 'Local babus want me to fail, I won't give up, asserts MBA sarpanch Chavvi Rajawat,' *The Economic Times*, 8 April 2012, https://economictimes.indiatimes.com/news/politics-and-nation/Local-babus-want-me-to-fail-I-wont-give-up-asserts-MBA-sarpanch-Chavvi-Rajawat/articleshow/12577831.cms. Accessed on 17 January 2022.
4. 'Meet India's First Woman Sarpanch: Chhavi Rajawat, Who Quit Her Corporate Career to Uplift a Village in Rajasthan', Yahoo! https://www.yahoo.com/news/meet-indias-first-woman-sarpanch-chhavi-rajawat-who-quit-her-corporate-career-to-uplift-a-village-in-rajasthan-090434728.html. Accessed on 17 January 2022.
5. Ainee Nizami, 'Here's Why You Need to Know the Story of Chhavi Rajawat, India's Youngest Village Sarpanch', *iDiva*, 8 March 2017, https://www.idiva.com/career/advice/heres-why-you-need-to-know-the-story-of-chhavi-rajawat-indias-youngest-village-sarpanch/17030648. Accessed on 17 January 2022.
6. Binjal Shah, 'This "jeans-clad" city-girl used her MBA and corporate career to become the sarpanch of her village', *OutLook Business Wow*, https://wow.outlookbusiness.com/chhavi-rajawat/. Accessed on 16 January 2022.
7. Ibid.
8. Chavvi Bhatia, 'Chhavi Rajawat's next aim: do away with mrityu bhoj', *DNA India*, 14 April 2017, https://www.dnaindia.com/delhi/report-chhavi-rajawat-s-next-aim-do-away-with-mrityu-bhoj-2401375. Accessed on 17 January 2022.
9. 'Grassroots level work is the key: Chhavi Rajawat', *The Bridge Chronicle*, https://www.thebridgechronicle.com/art-culture/grassroots-level-work-key-chhavi-rajawat-6107. Accessed on 17 January 2022.

10. 'MBA sarpanch Chhavi Rajawat dazzles at UN meet', *The Economic Times*, 28 March 2011, https://economictimes.indiatimes.com/news/politics-and-nation/mba-sarpanch-chhavi-rajawat-dazzles-at-un meet/articleshow/7798549.cms?utm_source=contentofinterest&utm_medium=text&utm_campaign=cppst. Accessed on 17 January 2022.
11. 'Sarpanch Chhavi Rajawat attacked over land dispute, seven arrested', *The Times of India*, 8 July 2019, https://timesofindia.indiatimes.com/city/jaipur/Sarpanch-Chhavi-Rajawat-attacked-over-land-dispute-seven-arrested/articleshow/38003327.cms. Accessed on 17 January 2022.
12. 'Chhavi Rajawat, MBA sarpanch from Rajasthan inspires all', *Hindustan Times*, 21 January 2015, https://www.hindustantimes.com/punjab/chhavi-rajawat-mba-sarpanch-from-rajasthan-inspires-all/story-wDjikdmZ8F48ei6VBcwYaM.html. Accessed on 17 January 2022.

16

KARNAM MALLESWARI

FIGHTING IRON WITH IRON

This story begins in a small village of Andhra Pradesh in the 1980s and goes to the podium of the 2000 Sydney Olympics, a journey spanning thousands of kilometres. It is the story of sweat, blood and tears, the story of sheer grit and determination. Karnam Malleswari, born on 1 June 1975, in Voosavanipeta village, was a feisty one. One of five sisters, she was barely in class 5 when she began bunking the last class of the school day, which was physical education, to wander around the village.

In the course of her wanderings, she came across a local gymnasium where some men were lifting weights. It fascinated her and she stopped to watch them for a while. She decided to become a weightlifter. The young Karnam marched up to the owner and trainer at the small gym and declared her intention to become a weightlifter. The coach thought that she wouldn't have the physical strength needed, that she was too scrawny. She went away smarting from the rejection. She decided she would train to become a weightlifter. Along with some of her friends, Karnam began scouting around for a place, any place, with equipment she could use to train with. They found a disused gym, a place which had gone to seed. This dilapidated space is where Karnam Malleswari, India's first woman to win an individual medal at the Olympics, would begin her journey.

Her father worked in the Railways and her mother was a housewife. Word got around that the young Karnam was busy lifting weights during the time she was supposed to be at school. Her mother, wonderfully forward thinking for the times, was very supportive about it. Her father worried about it affecting her studies. She would begin training formally in weightlifting when she was barely 12, under Coach Neelamshetty Appanna.[1]

The relatives were detractors. Who will marry girls who lift weights? they asked her parents. She recalls her parents being invested in their daughters' sports careers, they allowed their girls to go to camp at a time when most parents wouldn't have allowed it, especially for a sport like weightlifting. Perhaps this came from the fact that her father himself had been a college-level football player and valued sports, encouraging his daughters too in their pursuit of a sport of their choice.

Her father was very insistent that his daughters did not neglect their education for sports. All five daughters would eventually pump iron professionally, but Karnam was the one to bring laurels, not just for her family and village but also the country. Karnam's rise in the weightlifting circuit was meteoric. She began her journey in competitive weightlifting in 1990, when she joined the national camp and four years later, she was a world champion in the 54-kg category.[2]

Her moment of reckoning came when India's Russian weightlifting coach spotted her when she had accompanied her sister Krishna Kumari, who was training at a national camp in Bangalore in preparation for the 1990 Asian Games. Karnam had not competed so far, not even at the state level. The Russian coach got talking with her. On learning that she had been training by herself, he asked her to show them her skills. He recommended her to the director of the institute. She would train under the Russian coach for almost a year, it was the soundest grounding she would receive in the technicalities of weightlifting.[3]

Malleswari's first junior nationals in 1990 at Udaipur saw her break nine national records whilst competing in the 52-kg category. In 1991, she won a silver at the senior nationals staged in Ambala. It was a sign of things to come. From 1993, she began making her mark on the world stage. In the period from 1993 to 1998, she would win four World Championship medals and two Asian Games medals. In 1993, she won bronze at the World Championships in Melbourne. She was competing in the 54-kg category. She would go back to her village after winning the bronze, and meet her first coach, it was an emotional reunion.[4] In 1994, at the Istanbul World Championships, she won a gold and with it became the first Indian woman to win a gold medal at the World Championships. In the same year, she won a silver at the Hiroshima Asian Games. In 1995, she retained her gold at the World Championships in Guangzhou. In 1996, she won a bronze at the World Championships at Guangzhou.

The 2000 Olympics at Sydney was the first edition where women's weightlifting was introduced. She was told to move from the 63-kg weight category to the 69-kg, a category she had never competed earlier internationally. There wasn't much hope or expectations from her; of the 42-strong media contingent that had accompanied the Indian delegation to the Olympics, only four came to cover her event, but she surprised everyone by winning the bronze.[5] Karnam Malleswari would be the only athlete in a 65-member Indian contingent to win a medal. She still rues the gold that slipped her by, but cherishes the bronze she had to settle for.

After her victory, it took 12 years for the next Indian woman athlete to win an individual medal at the Olympics and 20 years for the next individual medal by a woman in weightlifting, with Mirabai Chanu winning a silver at the 2020 Tokyo Olympics. Karnam was the one who shattered the glass ceiling, and since then, Mary Kom, Saina Nehwal, P.V. Sindhu, Sakshi Malik, Mirabai Chanu and Lovlina Borgohain have all won Olympic medals for the country. Twenty years on, people are yet to grasp the enormity of Karnam's achievement.

Sydney 2000 would be her final moment on the podium. The sudden demise of her father just before the 2002 Commonwealth Games in Manchester left her emotionally distraught and incapable of participating. At the 2004 Athens Summer Olympics, she suffered a back injury which compelled her to retire from competitive sport.

In 1995, she was awarded the Rajiv Gandhi Khel Ratna Award, India's highest sporting honour, and in 1999, the Padma Shri award. In 1997, she got married to a fellow weightlifter, Rajesh Tyagi and had a son in 2001. Now retired from sports, she seeks to give back through an academy for female weightlifters she is setting up in Yamunanagar (Haryana). According to her website, the K. Malleswari Foundation was to be the first women weightlifting, fitness and wellness non-governmental organization in India, registered in Delhi in 2017. She is employed at the Food Corporation of India as chief general manager (General Administration). She was also recently appointed the vice chancellor of the forthcoming Delhi Sports University.

There was also to be a biopic on her life, which she is clear will not be a love story. It will be about her entire journey, right from the start till the point where her back injury compelled her to retire from the sport.[6] This biopic has apparently been put on the back burner for a while, although hers is definitely a compelling story that needs to be told on the big screen.

Excerpts from a conversation with her:

As a young girl, how did you and your sisters decide to take up weightlifting as a sport, given that it is traditionally considered to be a male sport? How did you first come across this sport and what was it that appealed to you about it?

This goes back over 35 years ago, to Andhra Pradesh. I was in class 5, and school was from 8.30 a.m. to 3.30 p.m. The last period was sports education and I would invariably bunk it. I quite enjoyed sports such as javelin, which were more popular, but I had no awareness about weightlifting as such. I would pass a gym on my way to school and see those inside training with weights. I think when I was in class six, I went inside and asked the coach to train me. You have to keep in mind that I was very thin and tiny at the time. Naturally, he took one good look at me and told me there was no way I could become a weightlifter. I was extremely hurt and upset. *How could someone else decide what I could be good at*? I thought to myself. I think I must have been 10 or 11 at the time. I went every day after school and watched them train, and after a point, I thought to myself, *I want to try this out myself. Where can I do it?* Now, near a pond there was a rundown gym, a small 25 ft x 25 ft room. The owner of that gym had a daughter who studied in my school and she heard about my search for a space in which to train and told me I could use that space. I was overjoyed. She brought the key with her one day and we skipped the last period of the day to go there. I would copy whatever I had seen the others doing at the gym. It was risky, the roof could fall in, the equipment was old and disused, but all these thoughts never crossed my mind. I had absolutely no idea that there could be serious injuries if I did this training without proper supervision. I wanted to do it so I just went ahead and did it. I didn't really think of the consequences, it didn't even occur to me that if I did something wrong, it could result in a serious injury. I just watched what the others were doing and went and imitated them.

You were one of five sisters, and you and your sisters trained in weightlifting. Could you tell us something about how your parents were open-minded enough to let you all train in this sport, and how they supported you despite the financial burden they may have faced?

Well, someone told my parents about what I was doing. My older sister was also training in weightlifting and my parents were surprisingly very supportive of this. My father did worry and insist that we also focus on our studies, but my mother was very cool. It's okay, she would say, do it if you want to. My father was a Railway police employee and the salary, as you can imagine, wasn't enough for a large family. He also had other family responsibilities: two brothers to get settled, two sisters to get married off and our school expenses; naturally, there was a limit on how much he could afford for our training and diet.

Your mother has been one of the main forces behind your getting into weight training. Could you tell us more about her and how she influenced you?

My mother was a very progressive thinker. She was not educated, she came from a small village in Andhra Pradesh, she was married early and had five daughters, but to me, she is the biggest role model I've ever had. She was very progressive for the time, especially given the fact that she came from a small village, was not educated and didn't have much exposure to sports. Despite her limited resources, my mother managed to feed us well enough so we could pursue this sport. And there were always relatives who would visit and make comments such as: What about their marriage? Who will want to get married to a weightlifter? Such remarks didn't faze my mother at all. She always said, whatever you want to do, do it from your heart and give it your 100 per cent.

You started practising at the age of 12. Could you tell us about your daily training schedule and your diet. Also, what other challenges did you encounter?

Back then, weightlifting wasn't even known as a sport, and those who did train were mainly men. Women who trained in weightlifting were very rare. We had no personal equipment, no kits, no shoes, no belts. We trained on mud floors. Our barbell would curve and we would just straighten it and continue training. Those were simpler times. We didn't have the kind of support that athletes get these days. No protein supplements, no nutritionist-prescribed diet. My mother made sure my diet, on our limited means, was highly nutritious and strengthening. I had a lot of ragi custard, dals and dahi. We had a patch of garden in our residential quarters allotted to my father where we grew spinach, drumsticks and other seasonal vegetables. Our diet was natural and wholesome, and most importantly, cheap. Fruits, vegetables, cereals and pulses, we had it all. There was no funding for specialized diets back then, we ate what we could afford. We trained almost 12 hours a day sometimes. It was like one had to constantly keep upping one's target. I had trained myself mentally to focus on my target, every night before going to bed I would determine the achievements of the day and focus on my target for the next meet.

Can you tell us about the Sydney 2000 experience, your reaction to the tournament, the challenges, the emotional highs and lows?

For Sydney I was 100 per cent ready. We had trained for 10 to 12 hours every single day. Our day started at 5.30 a.m. and we would continue to train till 8.30 a.m, after which we would take a short break. We would them resume training at 10.00 a.m. right till 1.00 p.m. After lunch, we would start practising at 4.00 p.m. and continue till 8.30 p.m. It was a relentlessly tough training. I had done the hard work, now was the time to deliver. Of course, there was pressure to deliver not just for those who had believed in me and supported me all these years, but also for myself. On the day of my event, I prayed to my Ganesha idol and offered some flowers, went to the competition venue, gave my body weight, waited for my recovery, ate a bit, rested and kept my mind as clear as I could.

We had a Russian coach and an Indian coach, and our job was to follow what they told us to do, they would do all the analysing of our competitors: their strengths, their weaknesses. We were not really aware of our competitors. I had prepared for a gold, I had worked hard for that. I hadn't gone there for a bronze; I was capable of winning a gold. That's why it still rankles, I lost the gold because of a miscalculation. A girl won an Olympic medal. It shocked everyone.

When you won the Olympic medal, what were the thoughts going through your mind at the moment?

The feeling when you stand on the podium at the international level is incomparable. The pride, the joy, the years of struggle and hard work, they're all vindicated in that one moment, it is something one cannot explain. Only those who have been there, have stood on the podium at that moment can understand what that means to a sportsperson.

What do you think women weightlifters in India need to win at international podiums?

Back then, cricket was all important, and there wasn't much awareness about other sports. For the first time, an Indian woman had won a medal at the Olympics but not many people understood how important that achievement was. Honestly, I don't think people still understand what a great achievement it was back then. You have to become iron, make yourself iron in order to fight with iron every day. It was always a struggle. Whatever one did, one did on one's own. At that time, there wasn't enough support from the government, there wasn't as much focus on sports as there is today. Of course, we went to camp at the SAI [Sports Authority of India] in Patiala and Bangalore, and we trained on our own, but things have changed now. Back then, weightlifting was never considered an important sport, it didn't get as much attention.

How do you think motherhood has changed you or impacted your training as a sportswoman?

I believe in handling everything I have to do in all my roles to the best of my capacity: whether at my job, whether as a mother or as a housewife, or whether as a sportsperson. I believe that whatever you do, you must give it your 100 per cent.

As someone who has retired from a competitive, international-level sport, what is it that you miss most about your training days and how do you give back to young girls and women who would like to take up this sport?

We have a lot of talent in India and the raw talent in weightlifting comes from the grass-root level. They have a hunger to achieve, a hunger to prove themselves. But they come from impoverished families; how can their families invest in their training and nutrition when they barely have enough to survive? You won't find weightlifting as a sport in friendly tournaments or showcase events. It is rough and gritty, it is a sport that only those under dire circumstances take up. By doing well in sports they can uplift themselves and their families from dire poverty. Our girls are doing so well, it is the girls who are keeping our hopes alive in the international arena.

Whatever your dreams or your goals for yourself, be very clear about what you want to achieve. Define them. In life, discipline is very important, as is focus and concentration. You will have detractors telling you that you can't achieve it, that you're a girl, that you cannot do what you want to do. Don't set out to prove them wrong, set out to make your dreams come true, to achieve the goals you set for yourself. The girls in Indian sports are proving themselves across disciplines. We need to get the equipment and training to deserving sportswomen who don't have access to them. During our time, we just had NIS [National Institute of Sports] Patiala and now we have so many more options for deserving sportspersons. Today, the government is a lot more supportive, our sports minister is very proactive in addressing all our requirements and even the private sector is supporting them. If I could do it, if I could win an Olympic medal back then, a young girl from a small village, with no backing, no background in sports, anyone with talent and determination can. I promise that one of my students will bring home the Olympic gold in weightlifting that I missed out on.

NOTES

1. Nicolai Nayak, 'Karnam Malleswari interview: "That a girl could win an Olympic medal came as a shock to everyone"', *Scroll.in*, 4 May 2020, https://scroll.in/field/960674/karnam-malleswari-interview-that-a-girl-could-win-an-olympic-medal-came-as-a-shock-to-everyone. Accessed on 17 January 2022; Somak Adhikari, 'Lifting Weights in a Thatched Hut to Being Our 1st Female Olympic Medallist: Karnam's Story Is Inspiring', https://www.indiatimes.com/sports/from-lifting-weights-in-a-thatched-hut-to-being-india-s-first-female-olympic-medallist-karnam-malleswari-s-story-is-one-of-determination-378400.html. Accessed on 17 January 2022.
2. 'Karnam Malleswari's bronze at Sydney 2000 lifts Indian women up', https://olympics.com/en/featured-news/karnam-malleswari-india-weightlifting. Accessed on 18 January 2022.
3. Nicolai Nayak, 'Karnam Malleswari interview: "That a girl could win an Olympic medal came as a shock to everyone"', *Scroll.in*, 4 May 2020, https://scroll.in/field/960674/karnam-malleswari-interview-that-a-girl-could-win-an-olympic-medal-came-as-a-shock-to-everyone. Accessed on 17 January 2022.
4. 'Karnam Malleswari's bronze at Sydney 2000 lifts Indian women up', https://olympics.com/en/featured-news/karnam-malleswari-india-weightlifting. Accessed on 18 January 2022.

5. Sanjeev Anand, 'Karnam Malleswari: The forgotten sports story awaiting the silver screen', *Sportskeeda*, 16 May 2018, https://www.sportskeeda.com/weight-lifting/one-forgotten-sport-story-awaiting-the-silver-screen. Accessed on 17 January 2022.
6. Ibid.

17

SHAILAJA TEACHER
VIRUS SLAYER

In her starched cotton sarees, hair tied back matter of factly and spectacles perched firmly on the bridge of her nose, Shailaja Teacher, as Shailaja K.K. is popularly known, is an unlikely hero, one who got thrust into the limelight during the COVID-19 pandemic.

Born on 20 November 1956 to K. Kundan and K.K. Shantha, she is originally from the Kannur district of Kerala. The influence of her family, specifically her maternal grandmother M.K. Kalyani, as well as her grand uncles led her into the communist ideology. Her maternal great-grandfather was a supervisor on a British-owned tea estate and the family was amongst the wealthiest in the district. They went through hard times though when her grandmother, M.K. Kalyani, was widowed at a young age. Shailaja grew up watching her grandmother, a respected social worker, campaign against untouchability. Her grandmother was often called upon to help resolve disputes and she was so highly respected in the village of Iritty that not only was she sought to intercede in village matters but even given a chair at the head of the proceedings. The young Shailaja was in awe of the respect her grandmother commanded, even the alcoholics in the village were afraid of her grandmother.

In an interview to *The News Minute*, she recollects being raised by three matriarchs: her grandmother, her mother and her maternal aunt.[1] This early interest and involvement in politics can be attributed to the family influence, as her son reveals, in an interview to *Gulf News*. 'She was born into a political family. Her great-grandmother was a popular social worker at the time of the formation of the communist party in India.'[2]

A good and sincere student, she graduated in science from the Pazhassi Raja NSS College in Mattannur and completed her bachelor's degree from the Visvesvaraya College in 1980. While in college, she had joined the Students' Federation of India, later to be called the Democratic Youth Federation of India, a student wing associated with the Communist Party of India (Marxist), CPI(M). It was here that she met her husband, K. Bhaskaran. She was a member of the committee, while he was the district committee president. On 19 April 1981, they got married and moved close to Pazhassi school in Mattannur. Her husband taught in this school until he retired from there as headmaster.

The couple has two sons. After completing her BEd, she took up a science teacher's job in Sivapuram High School in Kannur while continuing to be active in local party politics. She rose through the ranks quickly, thanks to her hard work, bolstered by her good oratory skills, her ability to connect with people and empathize with their concerns and work towards resolving their issues. She was the Central Committee Member of the CPI(M), the Janadhipathya Mahila Association's state secretary and was also elected to the Koothuparamba and Peravoor constituencies in 1996 and 2006, respectively. She represented both these constituencies in the Kerala Legislative Assembly. In her first stint after being elected as a Member of the Legislative Assembly (MLA) in 1996, she took leave from her teaching job. However, in 2004, she took voluntary retirement to focus completely on politics. She would win from Peravoor in 2006, lose the seat in 2011 to the Congress and win Koothuparamba in 2016, after which she was made health minister in the Pinarayi state government.

The 'teacher' appended to her name comes from her being popularly known as Shailaja Teacher from her teaching days. To her work as a minister, she brought the scientific temperament that comes from the territory of having been a science teacher. The background in science and the scientific temperament would come in handy when dealing with deadly viruses and a global, once-in-a-century pandemic in her political career, but more on that later. One of her colleagues at the Sivapuram Higher Secondary School in the 1990s recounts an incident when a girl student began behaving strangely in class. Back then, there was strong belief in ghosts and possessions, and all the teachers in the school wondered how they were to handle a possessed student, but Shailaja Teacher was clear that the child needed to see a psychiatrist and convinced the parents that they needed to take her to a mental health specialist rather than an exorcist. Her grounding in science showed itself in the way she handled first the Nipah virus crisis in Kerala in 2018 and after that, the COVID-19 pandemic. This is when she got the nickname 'Virus Slayer'.

In fact, so inspirational was her response to the Nipah virus as health minister of Kerala that a movie was made on it, titled, rather self explanatorily, *Virus*.[3]

She was elected to the Kerala Legislative Assembly from the Koothuparamba constituency of the Kerala State Assembly, and was one of the two women ministers in the first Cabinet of Pinarayi Vijayan.[4] In the second Cabinet, she was dropped from the ministry, thanks to a rule set by the party to have fresh faces as ministers and former journalist Veena George took over as the health minister. K.K. Shailaja would now serve as the party whip in the state assembly.

Apart from her political successes, she was also the editor of the Shylaja Mahila Association's Shrine Mahila Association, the chief editor of *Sthree Sabdam*, a district secretary, state secretary and secretary of the All India Democratic Women's Association.

She has also authored two books, *Indian Varthamanavum Sthreesamoohavum* (Chintha Publishers, 2014) and *China Rashtram, Rashtreeyam, Kazhchakal* (Chintha Publishers, 2015), both in her mother tongue, Malayalam.

In her term as health minister, she focused on setting up a robust and proactive healthcare system in the state. Hers was a baptism by fire when she was first given the state health portfolio with the Nipah virus outbreak coming into Kerala. During the Nipah outbreak, she herself went to the village which was the focal point of the Nipah outbreak to convince the villagers not to flee the village. She told *The Guardian*, 'I rushed there with my doctors, we organised a meeting in the panchayat [village council] office and I explained that there was no need to leave, because the virus could only spread through direct contact.'[5]

Nipah was training ground for COVID-19, which was yet to come. There were some similarities between the Nipah outbreak and COVID-19, although the scale of both was vastly different. There were important lessons learnt from earlier outbreaks like chikungunya, H1N1 flu and finally the Nipah outbreak of 2018. The Kerala Health Ministry, under the leadership of Shailaja Teacher, set up an aggressive protocol of testing, contact tracing and hospitalization, and finally the total death toll from the Nipah virus was below 20. The Nipah outbreak was a 'big lesson,' she says, which came in handy when the COVID-19 pandemic hit us. She had been tracking the news that was filtering in from Wuhan. On 20 January 2020, she called one of her deputies who had a medical background. She asked him if this dangerous new virus in China could come to India, specifically to Kerala. Most certainly, he had replied. What she also realized was that there were many students from Kerala in Wuhan, and the state was also one that had a lot of expatriates, with many in the Gulf countries. These people, numbering over six lakh, would definitely return if the virus was to spread, and the government needed to be prepared for all eventualities.

Barely three days after she had read up about this new virus, Shailaja Teacher had her rapid response team in place and already had the first meeting with the team. On 24 January 2020, the very next day after the first meeting, she had the team set up a control room and instructed all the medical officers in the 14 districts of the state to set up similar control rooms. On 27 January, the first case landed in Kerala via a flight from Wuhan. Thanks to her foresight, Kerala had also put in place the World Health Organization's recommendations of the test, trace, isolate and support protocol and was implementing it strictly. They had a central control room, isolation and home quarantine facilities, and sufficient stocks of N95 masks as well as personal protective equipment (PPE) kits. The passengers coming off the flight from Wuhan were checked. Those who had a fever were isolated, the rest sent into home quarantine, with enough information about the restrictions they had to maintain. Pamphlets stating the dos and don'ts were printed in Malayalam for distribution. Three days after the flight landed, they confirmed India's first COVID-19 patient on 30 January 2020, a student who had come back home from Wuhan in China, where it had all began.

They faced a crisis at the end of February 2020, when a family returning from a trip to Italy did not disclose their travel history and went home without adhering to the isolation-quarantine protocols. When the medical teams found a case of COVID-19 and traced it back to this family, the infected had already come in contact with hundreds of people. Each person was tracked down by the team through an all-out media and social media publicity blitzkrieg and all the contacts were placed in quarantine. Her focus now was on the large number of expatriates returning from the Middle East, and to put them in quarantine and home isolation depending on the status of each person. On 24 March, all flights in and out of India had been shut down and the entire nation was in lockdown.

One of the students who had come back from Wuhan and tested positive for COVID-19 spoke about how Shailaja Teacher herself called and wished them a speedy recovery. The husband of the nurse who passed away from Nipah went on record to say how Shailaja Teacher had been like a family member to them when they were bereaved. The human touch has been evident in the way the COVID-19 crisis has been handled in Kerala. Mid-day meals were delivered to students at their homes after schools were shut down, ration kits delivered to those in home quarantine, prisoners given the task of stitching masks and public companies roped in to make sanitizers.[6]

The country, she feels, needs to invest more in public-sector health infrastructure. To quote her from *The Week*,

> Kerala's strength lies in the strong foundation of the public health system, laid in 1957. In the last four years, our focus has been on transforming primary health centres (PHCs) into family health centres. Our taluk hospitals have been bought advanced machines, high-tech buildings are under construction in district hospitals. Our medical colleges have been upgraded with the latest machines, multi-specialty blocks and ICUs. This helped a lot during the corona crisis.[7]

Her efforts in containing the spread of COVID-19 in Kerala received much international acclaim. In June 2020, she was invited as a speaker to the UN Public Service Day, a function held to celebrate public servants working on the frontline of the COVID-19 pandemic. She was featured on BBC News along with South Korea's Jung Eun-Kyeong and China's Sun Chunlan, Chen Wei, Li Lanjuan, Ai Fen and Xie Linka as the women who were at the forefront of the battle against coronavirus. *Vogue* magazine also featured her as a 'Corona Warrior'.

While she may no longer be the health minister of Kerala, she continues to inspire young women looking for role models in the field of public health and leadership. She knows that the virus is not done with humankind yet. To quote her, 'The [corona]virus has become a global threat. It is with collective effort that we could fight this. The job is not done.'[8]

NOTES

1. Dhanya Rajendran, 'The making of KK Shailaja: From school teacher to Kerala minister', *The News Minute*, 18 March 2021, https://www.thenewsminute.com/article/making-kk-shailaja-school-teacher-kerala-minister-145473. Accessed on 17 January 2022.
2. Sajila Saseendran, 'Meet the UAE resident whose mother is leading Kerala's coronavirus battle', *Gulf News*, 26 April 2020, https://gulfnews.com/uae/meet-the-uae-resident-whose-mother-is-leading-keralas-coronavirus-battle-1.71186519. Accessed on 17 January 2022.
3. Shriti Ganguly, '"Virus": A Fitting Ode to Kerala's Battle Against the 2018 Nipah Outbreak', *The Wire*, 1 June 2020, https://thewire.in/film/2019-film-virus-nipah-kerala. Accessed on 18 January 2022.
4. K K Shailaja Teacher: Biography, https://www.oneindia.com/politicians/k-k-shailaja-teacher-3592.html. Accessed on 18 January 2022.
5. Laura Spinney, 'The coronavirus slayer! How Kerala's rock star health minister helped save it from Covid-19', *The Guardian*, 14 May 2020, https://www.theguardian.com/world/2020/may/14/the-coronavirus-slayer-how-keralas-rock-star-health-minister-helped-save-it-from-covid-19. Accessed on 18 January 2022.
6. Miriam Chandy, '"Corona Slayer In God's Own Country": How Shailaja Teacher Is Tackling Pandemic', *The Logical Indian*, 14 May 2020, https://thelogicalindian.com/story-feed/awareness/kk-shailaja-kerala-covid-19-pandemic-20775. Accessed on 18 January 2022.

7. Cithara Paul, 'Kerala health minister invited to speak at UN event', *The Week*, 23 June 2020, https://www.theweek.in/news/india/2020/06/23/kerala-health-minister-invited-to-speak-at-un-event.html. Accessed on 18 January 2022.
8. Aekta Kapoor, 'Humble Roots to Global Fame, Covid Warrior KK Shailaja's Extraordinary Story', *She the Gaze*, 2 October 2020, https://eshe.in/2020/10/02/kk-shailaja/. Accessed on 18 January 2022.

18

HIMA DAS

WINGS ON HER FEET

There's an iconic photograph that encapsulates Hima Das. Her eyes are twinkling with joy, she's holding the Indian flag aloft behind her, an Assamese gamusa (a piece of red and white cloth, a cultural identifier) draped around her neck. It had been a long journey from the muddy fields she started training in back in her village near Dhing, in Assam. Back then, she ran barefoot. Basic running shoes was an indulgence, branded shoes were a dream. She ran first for her school, then her district and when she reached the state level, she got her first pair of real sports shoes. They were an ordinary pair of running shoes, but she wrote 'Adidas' on them, along with its logo. One day, she would be able to buy herself a pair of Adidas shoes. Years later, Adidas would name an entire line of shoes after her, but she had to earn that, through struggle, sweat and blood.

This is the story of Hima Das, who rose from obscurity to international acclaim, a journey that took her from a small village in Assam to the podium of international athletic meets.

Born on 9 January 2000 into a family with very humble circumstances, Hima grew up in the Kandhulimari village, part of a sprawling joint family of traditional farmers, with over 17 members living together. The closest town for the young Hima to study in was Dhing, where she attended the Dhing Public High School. One of the first things she did as a young girl was to run. She never stopped running: in school races, across tracks in Assam and in coaching camps. She got her athletic genes from her father, who was a former football player. 'My father would play football and that's where I got my inspiration. So initially, I started playing football like him. But then, I developed a passion for athletics. My dad's brother had three sons. I would join them whenever they played. When I started receiving training for football, there were no opportunities for women players.'[1]

While she wasn't destined to continue as a footballer, what did beckon her was running and athletics. In 2014, Shamshul Haq, a sports teacher at the Navodaya School, saw the potential in her at an inter-school running competition. He took her to meet Gauri Shankar Roy, a noted sports trainer at the Nagaon School. Roy agreed to coach her, and it was under his training and mentorship that Hima won the gold in the interdistrict running championships in 2016, barely a couple of years after she had begun. At the Assam State Championships the same year, she won a silver.[2]

She would practise in muddy fields, barefoot, waking up at the crack of dawn to run in the fields before the farmers got their cattle to graze.[3]

Roy realized that Hima had immense potential and could go far; he introduced her to coaches Nipon Das and Nabajit Malakar of the Directorate Sports and Youth Welfare in Guwahati. They recommended that she move to Guwahati to train full-time at the academy. She was barely 17 and wasn't sure if she could live alone in camp so far away from her family. She had always been surrounded by a full house in a huge, joint family. It was at this time that her father had a long conversation with her, allaying her fears and encouraging her to step out of her comfort zone. She left her home and her village and travelled all the way to Guwahati to begin training formally at the Directorate Sports and Youth Welfare. She missed home and hated being alone in a new city, but she kept soldiering on. They would wake before dawn, train and then break for lunch and some rest, only to get to training again in the evening. But here, too, in Guwahati, she would prefer to train with the boys, so she could push herself harder.

The training was relentless and excrutiatingly tough, but it got her the timings required to qualify for the Asian Youth Championships, where she came seventh. After that was the 2017 World Youth Championships in Kenya. Her coaches, Nipon and Nabajit, had both taken personal loans to finance her trip to Kenya, such was their faith in her abilities. She competed in the 200-metre sprint there and came fifth. She moved onto distance running, competing at the Patiala Federation Cup for the 400 metres. She gave her trials for the Gold Coast Commonwealth Games and, in April 2018, qualified to be part of the Indian contingent for the 2018 Commonwealth Games at Gold Coast in the 400 metres and the 4×400 metres relay. While she reached the finals in the 400 metres, she would end up finishing sixth with a timing of 51.32 seconds.

What shot Hima into the spotlight was the IAAF World U20 Championships in Finland, barely a few months after the Commonwealth Games. In July 2018, Hima took her mark at the start point in the small Finnish town of Tampere. Back in Assam, her parents were watching on their tiny television set, the room crowded, the entire village too was watching the race with bated breath. There were absolutely no expectations from Hima, she was the outlier from India. Running behind the top medal contendor, Hima produced a spectacular burst in the last 50 metres and breasted the finishing line to bag a gold. The commentator exclaimed, 'Here comes Hima Das. The Indian can see the line. She can see history. India's never won any medal in a track event. But Das has done it here!'[4]

With this incredible win, Hima had done the unthinkable. She had become the first Indian track athlete to win an international medal at a world championship. She was now the fourth Indian ever to win a medal at the Under-20 World Championships, and only the second to win a gold after Neeraj Chopra, who had won the javelin throw at Bydgoszcz (Poland) in 2016. Neeraj, of course, would go on to win the gold at the 2020 Tokyo Olympics. This was India's first-ever gold at a track event at the athletics world championships and the nation was delirious with joy.[5] As she ran around the stadium in her victory lap, the Assamese gamusa around her neck, holding the Indian Tricolor aloft, the small village she had left behind celebrated with her. Prayers were offered in thanksgiving at the local *namghar* (temple) and villagers played the dhol in a victory procession through the village. After all, a girl from their little village had won the U20 World Championships.

The photograph of her with the traditional gamusa and the Indian flag after her victory in Tampere would become iconic. It had always been precious to her, the gamusa, and the identification with Assamese pride. She was quoted saying, 'I always carry the *gamocha* with me which is my identity. I just want the people of Assam and India to bless me so that I can represent the country in more important sporting events abroad and also showcase the *gamocha* which is the pride of the people of Assam.'[6]

Later that same year, she set an Indian national record in the 400 metres with the timing of 50.79 seconds at the 2018 Asian Games in Jakarta. This timing got her the silver medal. She was part of the women's 4×400 metres relay clocking 3:28.72, which won the silver. Sadly, a false start in the 200 metres semi-final led to her being disqualified, losing out on the chance she had in the category. However, she won a silver medal as part of the 4×400 metres mixed relay, which was held for the first time at the Asian Games that year. She had been away from the country and her family for a long stint, participating in all these international events and training, and had no inclination of the popularity she had achieved back home. When she landed at the Guwahati airport, she was completely taken aback by the sheer number of people who had come to welcome her.

Further realization of how popular she had become came a few months later when the German sports brand Adidas signed an endorsement deal with her. It was an intensely emotional moment for her. Speaking about it, she said, 'Once I scribbled Adidas on my shoes, now they make them with my name.' The custom-made shoes for her by Adidas have her name on one side and the words 'Create history' on the other.[7]

Her performance in 2018 saw her being conferred with the Arjuna Award, the nation's highest award for a sportsperson, on 25 September 2018 by President Ram Nath Kovind. She was appointed the first-ever youth ambassador of UNICEF-India on 14 November 2018. The Government of Assam appointed her as Assam's brand ambassador for sports. The Bannerghatta Biological Park named a Royal Bengal tigress cub as 'Hima' to honour her.

The year 2019 continued to be peppered with medals for her. She won the 200 metres gold in Poznań Athletics Grand Prix and 200 metres gold at the Kutno Athletics Meet a few days later, both were held in Poland in July 2019. A week later, she clinched a gold in the 200 metres at the Kladno Memorial Athletics Meet and the 200 metres gold at the Tabor Athletics Meet, both in the Czech Republic. She won her fifth gold in a month at Nové Mêsto (Czech Republic) in the 400 metres. However, while she qualified for the World Athletics Championships in Doha scheduled for October 2019, she was ruled out because of a back problem that had cropped up.

She missed the Tokyo Olympics due to an injury received during training, but is upbeat and confident that she will make a comeback in the Commonwealth Games scheduled for 2022. After all, it was hope and a dream that got her so far, and it is hope and a dream that will get her to the podiums that have evaded her thus far.

NOTES

1. Barry Rodgers, 'Hima Das Is Steadily on Her Way to Making History', *Grazia*, 25 July 2019, https://www.grazia.co.in/people/hima-das-is-steadily-on-her-way-to-making-history-4064-2.html. Accessed on 18 January 2022.
2. 'Gamocha Girl', *Magzter*, 30 July 2018, https://www.magzter.com/stories/5/292003/5b51ec2318885. Accessed on 17 January 2022.
3. 'Gamocha is my identity, my soul, says Assam's Hima Das', *Northeast Now News*, 19 July 2018, https://nenow.in/northeast-news/assam/gamocha-identity-soul-says-assams-hima-das.html. Accessed on 17 January 2022.
4. 'Pause, rewind, play: "Here comes Hima Das"– when the Indian won a historic gold medal at U20 Worlds', *Scroll.in*, 12 July 2020, https://scroll.in/field/967270/pause-rewind-play-here-comes-hima-das-when-the-indian-won-a-historic-gold-medal-at-u20-worlds. Accessed on 17 January 2022.
5. Sagnik Kindu, 'IAAF World U-20 Championships 2018: India's Hima Das wins historic gold medal; watch video', *Sportskeeda*, 13 July 2018, https://www.sportskeeda.com/athletics/iaaf-world-u-20-championships-2018-india-s-hima-das-wins-historic-gold-medal-watch-video. Accessed on 17 January 2022.
6. 'Gamocha is my identity, my soul, says Assam's Hima Das', *Northeast Now News*, 19 July 2018, https://nenow.in/northeast-news/assam/gamocha-identity-soul-says-assams-hima-das.html. Accessed on 17 January 2022.
7. '"Once I scribbled Adidas on my shoes, now they make them with my name": Hima Das', *The Indian Express*, 27 April 2020, https://indianexpress.com/article/sports/sport-others/hima-das-scribbled-adidas-shoes-tells-suresh-raina-6380422/. Accessed on 17 January 2022.

19

NAINA LAL KIDWAI

SMASHING THE GLASS CEILING

As a young girl, she loved to go with her father to his office. These were special occasions, visiting the headquarters of one of the largest insurance companies in the country, located on the bustling M.G. Road in Mumbai's Fort area. It was a treat to visit his office, to sit in his swivelling leather chair, to see the awe and respect he commanded. *Someday perhaps*, she must have thought to herself, *I too will have a chair in an office like this. Someday, I too will walk the corridors of power and command the same respect my father does.*

The young girl had a regular upbringing. She went to boarding school, then to college. The seeds of the dream of earning the respect her father commanded were planted, and she grew up emulating his principles and values of hard work, fairness and humility.

Girls, especially those from North Indian families, were not expected to dream of having a career. They were allowed an education, the best the family could provide, but beyond that they were expected to toe the line, to become wives and mothers, and to be the bulwarks behind the men in their lives. That was not this young girl's dream and her dream was not in vain: she would go on to become one of the most powerful women in corporate India, the first of three women to be hired by PricewaterhouseCoopers (now PwC), the first Indian woman to graduate from Harvard Business School, the first woman to head an investment bank and then to become the chief executive officer (CEO) of a foreign or private bank in India, and the first woman to be the president of the venerable Federation of Indian Chambers of Commerce and Industry (FICCI) after 85 years of its inception. It didn't come easy, but for the young girl who dreamed on and was encouraged to achieve, the end result was anything but surprising.

Many years later, Naina Lal Kidwai is a gentle, yet formidable presence in a room when she enters. She is soft spoken and gracious, but with the assurance of one who weighs her words and uses them wisely. She is always understatedly elegant in a saree, silk or handloom cotton always, with not a hair out of place, looking as unflappable as she definitely is. It is an unflappability that comes from a lifetime of being an achiever in every sphere, one who has broken glass ceilings before the word even found its way into our everyday lexicon. It however never occurred to her that she was breaking the proverbial glass ceiling. She was simply doing what she had always wanted to do: carve her space in a corporate world that hitherto had been dominated by men, and in doing so, pave the path ahead for countless women after her. She wears her achievements lightly, with a humility that comes from within.

The young Naina was a super achiever from the time she was in school: topper, school captain, college president. She came from a family that was rather well established. Her maternal grandfather, Karam Chand Thapar, supported the struggle for India's freedom from the British and founded the Thapar Group. Her father, Surendr Lall, was the CEO of one of the biggest insurance companies in the country, and her mother, Prem Mohini Lall, was a social worker. They had two daughters, Naina and Nonita.[1] Born in Calcutta in 1957, Naina grew up in an atmosphere that was conducive to learning with both her parents setting a great store by education and achievement. They lived in Mumbai and the influences at home—of their father's love of nature and life lessons firmly grounded in the teachings of the Bhagavad Gita, and their mother's strong family values and spiritual pursuits—were a great influence on Naina and Nonita. Conversations at home were about the corporate world, golf and wildlife. Both sisters today are at the top of their game. Naina, with all the accolades she has achieved in the corporate world, and the glass ceilings she shattered in the course of her career, is also a Padma Shri awardee. Nonita is one of the country's leading golfers, having represented India in international tournaments and now a renowned golf coach and an Arjuna awardee. Both sisters and their families are avid wildlife enthusiasts.

When she was 11, her parents decided to send her to a boarding school for a better all-round education. She was shifted from Walsingham House School in Bombay to Loreto Convent, Tara Hall, in Shimla. It was here that she would find someone who would go on to become one of the early influences on her life, an Irish nun and her teacher, Sister Cyril Mooney. Loreto also brought another life-long influence and a dear friend into her life, the acclaimed filmmaker, Mira Nair, who was a classmate. They would go through their lives with incredible parallels. To quote Mira from an interview, 'In our case, it's quite amazing. We were born in the same year, went to the same school, both ended up at Harvard, were married in the same year, and our kids were born a couple of months apart.' Nair says Naina was always destined for great things. 'When I first met Naina,' Mira said in the same interview, 'She was already something of a legend. She'd stand first every year, was a brilliant debater, and represented the school in every sport.'[2]

The quintessential golden girl at school, Naina was a class topper who also aced basketball and badminton to represent the school in inter-school tournaments, played lead roles in school plays and was class prefect, house captain and in her final year, the head girl. She has always been a natural leader. What she did learn from friends like Mira, though, was that being constantly competitive wasn't a good way to be. She learnt how to temper her competitive streak, and yet constantly keep challenging herself. Loreto was where she came into her own, where she developed the confidence in her abilities, learnt how to be part of a team and yet shine, and how to present her arguments through public speaking and representing the school in debates, something that proved immensely helpful through her corporate career.

She continued being an achiever through college. At Lady Shri Ram College, New Delhi, she graduated with Economics as her major in 1977 and lived up to the golden girl reputation. She was the president of the students' union and the organizer of the college's first annual all-India intercollegiate festival, a tradition which continues till today. She had to organize the funding for the event and the trophies, and persuade the college principal to allow the boys' colleges on campus so they could participate—a first for the college!

Naturally, when she graduated, she wasn't going to be content doing the easy thing, something that everyone else was doing. She was keen to study business management in the United States; her father though had set his heart on her becoming a chartered accountant (CA). Besides, at the time, people went abroad to study only after a few years of work experience under their belt. She drew inspiration from her friend from school, Mira Nair, who had gone to Harvard for her undergraduate studies. *If she could do it*, Naina thought, *I should at least try*. And she looked at the boys around her who were going abroad for their postgraduate studies and thought to herself, *How am I any less than them?* She was smarter than them, better at studies too, so why wasn't she being allowed to go when they were?[3]

Consequently, she applied to PwC for the position of articled trainee. This was when she first came across the glass ceiling. While her interview went well and she had all the qualifications required for the job, she was told that the firm did not hire women. She was shocked, but Naina being Naina wouldn't accept no for an answer. She kept calling and asking and getting people to intervene till finally the firm relented. They reviewed their recruiting policy and she was finally offered an internship there, along with two other women. This was her first step into corporate India, and she was already smashing the glass ceiling at the entry level itself, and by doing so opening the doors for other women as well. In interviews years later, she would say that in retrospect, she understood the firm's concerns. Sending an audit team out with a woman in an all-male environment to audit factories in the hinterlands for a couple of months could have been a legitimate concern.[4] The good news is the firm today has a near 50/50 ratio of men and women. Her three years at PwC were invaluable. Despite the initial hurdle in getting in, Naina was determined to learn all she could from the opportunities the training presented.

In her third year at PwC, she picked up the threads of her ambition to get an MBA from a university abroad. Her extended family was quite against the idea, but her parents relented and told her they would allow her to go only if she made it into one of the top three colleges in the US. She applied to both Harvard and Wharton for their MBA programme and was overjoyed when she was selected for the one at Harvard. It was a struggle to be allowed to do an MBA abroad—something most families wouldn't think twice about letting a son opt for. Her father was keen she complete her CA, but the date to join Harvard was two months before she was eligible to take the final exam for the CA. Naina took the hard decision to drop her CA exams and fly to the US to join her batch at Harvard Business School in September 1980. She would take her CA exams later, she promised herself and her father.

All around her, she could see boys being given the opportunities that she had to fight so hard for, and it rankled.

Besides, there were no other women she could look up to, as female role models were few and far between. She would go on, with the support of her family, to challenge male bastions, but through it all, Naina Lal Kidwai has retained that groundedness that makes her so accessible to all. It hasn't been an easy journey, but she underplays it with her signature graciousness.

Travelling to the US for the first time to live and study at Harvard was a culture shock. The youngest in her class at 23, studying at Harvard and living in the US opened up a completely new set of challenges for Naina. She had travelled abroad only once before, making the most of a Eurorail pass to see the length and breadth of Europe, learning and satiating her curiosity about different cultures she had only read about. But living alone in a foreign country was both exhilarating and intimidating. The climate and having to cope with snow and cold, shopping at the supermarket, using an ATM for the first time, managing on meagre remittances from home and a job in the library as foreign exchange remittances were permitted on a budget dictated by the Reserve Bank of India and sent out quarterly—all these were new learning experiences. Speaking up in class was a challenge too initially, one that she had to overcome.

Naina graduated from Harvard in 1982, becoming the first Indian woman to graduate from the Harvard Business School, a sad social commentary she says, given the fact that Indian men had been going to Harvard for three decades before her. Though she did receive some tempting job offers in the US, her heart was set on returning to India, because that was where the challenge lay, in making a difference. The Indian market was opening up, privatization was being ushered in, and entrepreneurship and the free market were being encouraged. She believed India was the right place to be at the time. She returned to India and joined the investment banking division at Grindlays Bank, which back then was the largest of the foreign investment banks in India. It was a tough decision, but one, which in retrospect, stood her in good stead for the landmarks she was going to achieve in her professional career. India was where the firsts were happening back then: the first listings of Indian companies abroad on the New York Stock Exchange, NASDAQ and London stock exchanges, new entrepreneurship ventures seeing the birth of information technology (IT) companies such as Infosys, setting up of Securities and Exchange Board of India (SEBI) (the regulator) and the National Stock Exchange and framing the new insider trading norms. Naina was in the thick of things. Even a small deal she closed here would have much more impact than a larger one in the US. Here was an opportunity to make a difference.

When she sat in the cabin she shared with a colleague in the Grindlays Bank office on Mumbai's M.G. Road, Fort area, the hub of the commercial centre in the city, she could look out of the window, across the road, to the building where her father had worked, the office she had visited as a child, that had first planted the desire to find her destiny in the corporate world. From 1982 to 1994, she worked at Grindlays, heading the Investment section and then setting up the global NRI services division for the retail section. Not to mention the stress of constantly being on her toes, trying to avoid a slip-up, lest the others pounced on her. She was like a goldfish in a glass bowl. Once established in her profession, she began to realize that gender didn't really matter when it came to performance. Bosses, she says, can be good or bad, whether male or female.

Naina would go on to become one of the select few powerful women to smash the glass ceiling in the male-dominated field of banking and high finance in India. She went on to head Hongkong and Shanghai Banking Corporation (HSBC) in India in 2006, thus paving the way for many to follow: Arundhati Bhattacharya of the State Bank of India, Shikha Sharma of Axis Bank, Kalpana Morparia of JP Morgan India and Chanda Kochhar of ICICI Bank.

The impeccably draped saree in tussar silk or handloom, which has become the look we associate Naina with, is something that she worked hard at. When she returned from the US, she had no clue about how to drape a saree but saw that all the women in positions of eminence, mainly in politics, wore them. She took it upon herself to wear a saree to work every day and the traditional weaves of India became a passion since.

She worked at Grindlays for 12 years and rose swiftly through the ranks. She took some hard career decisions during her stint there. She passed over a posting to Calcutta to head the investment bank for eastern India, preferring to wait for an opening to head North India as it was a bigger and a more diverse market. Her gamble paid off, and in 1987, she was appointed head of investment banking for North India. This was the ideal time to be posted in Delhi as privatizations were starting and the political capital of India was where the power deals and negotiations were happening. Naina was right in the thick of things and the Delhi branch soon overtook Bombay in terms of scale.

Her move to Delhi also led her to meeting Rashid Kidwai, the regional head of Clarion Advertising, whom she would marry. She moved back to Bombay when she was appointed the country head of the investment bank in 1989, the first woman to head an investment bank in India, she was all of 32 at the time. Her next move up the ladder would have been a foreign posting but she took a call to make her mark in India and asked for a transfer to the retail bank in Grindlays. This decision would broaden her experience base and give her the required credentials to eventually become the CEO of a bank. Soon thereafter, Bob Edgar, the then CEO of ANZ Grindlays, asked her to set up and head the global NRI services for the retail bank of Grindlays, a job profile which would necessitate her to travel to West Asia, the US, the UK, Singapore and other centres to set up new offices. On the day she was made this offer, she learnt she was pregnant. However, she decided to give it a shot, working all through her pregnancy and travelling too. She had her daughter, Kemaya, in 1991. It was a challenging time, but she was certain she could not let Bob and her organization down given the trust they had in her. And as luck would have it, Saddam Hussein's invasion of Kuwait in 1990 and India's own financial needs led to NRI money flooding into the country and NRI deposits were now over 50 per cent of the total deposits at the bank.

Naina moved to Morgan Stanley in 1994 and became the vice chairman and the head of investment banking. It was a move that catapulted her into the limelight. She was negotiating powerful and important deals in that position. She was also instrumental in taking Morgan Stanley into the partnership with Nimesh Kampani's JM Financial group of companies, thus leading to the creation of JM Morgan Stanley in 1997. In 2000, *Fortune* magazine declared her the third-most powerful woman in business in Asia and she continued to appear for many years in their international list of the Most Powerful Women in Business. *Time* magazine listed her as their 15 Global Business Influentials for 2002.

Naina moved to HSBC in 2002 as the vice chairman and managing director of HSBC Securities and Capital Markets (India), where she was in charge of the investment bank, securities trading and research. In 2004, she became its deputy CEO. In 2005, she joined the global board of Nestlé as a non-executive director where she remained for the full term of 12 years. The experience and knowledge gleaned from such a board were invaluable and supported her rise through HSBC. Soon after, she was named group general manager of the bank and CEO of HSBC in India, becoming the second woman country head in the HSBC world and only the second Indian to head HSBC in India. She also became the first woman to be at the helm of a private or foreign bank in India. In 2009, she was elevated to executive chairman for India, overseeing 35,000 people employed in the multiple businesses of HSBC in India including the two businesses she had already headed. This was in addition to asset management, a general insurance brokerage, a life insurance joint venture which she set up, and the technology and global back-office operations of the bank. She also joined the HSBC Asia-Pacific board, which was responsible for over 80 per cent of HSBC's business.

In 2006, she was in *The Wall Street Journal*'s global list of 'Women to Watch Out for'. She was awarded the Padma Shri in 2007 by President A.P.J. Abdul Kalam for her contribution to trade and industry, and in a lovely serendipitous coincidence, Sister Cyril Mooney, who had been her teacher and a strong influence from her school days, was also awarded the Padma Shri the very same day for her work educating underprivileged children.

In 2013, Naina went on to break another male bastion by being elected as the first woman president of FICCI. On this, the then Prime Minister of India, Dr Manmohan Singh, would say, 'I would like to note that FICCI is going to have its first-ever lady president... She has been an icon to many young ladies in our country and has been a role model for women to aspire to reach the top. I am sure she will steer the ship of FICCI well.'[5]

Her leadership style has always been inclusive. She believes in being respectful and fair to all and being receptive to inputs and opinions, regardless of age, gender or seniority—something she learnt from her father. She is also a firm believer in teamwork and delegation. Having climbed up the corporate ladder, she now mentors women in the corporate space to achieve their goals. Her focus is also on giving back to society. She has been engaged in social work, especially women's empowerment and the environment. She was able to deepen her understanding of climate change and water conservation through the exposure HSBC provided her at the global level. While attending the

World Economic Forum and leading their Councils on these subjects, she honed her knowledge and helped develop global frameworks for green financing with the United Nations Environment Programme (UNEP) and as a global commissioner for the New Climate Economy. She also set up the Water Mission at FICCI, an initiative that she continues to lead.

Her husband Rashid K. Kidwai, after a stellar career in marketing and advertising, was then heading an NGO called Grassroot Trading Network for Women, promoted by SEWA, and a not-for-profit organization called Digital Partners. His background in the social sector since the early 2000s provided her important insights into the social sector. They jointly set up the India Sanitation Coalition in 2014 to work on sanitation. He, sadly, passed away in 2021 from post-COVID-19-related complications.

A big nature buff, unwinding for Naina is going to wildlife sanctuaries in the country and abroad. She also has three books to her credit: *Survive or Sink, An Action Agenda for Sanitation, Water, Pollution and Green Finance* (Rupa Publications, 2018), *30 Women in Power: Their Voices, Their Stories* (Rupa Publications, 2015) and *Contemporary Banking in India* (Businessworld, 2012).

And finally, now that she's sat on her very own leather upholstered swivel chair and led organizations and achieved what she set her heart on as a young girl, she is yet not ready to rest on her laurels. Even though she retired from HSBC in 2015, she continues to be active at FICCI and as a non-executive director on global and Indian corporate boards. She has committed half her time to the non-profit sector in the areas of women's empowerment, water and sanitation, green finance and the environment, working with global think tanks and the India Sanitation Coalition, which she founded and chairs. She continues to have a very busy schedule. And in her words, 'I enjoy every minute of what I do as I have chosen to do what

I do, knowing I have the freedom today to stop doing what I don't want to do.'

Excerpts from an interview with her.

Beginning right from your childhood, what were the expectations you had from yourself, and what were the influences that shaped you when you were young?

The issue, if at all there was one, was the lack of expectations. Women, and particularly as a young girl growing up in a North Indian family, there was no expectation that I should have a career. In the early days, I was developing an interest in doing less conventional things and the first real struggle that became apparent was when I had set my heart on studying abroad. I got my undergraduate degree in economics from Lady Shri Ram College, Delhi, after which I was hell-bent on going abroad for an MBA. I went on to do my CA, but I didn't complete it because I was determined to do an MBA in one of the best schools in the US. And once I got admission, I didn't want to lose a year to give my final CA exam, knowing I could return to do it. At every stage, there wasn't wholehearted support for my decisions; education abroad wasn't seen as something important and necessary for women at that time. My uncles didn't help as they believed this was a waste of money and I should be married off! The Indians who went to Harvard Business School were typically IIT [Indian Institute of Technology] graduates who had some work experience. They went on to do their MBAs abroad and eventually settled there.

Every level was a negotiation. My father was keen that I complete my CA and take my exams. I didn't want to lose the opportunity of going to Harvard. Finally, I persuaded him that I would go to Harvard, complete my MBA and then come back and write the CA exam. Once I came back after completing my MBA and started to work in India, I had full support of my family. I could never have succeeded in balancing work and home and bringing up our daughter without the support of my mother, my mother-in-law and of course my husband. My father passed away before my daughter's first birthday; I so missed his sage advice and discussions.

You have a formidable career with a number of firsts to your credit. When you were the first woman from India at Harvard Business School, did you realize the legacy you had just built? And what were the pressures that came with these firsts that we don't often realize?

I had reason to believe that there were a few Indians who had been to Harvard before me, but it had never crossed my mind to think if any other Indian women had been there before me. It was Harvard that approached me after the term started. I was told that I am the first woman from India to be at Harvard for an MBA and they gave me a scholarship. It was their way of letting me know that they were glad. I was the youngest in my class, and I had to learn to speak up. However, adjusting was easy as language and coping with a rigorous schedule was not an issue. And then there was the excitement of being at Harvard and living in the dorm on campus which made life very simple. I had never been to America before though, and my idea of life abroad was through this one trip that I had taken to Europe. But I had the exposure to the world outside India through books, music and movies and that made the transition easier. Academically, coming from a background of economics and chartered accountancy helped, and as such I didn't have any problem coping with studies. What was hard was not coming back home for over two years as the travel was very expensive, and at that time making a call home was difficult, full of interruptions and costly.

As for the 'firsts', you don't set that as your target, you rather set out to achieve your goals and be strategic in your career choices. When I look back, I did carry the pressure of feeling I was being watched all the time, treated as a bit of a curiosity.

You chose to come back to India after Harvard, at a time when you had opportunities available to you in the US. What were your motivations to come back and were there, at that point, any doubts about whether you were making the right decision?

Coming back to India after I completed my MBA was the plan all along but just to make sure that I wasn't taking the easy way out I applied and got a couple of great jobs in Manhattan, New York. If I had wanted to work in the US, Manhattan is where I wanted to be and it was a lot more money than what I would earn in India. I thought over it for a while; it was a difficult decision. India was where the action was and also where my heart was. I was told a couple of years in the US was not going to be given credit as when I returned, I would have to start at the bottom in any case. The leading organizations those days had well-entrenched programmes where they hired management trainees and groomed them to take on leadership roles. Weighing all this, the decision to return straightaway made the most sense.

Back then, women did not choose finance and banking as a career. What was the kind of sexism you encountered when you started out and how did you deal with it?

Well, I wasn't expecting it to be otherwise. We were a handful of women in the business world and it was like if you made mistakes, we all got noticed and if you succeeded, you had to ensure that you got acknowledged. There were times when I had to have a tough discussion with the organization to make sure I got what I believed was a fair deal. In this respect, I was fortunate to start in investment banking as it is difficult to go unnoticed. It is hard for an organization to say you haven't done your bit as you shine or die depending on the deals you are working on. Yes, there were times when I had to fight to be treated fairly. One thing to be noted is also that women were in leadership positions in investment banking long before we were CEOs of banks. I was head of the largest foreign investment bank in 1989 and it took 17 years till I became the CEO of HSBC bank in 2006. At the time, there was only one other woman heading a bank, Tarjani Vakil, who had recently been appointed as head of the troubled public-sector Indian Bank.

As for discrimination, whether a man or woman, when you rise, it is normal for your peers to feel the pressure and competition. But once you establish yourself, teams want you, as you contribute to their performance. The only distinction I would draw between a man and a woman is that in the latter failures get easily noticed and they are blamed more too often. Many times, I felt that I had to deliver and not fail, not just for me but for all of womankind!

Who were the mentors and the influences that shaped and guided your path?

I had people I would go to for support and advice depending on the situation. All of them were men. I turned to different people for different things at different points. For instance, one such mentor in my career was the then CEO of ANZ Grindlays Bank, Bob Edgar, while I was heading the investment bank. After a discussion with him regarding what he believed I needed to do, I asked him if I could work in retail banking to one day head the bank. Then one fine day, he offered me a job to start NRI services for the retail bank. I had just, at the time, found out that I was pregnant and the job would include a lot of travel. With some trepidation I went to him and told him I was pregnant and I want to do the job but am not sure if I will be able to travel, given my condition. To this (after he recovered from the shock!) he just asked me, 'What would you like to do?' And I replied, 'I would like to give it a shot,' and he said, 'Let's do it, the job is yours.'

I worked my butt off as I didn't want to let him down. Many people looked out for me and sometimes it came from unexpected quarters in unexpected ways.

We have read of high-powered women in the corporate world who still need to achieve work-life balance, and the parenting guilt they deal with. I am sure you have had times when it had to be a hard call between work and home. How did you handle these situations, and how do you think women can reach this elusive balance?

I believe we have three balls that we constantly keep juggling. One is the work ball, the other is the family ball and the third one is the me ball. The work and family balls are crystal balls and we have to keep juggling them in the air and not let them fall and shatter. The me ball is a rubber ball which can be dropped from time to time. I had a very supportive husband and mother-in-law. My mom would fly down from Delhi to Mumbai whenever needed. We in India also benefit from domestic help in addition to the family network. The one thing which is not easy is the social system around us which is not as supportive of working women and is steeped in traditional beliefs. We women need to get over that feeling of guilt; of not being the perfect mother, the perfect wife, the perfect daughter and the perfect daughter-in-law. We wear ourselves down; we worry about the choices that we make. Men don't feel guilty the way we do because of society's expectations, after all they have the same kids and aged parents to look after!

You are now closely involved with social causes—the environment, sanitation, water, women's empowerment. Tell us what drives you to a cause, and compels you to take it up. What are the challenges you have faced in this journey?

Women's empowerment has always been very close to my heart and Rashid had worked with SEWA and others in this area providing me invaluable insights. I have visited many projects HSBC supported in microfinance where women self-help groups are the beneficiaries and we set up livelihood training centres for women. HSBC began to look into issues to do with the environment, and I volunteered my time towards the work they were doing. As CEO, I had a significant role in the implementation of projects related to cleaning up of water bodies and rivers, and preserving biodiversity. These learnings at the domestic and global level gave me the courage and insights to work in these areas. There is still so much that needs to be done. I have continued to work in water and founded the India Sanitation Coalition. When at international forums, India was always spoken of as an abject failure in water conservation and sanitation, and I thought I could do my bit to help the cause. We lucked out with the direction set by Prime Minister Narendra Modi and the Swachh Bharat mission helping the India Sanitation Coalition align with a huge national agenda. Challenges abound regarding funding and talent. The not-for-profit sectors require much hand-holding and personal engagement. The outcomes are slow, but it is worth every minute and every drop of blood, sweat and tears.

You have chosen to be an active mentor to many women in corporate India. What advice would you give to other women? How can women help other women to move up the corporate ladder to help redress the gender inequity we see in the workspace?

We need to get over the inhibitions we impose on ourselves, we see glass ceilings where they may not exist. We need to break through these glass ceilings. There is also a need to connect outside the work environment and also network at work. I found my participation in my investment banking days and then chairing the capital markets committee at FICCI, created work-related networks outside the office which helped my work and enabled me to contribute to building India's capital markets infrastructure and frameworks. There is an opportunity to meet other women, and to discuss leadership issues. Building and being part of networks in today's world is helpful and many companies have set up women's networks. At FICCI, we started a women corporate board initiative providing training and getting women board-ready. This also enabled a network and helped companies find their independent board members. We try to create an easy way for women to go up the ladder and achieve what they dream of. Ideally, we need an ecosystem wherein women rise to their full potential assisted by men and women at the helm.

And finally, as a woman who has shattered the glass ceiling much before the word even came into our everyday lexicon, what would you like your legacy to be?

I would like to be remembered as someone who helped others achieve their potential, their dreams. As someone who worked hard and wisely and was fair and good to work with. We all have it in us to be a winner and ensure we don't give up when developments get us down. If I can do it, then every other woman (or man) out there can do it.

NOTES

1. 'Naina Lal Kidwai: Banking on wonder women', *LiveMint*, 4 May 2018, https://www.livemint.com/Companies/u1NkBKJeXXxMzF4daVmFkL/Naina-Lal-Kidwai-Banking-on-wonder-women.html. Accessed on 17 January 2022.
2. 'Two women, two friends', *The Times of India*, 23 March 2003, https://timesofindia.indiatimes.com/Two-women-Two-friends-/articleshow/41053032.cms. Accessed on 18 January 2022.
3. 'How am I any less?' *DNA India*, 21 November 2013, https://www.dnaindia.com/lifestyle/special-how-am-i-any-less-1060702. Accessed on 17 January 2022.
4. Ibid.
5. Gunjan Jain, *She Walks, She Leads,* Penguin Random House India; Latest edition (2016).

20

SHAKUNTALA DEVI

MORE THAN A HUMAN CALCULATOR

In the 1970s, a young woman in a sharply draped saree engaged in witty repartee with the studio audience on our television screens. Shakuntala Devi, the Human Calculator as they called her, was an acknowledged genius, her mathematical abilities having been on display around the world, and tested under laboratory conditions. She was an international celebrity. Slowly, she all but faded from the public mind. Come 2020 and Shakuntala Devi shot back into the limelight, and it took Bollywood and a biopic on her life to make this happen.

Who was Shakuntala Devi? Born into an impoverished Kannada Brahmin household on 4 November 1929 in Bangalore, then part of the princely state of Mysore in pre-Independence India, Shakuntala Devi had eight siblings. Her youngest sister Vasanthalakshmi claims that all the siblings had some mathematical ability but Shakuntala topped them all. Shakuntala Devi was a precocious child and received almost little or no formal education. Her father realized that his little daughter was something of a savant during a game of cards, when she was consistently beating him. She was barely three at the time. Her father thought she was sneaking a peek at his cards but realized that the young Shakuntala was actually memorizing the cards and calculating the odds. Astounded by this discovery, he took her on roadshows to demonstrate her superhuman skills with numbers. She hadn't learnt mathematics and calculations formally yet and what she was doing with numbers was completely instinctive.[1]

When she was barely six, she did a demonstration of her jaw-dropping abilities to calculate numbers at the University of Mysore. By now, Shakuntala Devi was on roadshows constantly. Years later, she would speak with regret and rancour about those early days. While she had been admitted to St Theresa's Convent in Chamarajpet in Bangalore, for Class One, she was compelled to drop out because the monthly fee of two rupees was too much for her parents to afford. She had become the sole breadwinner of her family. At the age of six, she gave her first major show at the University of Mysore. She didn't like to do the performances. 'When I was young, I didn't want to do the shows, because I didn't like them. My father would beat up my mother in anger, and my mother would beat me up.'[2]

She herself had no explanation for her ability to calculate huge numbers in her head. She called it 'God's gift. A divine quality.' It was a quality that no one in her family had, she claimed, 'Not even remotely, although my father was a stage magician.'[3]

In 1944, she moved to London with her father. But despite the international fame and acclaim, she lived a very frugal life. Her meals would often be mixing the tomato ketchup from free sachets in local cafeterias with hot water to make a quick tomato soup, so as to save on food costs. Through 1950, she toured Europe and in 1976, she did a tour of New York City. On her BBC appearance, her answer to a calculation differed from that of the interviewer's. When rechecked, it was found her answer was right and not that of the interviewer's. At the University of Rome, one of her answers was wrong according to the precalculated answers, but when they rechecked the problem, her answer was found to be right. When she toured New York in 1976, *The New York Times* gushed about her, 'She could give you the cube root of 188,132,517—or almost any other number—in the time it took to ask the question. If you gave her any date in the last century, she would tell you what day of the week it fell on.'[4]

On 18 June 1980 at the Imperial College in London, Shakuntala Devi set a world record, a feat that earned her a spot in the 1982 edition of *The Guiness Book of World Records*. She demonstrated the multiplication of two 13-digit numbers: 7,686,369,774,870 × 2,465,099,745,779 in her head. These 13-digit numbers were picked at random by the Department of Computing at Imperial College London. Her answer: 8,947,668,177,995,426,462,773,730 was given in 28 seconds, which wasn't only the time taken by her to compute the answer, but included the time she took to speak out the answer. This feat also earned her the moniker of the 'Human Computer', a title she disliked most vehemently.

In 1988, when Arthur R. Jensen, the professor of educational psychology and a researcher on human intelligence at the University of California, Berkeley, found out that she was to visit the San Francisco Bay Area. He requested her to visit his chronometric laboratory, so they could measure her basic speed of information processing on a battery of elementary cognitive tasks (ECTs) for which the results could be compared with the reaction time (RT) data they had obtained on the same ECTs in large samples of students and older adults. Shakuntala Devi agreed to do so and spent three hours taking various tests and two hours discussing her life and her work with Professor Jensen. In that session, he tested her abilities with many arithmetical problems including calculating the cube root of 61,629,875 and the seventh root of 170,859,375, and reported that she was able to give him the solution of the two mentioned problems before he was even able to copy down the numbers in his notebook.

He would go on to publish his findings in the academic journal *Intelligence* in 1990.

To quote him from the article in *Intelligence*,

> Shakuntala Devi, one of the world's most prodigious mental calculators on record, past or present, is especially remarkable for the incredible speed with which she performs mental calculations on very large numbers. This rare phenomenon prompted the question of whether such exceptional performance depends on the speed of elementary information processes. Devi's rather unexceptional reaction times on a battery of elementary cognitive tasks, which were compared with the mean RTs of college students and older adults on the same tasks, contrasts so markedly with her amazing speed of performing huge arithmetic calculations as to indicate that her skill with numbers must depend largely on the automatic encoding and retrieval of a wealth of declarative and procedural information in long-term memory rather than on any unusual basic capacities. Some kind of motivational factor that sustains enormous and prolonged interest and practice in a particular skill probably plays a larger part in extremely exceptional performance than does psychometric g or the speed of elementary information processes.[5]

While analysing her process, he revealed that Devi refused to accept large numbers marked off with commas, claiming that the commas break up a number artificially. He would say that she was very unlike the perception of the socially awkward autistic savant. To quote him, 'Devi comes across as alert, extroverted, affable and articulate.' He added that for Shakuntala Devi, 'the manipulation of numbers is apparently like a native language, whereas for most of us arithmetic calculation is at best like the foreign language we learned in school.'[6] A video filmed by the Canadian broadcast network ATN shows her coming up with answers to questions posed by a studio audience, confidently, in barely seconds after the questions have been asked. A panel of mathematicians is grilling her. One of the panellists says, 'These numbers are a bit nasty.' Never slow on the repartee, she replies with a huge grin, 'Come on, be nasty.'[7]

Her daughter, Anupama Banerji speaks about how social a person Shakuntala Devi was. To quote her, 'Having Shakuntala Devi as your mother meant there was never a dull moment! She had an amazing zest for life and lived it to the fullest and on her own terms.'[8] She was often annoyed that being a woman she was perceived as a limitation amongst those who saw mathematics as a 'masculine' subject. A journalist once asked her, 'What is it like being a female mathematician?' Devi instantly retorted, 'What is it like being a male journalist?'

In 1950, she had said, 'Marriage would only mean another of life's bondages. I do not want to give any man an opportunity to say that if I made a name, it was because of his help.' Nonetheless, she returned to India in the 1960s and then got married to Paritosh Banerji, an IAS officer from Kolkata, and the couple would have a daughter, Anupama. They met when Banerji was part of the audience at one of her performances. She refused to change her name, saying at the time, 'I believe in equality both ways…I do not even wear the traditional symbols of marriage.' In fact, this insistence on keeping her own name got her into a conflict with the authorities when in 1976 she refused to give her husband's name for identification while making a ration card for herself in Kolkata. She said at the time, 'I want the ration card to be made out in my own name, taking me as a full-fledged individual, a complete person in my own right.'

Unfortunately, the marriage was destined to be short-lived. They would get divorced in 1979. One of the reasons, reportedly, was that her husband possibly was homosexual, something that her daughter strongly refutes. Nonetheless, what emerged from this unhappy experience was a book which would study and advocate societal acceptance for homosexuality. She was possibly amongst the earliest gay rights activists in India, decades before LGBTQ (lesbian, gay, bisexual, transgender and queer or questioning) rights became part of our discourse.

Her book, *The World of Homosexuals*, was a pioneering effort to present homosexuality in India through an academic lens. Published in 1977, the book comprised interviews with homosexuals in India and a homosexual couple in Canada. Today, the book is considered a pioneering academic effort to understand and present a case for homosexuality in a country which back then criminalized homosexuality. She would continue to remain friends with her husband after the divorce, a rare feat, and be a single parent to their daughter. Says Anupama Banerji, 'It wasn't easy for her to bring up a child alone. As I grew older, we grew into a friendship. A few issues also started creeping up. But the thing was: she was my whole family.'[9]

Barely a day before her biopic was released, her daughter received the certificate from the *Guinness World Records* declaring her mother's feat at the Imperial College in London, back in 1980, as the fastest human computation. She had then multiplied random 13-digit numbers within 28 seconds at the Imperial College London. Banerji was barely 10 when her mother achieved the record. She said in an interview, 'I remember going to the Trocadero Centre (an entertainment complex on London's Coventry Street). They have a room there which has mummy's picture.'[10] In 2013, Shakuntala Devi fell severely ill with respiratory problems and was admitted to a hospital in Bangalore. She passed away on 21 April 2013 at the age of 83.

What made Shakuntala Devi the genius she was? Was it her skill with numbers, or her sheer delight at being a performer with these numbers? She had said to Professor Jensen that her career came out of her 'love of numbers and love of people'. She instantaneously corrected herself, 'Oh, I should say it the other way around: my love of people and my love of numbers.'[11]

That is perhaps where her magic lay. Energetic, vibrant, and bursting with life and vivacity, she did all she could through her life to tell us that mathematics was not something to be feared, but an exquisite language which would reveal its beauty to those who cared to listen to it very, very carefully.

NOTES

1. Nina C. George, 'Why Shakuntala's siblings gave up on maths', *Deccan Herald*, 8 August 2020, https://www.deccanherald.com/entertainment/why-shakuntala-s-siblings-gave-up-on-maths-871060.html. Accessed on 18 January 2022.
2. Amrita Dutta, 'Prime Woman: Why Shakuntala Devi was a woman who wanted it all', *The Indian Express*, 1 August 2020, https://indianexpress.com/article/express-sunday-eye/prime-woman-why-shakuntala-devi-was-a-woman-who-wanted-it-all-6532985/. Accessed on 17 January 2022
3. 'Obituary: India's "human computer" Shakuntala Devi', BBC, 22 April 2013, https://www.bbc.com/news/world-asia-india-22244118. Accessed on 18 January 2022.
4. *The New York Times*, https://www.nytimes.com/2013/04/24/world/asia/shakuntala-devi-human-computer-dies-in-india-at-83.html. Accessed on 17 January 2022.
5. Aurther R. Jensen, 'Speed of Information Processing in a Calculating Prodigy', University of California, Berkeley, https://arthurjensen.net/wp-content/uploads/2014/06/Speed-of-Information-Processing-in-a-Calculating-Prodigy-Shakuntala-Devi-1990-by-Arthur-Robert-Jensen.pdf. Accessed on 21 January 2022.
6. 'Shakuntala Devi, "Human Computer" Who Bested the Machines, Dies at 83', *The New York Times*, https://www.nytimes.com/2013/04/24/world/asia/shakuntala-devi-

human-computer-dies-in-india-at-83.html. Accessed on 18 January 2022.

7. Nandini Ramnath, 'More than maths: Shakuntala Devi biopic aims to reveal the woman who "lived life to the fullest"', *Scroll.in*, 25 July 2020, https://scroll.in/reel/968328/more-than-maths-shakuntala-devi-biopic-aims-to-reveal-the-woman-who-lived-life-to-the-fullest

8. 'She believed she was better than any computer: The incredible life and times of Shakuntala Devi', https://www.edexlive.com/news/2020/jul/30/she-believed-she-was-better-than-any-computer-the-incredible-life-and-times-of-shakuntala-devi-13568.html. Accessed on 18 January 2022.

9. Amria Dutta, 'Prime Woman: Why Shakuntala Devi was a woman who wanted it all', *The Indian Express*, 1 August 2020, https://indianexpress.com/article/express-sunday-eye/prime-woman-why-shakuntala-devi-was-a-woman-who-wanted-it-all-6532985/. Accessed on 17 January 2022.

10. https://www.outlookindia.com/newsscroll/guinness-world-records-awards-certificate-to-shakuntala-devi-for-fastest-human-computation/1905845. Accessed on 18 January 2022.

11. Abhinav Srinivasan, 'Remembering Shakuntala Devi, Who Did Much More than Solve Math Problems', *Science the Wire*, https://science.thewire.in/the-sciences/shakuntala-devi-arithmetic-world-of-homosexuals-humanity/. Accessed on 17 January 2022.

21

P.T. USHA

PAYYOLI EXPRESS

All lean muscle, long limbs and chiselled features, P.T. Usha was an instantly recognizable face on our television screens in the 1980s. All who had watched her compete in the 400 metres hurdles at the 1984 Los Angeles Olympics, where she came fourth by a heartbreaking fraction of a second, mourned the loss with her. This scintillating run might not have got her an Olympic medal but with her performance, P.T. Usha became the undisputed queen of Indian track and field.

Barely a year later, at the 1985 Asian Games at the Senayan Madya Stadium in Jakarta, she would win six medals: five gold and one bronze. This record haul was fuelled by Usha's desire to dethrone the then reigning track and field queen of Asia, Lydia de Vega of the Philippines, with whom she had a long-standing rivalry.[1] Theirs was a rivalry that lasted through the years, beginning way back in 1982 at the Asian Games.

Pilavullakandi Thekkeparambil Usha, or P.T. Usha as we know her, was born on 27 June 1964, in Kerala, into a family of seven. Her father owned a small clothing shop. Her parents were E.P.M. Paithal and T.V. Lakshmi, from the village of Koothali in the Kozhikode district of Kerala and she was brought up in Thrikkottur. The family would later settle in Payyoli. As a child, Usha was frail and weak, but as she grew up, she began showing incredible prowess in athletics at school.² She was a bright student, and her father wanted her to become a teacher, but her uncle encouraged her to pursue athletics. Her father, initially, was against the idea of her getting into competitive sports, but her uncle managed to prevail. O.M. Nambiar, a noted athletics coach from Kerala, spotted her at a sports prize-distribution ceremony in 1976, when she was barely 12 years old. Nambiar would recall that what impressed him at first sight about Usha was her lean shape and fast walking style. He knew that she would go on to become a very good sprinter. Usha was in class seven and topped her trials at both district and state level and was selected to join the Kannur sports division school where Coach Nambiar was amongst the faculty. He realized her potential and gave her special attention as well as facilitated the use of a nearby ground and beach for her to continue practice during her vacations at Payyoli.³

Coming from a humble background, Usha often didn't receive the nutritious diet required for an athlete. Being primarily a vegetarian who ate fish, it was Coach Nambiar who convinced her to begin eating eggs. She didn't like the smell and would put the boiled eggs he gave her in her bag. Her bag started smelling and her coach found out that she hadn't been eating the eggs he'd given her.

It wasn't long before the potential he had spotted began bearing fruit. She would win multiple medals in the 1979 National Games, and sweep the 1980 National interstate meet and set new records. She was the youngest Indian to go to the 1980 Moscow Olympics when she was barely 16.⁴

At the time, she had no clue that she was the youngest Olympian from the country at the Games. She was travelling alone, taking the very first international flight of her life from Delhi to Moscow, further stymied by the fact that she spoke only Malayalam while the other senior members of the squad spoke primarily Hindi or English. She felt overwhelmed and completely alone, having to go to the mess, the practice grounds and the event venues all alone and fend for herself at this huge international event. There was a Malayali basketball coach, she says, who was very encouraging but he too was busy with his allocated duties. However, the chief coach of the delegation, J.S. Saini, was very encouraging. He motivated her to participate in the 200 metres and she came sixth.[5]

At the 1981 interstate meet, held in Bangalore in 1981, she set national records in both the 100 metres and the 200 metres. From here, her next stop was at the 1982 Asian Games, held in New Delhi, where she won silver in both the 100 metres and the 200 metres. She was barely 18 when she became a national sporting icon. At the 1983 Open National Championship, held at Jamshedpur, she would break the 200 metres national record again, clocking 23.9 seconds, against the 25.32 seconds she herself had set the previous year. She would also set a new national record in the 400 metres at 53.6 seconds. She was also the first Indian athlete to have a personal coach.

The next big thing looming on the horizon was the 1984 Los Angeles Olympics. In the run-up to the Olympics, Usha had a spate of great performances at the New Delhi interstate meet and the Mumbai Open National Championship. The Moscow World Championships though, saw her perform poorly in the 100 metres and 200 metres, and she then decided to focus on the 400 metres hurdles. It was Coach Nambiar who realized that her stride was suited to the hurdles which was then a new event, and convinced her to make it her event. That year, she would go on to win the gold in the 400 metres at the Asian Championships held in Kuwait City. She had beaten the then current Asian Champion M.D. Valsamma to qualify for the Olympic Games. At the time, Valsamma's coach had stated that if she had trained on a synthetic track, she would have beaten Usha. Usha kept the clipping of that news report under her pillow to motivate herself in the run-up to the 1984 Olympics.

At the pre-Olympics trial in Inglewood, California, she beat the top sprinter from the United States, Judi Brown, with a time of 55.7 seconds. This set the eyes of the world on her. At the Games itself, she would clock 56.81 seconds in the heats and 55.54 seconds in the semi-final. This timing in the semi-final was a new Commonwealth record in itself. All eyes were on Usha, who reached the final of the 400 metres hurdles. At the final, one of her competitors had a false start. It broke Usha's concentration and she clocked 55.42 seconds. Although this was better than her personal best, she narrowly missed the bronze, which went to the Romanian runner Cristieana Cojocaru. Usha's name was in the top three. They then decided to go through the slow-motion footage from the cameras and Usha was in the dope room when it was officially announced that the Romanian was in third place. Coach Nambiar reportedly began sobbing, but Usha assured him that they would win a medal at the next Olympics.

The Olympics final was just her sixth 400 metres hurdles race, perhaps if she had more experience of the event, she could have done better. 'We would jealously look at the athletes from other countries enjoying fabulous amenities; they had the latest equipment at their disposal. We wondered if we too would one day have access to such facilities.'[6]

In later interviews, she would say she had eaten just rice porridge with pickles at the Games Village, because there wasn't any food of her choice available, nor food supplements. 'I remember it—the pickle we [eat] in Kerala called "kadu manga achar". That and some sliced fruit. I was not accustomed to baked potatoes or half-boiled chicken with soya sauce and some other typical American food.'[7]

There are other regrets as well. She still feels that had she dipped her body at the finish, she could have easily won the medal. Her timing of 55.42 seconds for the 400 metres hurdles, set in the 1984 Los Angeles Olympics, was a national record and stayed so for over 35 years.[8]

She bounced back from this narrow miss though, and went on to win five golds and one bronze at the 1985 Jakarta Asian Championships. Winning the 100 metres, the 200 metres, the 400 metres with a new Asian record and the 400 metres hurdles, she reclaimed the glory she had lost the previous year at the Olympics. Her fifth gold would be in the 4x400 metres relay, and the bronze in the 4x100 metres relay. This spectacular performance would earn her a record for the most gold medals ever won at a single event in the entire history of the championships. She was given a house in Payyoli by the state government after her phenomenal performance at Jakarta.

She finds it annoying that her career seems to be defined by the 1984 Olympics' near miss: 'It was not a flash in the pan. Right through the '80s and for over a decade, I won gold medals for India.'[9]

The very next week, she would better her personal best timings of the 400 metres event at the 1985 Canberra World Cup, but even her personal best of 51.61 seconds would get her the seventh spot.

It was at the 1986 Seoul Asian Games that the entire 70,000-strong audience reverberated with 'Usha, Usha, Usha' as she lined up at the starting block. She vindicated herself and the loss of that bronze at the Olympics by winning four golds (200 metres, 400 metres, 400 metres hurdles and the 4x400 metres relay) and a silver (100 metres): a record for a single athlete at any international meet. She ran three races within the span of 110 minutes. It didn't allow her enough time to rest and warm up between events, but she had to do it in order to bring home the medals for India.

Her career between 1983 and 1989 saw her gather 13 gold medals at ATF meets (later rechristened Asian Championship). She decided to train at the Crystal Palace Sports Training Centre for a few months before the Asian Athletics Championships and went there with her coach and mentor, Nambiar. Here, she discovered the joy of having an English breakfast: 'I loved the bacon there. It was so juicy and tasty that I looked forward to breakfast. Eggs, toast, bacon and the salads, I hogged that.'[10]

While she won five golds and a bronze at the Meet, she cherishes most dearly the bronze, because it was the second time she beat Lydia de Vega at the meet.[11]

She made her comeback at the 1989 Asian Track and Field Meet, and won four golds. She ideally wanted to retire that very year, while still on the high of the four golds but decided against it and went on to compete at the 1990 Beijing Asian Games and won three medals there.

In 1991, Usha got married and had a son the next year. In 1993, she began training again, her eye on the 1996 Olympics. She returned to the track and won a silver at the Hiroshima Asian Games in 1994. The 1996 Atlanta Olympics were not too far away. But unfortunately, in 1995, she had knee injuries and her Olympic dream faded. She returned yet again to the track though, for the 1998 Asian Track and Field Meet in Japan and here she would set a new national record in the 200 metres race with a time of 23.27 seconds.[12] She quit soon after. She has now taken on the baton of coaching the next generation of potential athletes, setting up the Usha School of Athletics in Kerala to train young, deserving talent in India.[13]

The Government of India conferred Usha with the Arjuna Award, the highest national award for a sportsperson, in 1983 and the Padma Shri in 1985. She was named Sportsperson of the Century as well as Sportswoman of the Millennium by the Indian Olympic Association. In 2019, she was awarded the International Association of Athletic Federation's (IAAF) Veteran Pin for her outstanding service to sport.[14] Her rich haul of 101 medals is a towering achievement, making her a living legend and an inspiration for the next generation of female athletes.

NOTES

1. Rahul Venkat, 'Five golds, one bronze in three days: Why PT Usha was an Asian superwoman', 23 August 2020, https://www.olympicchannel.com/en/stories/features/detail/pt-usha-record-indian-sprinter-athletics-1985-asian-championships/. Accessed on 19 January 2022.
2. Rekha Balakrishnan, 'As PT Usha turns 54, 10 facts about the golden girl of Indian athletics', 27 June 2019, https://yourstory.com/herstory/2019/06/golden-girl-pt-usha-birthday-olympics. Accessed on 19 January 2022.
3. Manish Kumar, 'Crores of rupees being spent, but we are not getting closer to an Olympic medal in athletics, says PT Usha', *The Times of India*, 9 July 2020, https://timesofindia.indiatimes.com/sports/more-sports/athletics/crores-of-rupees-being-spent-but-we-are-not-getting-closer-to-an-olympic-medal-in-athletics-says-pt-usha/articleshow/76868914.cms?utm_source=contentofinterest&utm_medium=text&utm_campaign=cppst. Accessed on 18 January 2022.
4. Rahul Venkat, 'Five golds, one bronze in three days: Why PT Usha was an Asian superwoman', 23 August 2020, https://www.olympicchannel.com/en/stories/features/detail/pt-usha-record-indian-sprinter-athletics-1985-asian-championships/. Accessed on 19 January 2022.
5. Manish Kumar, 'Crores of rupees being spent, but we are not getting closer to an Olympic medal in athletics, says PT Usha', *The Times of India*, 9 July 2020, https://timesofindia.indiatimes.com/sports/more-sports/athletics/crores-of-rupees-being-spent-but-we-are-not-getting-closer-to-an-olympic-medal-in-athletics-says-pt-usha/articleshow/76868914.cms?utm_source=contentofinterest&utm_medium=text&utm_campaign=cppst. Accessed on 18 January 2022.

6 'Pause, rewind, play: When PT Usha missed an Olympic medal by a heartbreaking margin in 1984', *Scroll.in*, 27 June 2020, https://scroll.in/field/961274/pause-rewind-play-when-pt-usha-missed-an-olympic-medal-by-a-heartbreaking-margin-in-1984. Accessed on 19 January 2022.

7 Ibid.

8 Manish Kumar, 'Crores of rupees being spent, but we are not getting closer to an Olympic medal in athletics, says PT Usha', *The Times of India*, 9 July 2020, https://timesofindia.indiatimes.com/sports/more-sports/athletics/crores-of-rupees-being-spent-but-we-are-not-getting-closer-to-an-olympic-medal-in-athletics-says-pt-usha/articleshow/76868914.cms?utm_source=contentofinterest&utm_medium=text&utm_campaign=cppst. Accessed on 18 January 2022.

9 'I was not a one-race wonder: PT Usha opens up on "golden period"', 27 June 2020, https://www.olympicchannel.com/en/stories/news/detail/indian-athletics-pt-usha-running-olympics/. Accessed on 19 January 2022.

10 'I was not a one-race wonder: PT Usha opens up on "golden period"', 27 June 2020, https://www.olympicchannel.com/en/stories/news/detail/indian-athletics-pt-usha-running-olympics/. Accessed on 19 January 2022.

11 Rahul Venkat, 'Five golds, one bronze in three days: Why PT Usha was an Asian superwoman', 23 August 2020, https://www.olympicchannel.com/en/stories/features/detail/pt-usha-record-indian-sprinter-athletics-1985-asian-championships/. Accessed on 19 January 2022.

12 'PT Usha: India's Golden Girl of Athletics', *Hindustan Times*, 11 July 2019, https://www.hindustantimes.com/inspiring-lives/pt-usha-india-s-golden-girl-of-athletics/story-0z2343ZIdthFhoQJazqb4L.html. Accessed on 19 January 2022.

13 Manish Kumar, 'Crores of rupees being spent, but we are not getting closer to an Olympic medal in athletics,

says PT Usha', *The Times of India*, 9 July 2020, https://timesofindia.indiatimes.com/sports/more-sports/athletics/crores-of-rupees-being-spent-but-we-are-not-getting-closer-to-an-olympic-medal-in-athletics-says-pt-usha/articleshow/76868914.cms. Accessed on 19 January 2022.

14 PTI, 'Former athlete PT Usha nominated for IAAF's Veteran Pin', *The Hindu BusinessLine*, 18 July 2019, https://www.thehindubusinessline.com/news/sports/pt-usha-nominated-for-iaafs-veteran-pin/article28542508.ece. Accessed on 19 January 2022.

22

P.V. SINDHU

RACKET GIRL

2004. A slight eight-year-old, her hair cropped short, began training at a badminton academy. The academy, founded by Pullela Gopichand, was the best in the country for badminton. Gopichand himself was an All England Opens champion who had reached the quarter-finals of the 2000 Sydney Olympics, but became a coach after he had to cut short his promising career due to injury.

The eight-year-old was P.V. Sindhu. Back then, her day began at 3.30 a.m., with a long journey from her home in the railway colony at Secunderabad to the academy in Hyderabad, a journey she made by train every day to reach the academy at 4.30 a.m. sharp. She was never late, never slacked off or bunked. The head coach of the academy, Rajendra Kumar, told *The New Indian Express*, "'Until about 14 years of age, she used to suffer defeats against the top players of her age group quite regularly. That changed completely when she got tall. The same players were now finding it difficult to get past her since. She always had the build of an athlete since then."'[1]

Twelve years later, that determined little eight-year-old was a towering (5 ft 10 inch) 21-year-old dominating the court at the 2016 Rio Olympics. Her trademark powerful smashes reverberated through the closed confines of the court, decimating her opponents, only to lose in the final to Carolina Marin of

Spain, bagging a silver in a well-fought match. This is the story of P.V. Sindhu, the girl who made us proud at Rio and went on to become the World Champion in badminton barely a year later. And at Tokyo 2020, she would go on to win bronze, defeating He Bing Jiao of China, and with it becoming the first Indian woman to win two individual Olympic medals.

Perhaps it all began with her parents, P.V. Ramana and P. Vijaya, who were both national-level volleyball players themselves and understood the rigours and sacrifices needed to reach the top in any sport, and were completely supportive of her passion for badminton. Her father himself was a member of the Indian volleyball team that won the bronze at the 1986 Asian Games in Seoul. He was conferred with the prestigious Arjuna Award in 2000 for his contribution to the sport. Sindhu would get from her parents not just their height but also their sporting ethos and dedication. Sindhu is the second child of her parents. Her older sister, Divya, also played handball at the national level, but chose to drop out of a sporting career to pursue medicine.

Sindhu was a sincere student as well, as her mother Vijaya avers. She would diligently complete all her school work before going in for badminton practice. To quote Vijaya, 'Sindhu has always been very dedicated. She is the one who decided to learn badminton and make something of herself. It's not like we did anything special for her.'[2]

For Sindhu, the decision to choose badminton over volleyball, the sport that both her parents had excelled in, came from her fascination with the success of Gopichand, a Hyderabad lad who had won the 2001 All England Open Badminton Championships. She was very young when she began training in badminton. Her first coach was Mehboob Ali, who trained her at the badminton courts of the Indian Railway Institute of Signal Engineering and Telecommunication in Secunderabad. As she got better at the game, they took the decision to enrol her at the Pullela Gopichand Badminton Academy in Hyderabad. Every morning,

Sindhu would be at the training centre at 4.30 a.m. sharp. Never once, her coach says, did she ask if they could start at 4.45 a.m. or 5.00 a.m.—such was her dedication to her sport.

While Sindhu's hard work to reach where she did is important, it would have been impossible had her parents not been bulwarks behind her training and travelling. They would eventually move closer to the Academy so as to reduce the commute time.

What Gopichand saw in Sindhu was the potential to be a champion, along with the most requisite ingredient—the attitude to give the sport her all as well as a never-say-die spirit. She showed early promise. Competing in the under-10 category, she won the 5th Servo All India ranking championship in the doubles category and the singles title at the Ambuja Cement All India ranking. Moving up to the under-13 category, she won the sub-juniors in Puducherry, the doubles title at the Smt Krishna Khaitan All India Tournament, IOC All India Ranking, the Sub-Junior Nationals and the All India Ranking in Pune. Her first moment of national fame came when she shot into the spotlight, breaking into the Badminton World Federation (BWF) World Ranking way back in September 2012, when she was barely 17. In fact, in 2012, she even missed her sister's wedding because she had reached the finals of the Syed Modi International India Grand Prix Gold in Lucknow. From 2013 onwards, she would win a medal at every world championship, barring 2015.

In December 2015, she lost in the first round itself at the Australian Open against the then world number one, Yihan Wang. At that point, they were in Melbourne. For those few days, Gopichand let Sindhu enjoy her break from the daily routine of practice. Her sister was there too, and the girls made merry, with late nights and no food restrictions. The 2016 Rio Olympics were looming large and Gopichand wanted Sindhu to go for gold. When they returned to India, Gopichand summoned Sindhu to his office and handed her a letter with a list of dos and don'ts.

Amongst them, was a clause that required her to give up her phone completely till the Rio Olympics. She thought, he couldn't possibly be serious. Who would expect a young girl to give up her phone? But her coach couldn't have been more serious with his diktat, and so for the next many months, Sindhu, a young girl of barely 21, was without her phone. Another clause Gopichand had put in the letter was about the dietary restrictions Sindhu would have to abide by. He put Sindhu on the strictest diet to ensure she was in her best form for the Olympics.[3] When they reached Rio, Sindhu was initially nervous but in the best possible form, and she absolutely focused on her game. Though she had a shaky start, she soon came into her own and reached the finals where she played a blistering game against Spain's Carolina Marin, but lost. She won the silver. The first thing her coach did after she got her medal was to give her phone back, and the first thing she would do was to eat an ice cream.

It would be in 2016 again that she would win her first superseries title at the 2016 China Open. In April 2017, she reached a career high ranking of No 2. That year, she would win four more titles in Korea and India, silver medals at the 2018 Commonwealth and Asian Games, and two bronze medals at the Uber Cup. However, 2017 also saw her reach a few finals and lose. These losses began playing on her confidence and affecting her game. It was then that her coach decided she needed a drastic change in her on-court style. He urged her to become aggressive, to shout, to be attacking and vocal on court. The shift in style helped.

In August 2017, she played the World Championships final against Nozomi Okuhara and won a silver. That final encounter is widely regarded as one of the best-ever women's singles final. In the 2018 Commonwealth Games in Gold Coast, she won a silver in the women's singles and a gold in the mixed team. In December that year, she became the first Indian to win the season-ending BWF World Tour Finals tournament in

Guangzhou, China. At the Asian Games 2018, she won silver, losing to world number one Tai Tzu Ying in the final. She lost to Carolina Marin in the BWF World Championships in August that year, winning the silver. She was the only badminton player from India who had qualified for the prestigious BWF World Tour Finals, and created history by winning the title without losing a single match. At the Premier Badminton League (PBL) auctions in 2018, she was picked by Hyderabad Hunters and made the team captain. In 2019, she lost the Indian National Badminton Championships to Saina Nehwal.

Her next moment of glory after the Rio Olympics came on 25 August 2019, when she defeated Okuhara to win gold at the World Championships. It was a hard-fought match, it barely took Sindhu 32 minutes to play out Okuhara in a totally one-sided combat with 21-7, 21-7 to win the gold. With this she became the first Indian to win gold at the World Championships. She is the second woman after Zhang Ning to win over five medals at the World Championships.[4]

She has always credited her parents for their unstinting support on her journey. To quote her, 'Parents are the most important part of an athlete's success as they understand the psyche of a child better than the others.'[5]

Interestingly, while she is an Olympic individual medal winner, she has ensured that academically she is well qualified too. She holds multiple academic degrees: a bachelor's in commerce (BCom) degree, an honorary doctorate from Vels University and a master's in Business Administration (MBA) from St Ann's College for Women in Hyderabad.

In an interview, she revealed that she barely got any time to herself in the run-up to Tokyo 2020. To quote her,

> My training session starts at 7 in the morning and we do 7 to 8:30 and then we have a break. Then we start at 9:15 until 11. So that's on-court sessions almost every day. I do my training in Suchitra Academy, so that's like an hour away

from my house, so I leave at 2:30 so that I can get there by 3:30. At 3:45 start my session, so by the time I finish, it's like 6 o'clock. At 6, I leave from there. I finish my physiotherapy and do my stretching exercises, relax and everything. I leave from that academy around 6:30, 6:45 then I come home by 7:45-8. People ask me like Sindhu let's go here, let's go there but I actually don't have time.'[6]

In both 2018 and 2019, she made it to the Forbes list of the highest-paid female athletes. Before the All England Badminton Championships, she signed off from her endorsement deal with Yonex and signed up with the Chinese premium sports brand Li-Ning for four years, a mega deal worth $7.2 million. This is reported to be one of the biggest deals in world badminton.[7]

In March 2015, she was awarded the Padma Shri, the fourth-highest civilian award in India, and in August 2016, she was conferred with the Rajiv Gandhi Khel Ratna. In 2020, she was awarded the Padma Bhushan.

For the 2020 Tokyo Olympics, she initially trained under the Korean duo of Park Tae Sang and Kim Ji Hyun from 2019, and then under Park. Winning the bronze at the Olympics in 2021, in a tightly fought match against China's He Bing Jiao, made her the country's only female sportsperson to have two individual Olympic medals.

The journey that began way back in 2004 bore fruit in Rio 2016 and was reinforced in Tokyo 2020. From here, P.V. Sindhu has only the gold at the Olympic podium to look forward to now.

NOTES

1. 'No one at the Gopichand Academy thought P.V. Sindhu would be a world-beater until...' *The New Indian Express*, 26 August 2019, https://www.newindianexpress.com/sport/other/2019/aug/26/no-one-at-the-gopichand-academy-thought-sindhu-

would-be-a-world-beater-until-2024620.html. Accessed on 19 January 2022.
2. Ria Das, 'Behind PV Sindhu's Success Are Her Parents Who Worked Equally Hard', *She the People*, 28 August 2019, https://en-stage.shethepeople.tv/home-top-video/successful-sportsperson-parents-worked-hard/. Accessed on 19 January 2022.
3. 'The story of sacrifices, and hardwork behind PV Sindhu's Olympic medal', *The Times of India*, 20 October 2017, https://economictimes.indiatimes.com/news/sports/the-story-of-sacrifices-and-hardwork-behind-pv-sindhus-olympic-medal/articleshow/61157905.cms?from=mdr. Accessed on 19 January 2022.
4. 'No one at the Gopichand Academy thought P.V. Sindhu would be a world-beater until...' *The New Indian Express*, 26 August 2019, https://www.newindianexpress.com/sport/other/2019/aug/26/no-one-at-the-gopichand-academy-thought-sindhu-would-be-a-world-beater-until-2024620.html. Accessed on 19 January 2022.
5. 'Nothing compares to parents' support for P.V. Sindhu', https://www.olympicchannel.com/en/stories/news/detail/indian-badminton-pv-sindhu-parents-family-success-team/. Accessed on 19 January 2022.
6. 'I sit down sometimes and think I actually don't have time: PV Sindhu', *India Today*, 18 January 2020, https://www.indiatoday.in/sports/badminton/story/pv-sindhu-training-tokyo-olympics-diet-gopichand-1638125-2020-01-18. Accessed on 19 January 2022.
7. V.S. Biswas, 'P.V. Sindhu is now the highest-paid woman athlete in India', *Financial Express*, 9 September 2019, https://www.financialexpress.com/industry/brand-icon-sindhu-is-now-the-highest-paid-woman-athlete-in-india/1700175/. Accessed on 19 January 2022.

23

EKTA KAPOOR

THE QUEEN OF THE SCREEN

A little off the bustling Link Road in Andheri West, Mumbai, an entire stretch is known as the Balaji Lane. It is where the Balaji Telefilms office is located. And it all began in a garage in Juhu way back in the 1990s, when a young girl, barely out of her teens, began producing television content. The rest, as they say, is history.

That young girl was none other than Ekta Kapoor, and the production company she launched back then, Balaji Telefilms, is today one of the leading visual content-producing companies in the country. Born on 7 June 1975 to Hindi film superstar Jeetendra and Shobha Kapoor, then a homemaker, Ekta was brought up like any other regular kid. She attended school at Bombay Scottish, Mahim and then went to Mithibai College, immersing herself in the life of a typical collegian—bunking classes and partying. This carefree life came to an abrupt end when one day her father told her that she should either get married or earn her own money. Ekta then began interning with ad filmmaker Kailash Surendranath. At this point, a friend of her father's asked him to create content for TV Asia, a channel that was to target the non-resident Indian (NRI) audience.[1]

She took up the challenge, setting up her own television production company, Balaji Telefilms, in 1994. Their first office was in the garage of their bungalow. From these humble beginnings, grew the multistoried, glass-fronted building that is now the office of Balaji Telefilms.²

In the early days, she had to take her father with her to meetings so that she was taken seriously. She began with a seed capital of around ₹1.5 crore, which was spent in creating four pilot shows for a new London-based channel called TV Asia that catered to the Indian diaspora. But the fledgeling channel got sold off to the newly formed Zee TV. In a single stroke, the collaboration with TV Asia that they had been banking on was gone. She had to pitch her shows to Zee TV, begin from scratch. And that she did.

Her first show that debuted on Zee TV in 1995 was the supernatural *Mano Ya Na Mano*, which was a complete gamble. It didn't quite hit the mark. Perhaps, the Indian audiences were not yet ready for horror. Reportedly, after her initial investments were exhausted and none of her shows managed to hit that elusive high TRP (target rating point) mark, Ekta created a pilot for a show called *Hum Paanch*, which was about five sisters and their quirky escapades, and sold it to Zee TV.³ Running from 1995 to 2006, the show went on to become a mega success. *Hum Paanch* launched Ekta, all of 19, as the producer of a super successful sitcom on the silver screen. Back then, in the 'garage office', everyone—editors, cameramen, accountants, writers and the entire staff—worked out of the same room. Lunchtime had food coming from Ekta's home, cooked and supervised by her mother.

Hum Paanch was the springboard that launched Ekta's full-time television production career. By the time she was 20, she had multiple shows being aired on television. To quote her from an interview in *Outlook Business Wow*, 'I started enjoying production. Some shows were making a lot of money and some were not. But once I started enjoying the challenges, I became obsessed about production. I ate, drank, slept and married television.'³ This was also the time when Hindi general entertainment channels (GECs) were limited and she couldn't get a foothold into South Indian GECs. At this juncture, it was superstar Rajnikanth who came to her rescue. They had been introduced at a party and he was impressed by her, saying as much to her father. She requested him to put in a word for her at Sun TV, which he agreed to do. This call from Rajnikanth got her a non prime-time slot on the channel. She made the most of this opportunity, writing dialogues for the show *Kudumbbam* and getting her accounts head find her a translator. The show became a superhit and, a few years later, was remade in Hindi and aired on Sony TV in 1999 as *Ghar Ek Mandir*, a show that went on to top the TRP race.[4]

Then came Star Plus and the revolutionary partnership with it which was the first of its kind in the industry, with Balaji Telefilms signing up to produce exclusive content for them. In 2000, she launched three shows on Star Plus: *Kyunki... Saas Bhi Kabhi Bahu Thi*, *Kahaani Ghar Ghar Kii* and *Kasautii Zindagii Kay*. These three shows went on to become TRP toppers, as well as redefine television viewing in the Hindi GEC space. Ekta understood her viewer well and catered to the requirement of aspirational living and dressing with opulent sets and lavish costumes. She set up a writers' apartment years ago, a concept that has only recently become commonplace, and ran an all-India contest to find talented writers who were then trained in script writing. This nationwide talent hunt ran for four years and scouted over a hundred talented writers.

The 'K serials' ruled the Hindi GEC space for years. Her partnership with Star TV ensured her serials got prime time and Star gave the shows all the promotion needed to make them hits. But things started slipping in the late 2000s. The K serials began to lose their Midas touch and the TRPs started dipping. *Kahaani Ghar Ghar Kii* was pulled off air and *Kyunki... Saas Bhi Kabhi Bahu Thi* was sidelined by the channel. The seven-year partnership between Balaji and Star TV ended suddenly and antagonistically.

While she had big shows such as *Bade Achhe Lagte Hain* on the airwaves, nonetheless she took a hard call to recalibrate the direction the production house would take. She had already ventured into Bollywood movie production with *Kyo Kii...Main Jhuth Nahin Bolta* (2001), *Kucch To Hai* (2003) and *Krishna Cottage* (2004), the latter two based on supernatural themes. However, back then, her focus continued to be primarily the television business and it was only in 2008 that she began focusing on movies. She produced the comedy *Kya Kool Hain Hum* (2005) with her brother, Tusshar Kapoor. She also co-produced the gangster film *Shootout at Lokhandwala* (2007) and action thriller *Mission Istanbul* (2008). Between 2010 and 2014, her movie production division released films such as *Love Sex Aur Dhokha*, *Once Upon a Time in Mumbaai* and *Shor in the City*, amongst others but most of them flopped. It was a new low for her, she lost confidence in herself. Back in 2000, she had taken Balaji Telefilms public. However, despite the company going public, the family continues to retain control over it. Her father heads the company. Her mother remained the managing director and Ekta continued as joint managing director.

Shobha Kapoor is the wind beneath her wings. In an interview, Ekta says, 'From the beginning, mom would handle production and the finances, and I, the creative end, right from looks and designs to set management and the scene break-up. She has always been good at things such as managing budgets and being hard-nosed about money. These are things that I am absolutely terrible at.'[5] Another major shift came about after she attended a three-week owners/president management programme at Harvard University. There, she realized that family-run businesses could face setbacks if they failed to professionalize at the right time. When she returned to India, she set up an advisory council for Balaji Telefilms. She was hesitant to venture into the online streaming app business, it was a space dominated by big players with 'billions to burn', she felt. But her then CEO, Sameer Nair convinced her to make a less expensive app for the masses and she was grateful for his advice and her consequent decision to set up ALT Balaji, which she launched in April 2017.[6]

ALT Balaji also helped her recover from a financially disastrous 2016.[7] She's also backed women-centric productions. *The Dirty Picture* (2011), which she produced, unabashedly celebrated the life of a Southern sex symbol known for her oomph and her rather unconventional lifestyle. She has backed movies such as *Lipstick Under My Burkha* (2016) when it got caught up in controversy.[8] The one advantage of creating products for various platforms is that she connects to audiences across segments and demographics. To quote her, 'With the variety of shows, we are reaching to different generations. I came across girls who said that once they felt irritated watching daily soaps on TV with their mothers, they discovered their own stories in shows like *Broken But Beautiful*.'[9] She also has no qualms showing sex on screen; in fact, she is aware that if audiences do not get such content on television, they will shift to apps. 'Netflix caters to the urban niche audiences and I deal with the mass audience who pays ₹30 a month for the app. The day you curb the natural need of the audience, you spoil it. People ask me how I am so bold and I tell them "I have no problem with sex". I think it is a natural thing and people either see it or consume it.'[10]

Ekta chose to have her child late through surrogacy. Her son, Ravie, is named after her father, whose original name is Ravi Kapoor. She announced the birth of her baby boy on her social media on 27 January 2019. She is also strongly religious and is known to walk to Siddhivinayak Temple in Prabhadevi, Mumbai, from her home in Juhu on most Monday nights to have the first darshan early Tuesday morning. She is often known to have her staff join her on these walks to the temple, as well as on her jogs to discuss work.

She has other curious quirks and beliefs as well. One of them is her immense belief is numerology, and on the advice of her numerologist, she decided to have the names of her shows start with the letter 'K'. While numerology may or may not have had a role to play in her success, we cannot discount the sheer amount of hard work she has put in to reach where she has. She is also grateful to those who have given her a chance and had the faith in her ability to deliver. She tries to pay it forward. 'People such as Makarand Adhikari and Rajnikanth have been important to my success. Sameer Nair and Uday Shankar, who gave me a chance to come back to Star; Subhash Chandra, who gave me *Pavitra Rishta* in 2009 when even I didn't believe in myself...there are so many people I could be grateful for. To give back is to mentor. If you see a spark, give it a chance.'[11]

In 2020, she was awarded the fourth-highest civilian honour, the Padma Shri. She had earlier received the prestigious Dadasaheb Phalke Iconic Film & Television Producer Award in 2012. She was already among Forbes list of '50 most powerful women in Asia' and has received many other accolades for her work. While the film industry is known for being the old boys' club, television paradoxically is dominated by women at every level, right to the top, with even the content being created keeping the female audience in mind. To quote her, 'If there's a big-boys' club in movies, there's a big-girls' club in TV—the "Cashmere mafia". If there is a gender bias, it's not going to last.'[12] To this end, she's initiated Indian Women Rising: A Cinema Collective with producer Guneet Mongia and writer-director Tahira Kashyap to promote talented independent women filmmakers in India.

Ekta Kapoor has created and nurtured some of the biggest names in the business—actors, writers and directors, and she continues to create some of the most compelling and popular television shows and movies. It is the Indian audience that drives her to keep doing better, to make content that appeals to everyone and that which young and old alike can relate to, across demographies.

NOTES

1. Sonia Mariam Thomas, 'Drawn into TV production at the young age of 19, how Ekta Kapoor became India's "Soap Rani"', *Outlook Business Wow*, https://wow.outlookbusiness.com/ekta-kapoor/. Accessed on 19 January 2022.
2. Suhani Singh, 'Balaji Telefilms' journey from Jeetendra's garage to becoming one of India's most successful production house', *India Today*, 11 August 2017, https://www.indiatoday.in/magazine/cover-story/story/20170821-balaji-telefilms-ekta-kapoor-k-serials-production-house-1028860-2017-08-11/ Accessed on 19 January 2022.
3. Sonia Mariam Thomas, 'Drawn into TV production at the young age of 19, how Ekta Kapoor became India's "Soap Rani"', *Outlook Business Wow*, https://wow.outlookbusiness.com/ekta-kapoor/. Accessed on 19 January 2022.
4. Ibid.
5. Ibid.
6. Ekta Kapoor shares rare family photo featuring Jeetendra and Tusshar Kapoor, says 'we have come a long way"', *Hindustan Times*, https://www.hindustantimes.com/tv/ekta-kapoor-shares-rare-family-photo-featuring-jeetendra-and-tusshar-kapoor-says-we-have-come-a-long-way-story-HjXbfMEkoS5zvohvk8dEXJ.html. Accessed on 19 January 2022.
7. Ekta Kapoor: Primetime primadonna, *Live Mint*, 15 December 2017, https://www.livemint.com/Consumer/0sffLmm7LMlJTMqyTzlubL/Ekta-Kapoor-Primetime-primadonna.html. Accessed on 19 January 2022.
8. Shalini Ojha, '#WomensDay: How Ekta Kapoor touches lives of millions of women', *News Byte*, 8 March 2019, https://www.

	newsbytesapp.com/timeline/Entertainment/42909/192038/women-s-day-special-celebrating-the-icon-ekta-kapoor. Accessed on 19 January 2022.
9	'Ekta Kapoor: Making "Nagin" for TV as much fun as "Broken But Beautiful" for OTT', Sify, 16 November 2019, https://www.sify.com/movies/ekta-kapoor-making-nagin-for-tv-as-much-fun-as-broken-but-beautiful-for-ott-news-bollywood-tlqpEqdafhcdd.html. Accessed on 19 January 2022.
10	Priyanka Chandani, 'My shows are regressive: Ekta Kapoor', *Asian Age*, https://www.asianage.com/age-on-sunday/250519/my-shows-are-regressive-ekta-kapoor.html. Accessed on 19 January 2022.
11	Sonia Mariam Thomas, 'Drawn into TV production at the young age of 19, how Ekta Kapoor became India's "Soap Rani"', *Outlook Business Wow*, https://wow.outlookbusiness.com/ekta-kapoor/. Accessed on 19 January 2022.
12	Ibid.

24

KIRAN BEDI

CRANE BEDI

The first woman to join the Indian Police Service (IPS), Kiran Bedi has been a visible face of the Indian Police Force for the 35 years that she was in service before she opted for voluntary retirement in 2007.

Hers has been a tumultuous journey, filled with achievements, firsts, awards and some controversies, all in good measure. It all began on 9 June 1949, when she was born in Amritsar. Bedi was the second of three sisters. Her father Prakash worked in the family's textile business. Her father was also an avid tennis player, and the young Kiran developed a fascination for the sport watching him play. She started training in tennis from the age of nine. As a teenager, she cut her hair short because she felt long hair interfered with her game. Between 1965 and 1978, she would go on to win titles at the state level and national level. They were a tennis-playing family and had to get up early to do their fitness and practice. They valued education equally, something their mother instilled in them. Along with playing competitive tennis, the sisters were toppers of their respective classes.

She graduated with a BA in English in 1968 from the Government College for Women in Amritsar. In 1970, she would get her master's degree in political science from Panjab University, and would teach political science at the Khalsa

College for Women in Amritsar for the next two years. She would also continue with her education, getting a law degree from Delhi University in 1988 and her PhD from Indian Institute of Technology's (IIT), Department of Social Sciences, Delhi, in 1993. In 1972, she married Brij Bedi, a tennis player she had met on the tennis courts in Amritsar. The two had a simple wedding ceremony in a temple and would go on to have a daughter, Sukriti, who would later change her name to Saina. The marriage would be short-lived; Bedi and her husband would spend most of their married life separately.

In 1972, the year she got married, she also began training at the National Academy of Administration in Mussoorie for a career in the IPS; she was then the only woman in a batch of 80 trainees. She would graduate from this training programme, becoming the first woman IPS officer ever. Post a six-month foundation course, she did a further nine months of training in Rajasthan at Mount Abu. This was followed by further training with the Punjab Police in 1973. She was allocated the Union Territory cadre. She would be posted in Delhi, Goa, Chandigarh and Mizoram in the course of her career with the IPS. Her first posting was as an assistant superintendent of police in Chanakyapuri, Delhi. She would also become the first woman to lead the all-male contingent of Delhi Police at the Republic Day Parade in 1975.

Her posting in Chanakyapuri had put her in charge of one of the most prestigious areas in Delhi, including Parliament House, foreign embassies, the residences of both the president and the prime minister of India. The challenge in this posting was the number of political demonstrations in this area. In the 1970s, the conflict between the Akali and Nirankari factions of the Sikh community was at its peak. In November 1978, India Gate saw a huge congregation by the Nirankaris, and simultaneously a parallel contingent of the Akalis demonstrating against them. The situation was very volatile and Bedi charged at them with just her baton in hand, without hesitating even when protestors brandishing swords ran towards her. With only their batons to defend themselves, she and her unit managed to take control of the situation. She sustained injuries to her elbow and leg. She was barely 29 at the time.[1]

This act of bravery won her the President's Police Medal for Gallantry in 1979, which was awarded to her in 1980. In 1979 itself, she was posted to Delhi's West District, and in 1981, she was appointed Deputy Commissioner of Police (DCP, Traffic). Given this was the national capital with the government, ministers, civil servants and embassies all located here, she had the added pressure of the forthcoming 1982 Asian Games, and the construction of 19 stadiums concurrently in the city, along with several flyovers. The blockades and diversions were taking their toll on the smooth flow of traffic. She brought in the use of tow trucks (cranes) to tow away vehicles that were wrongly parked. This earned her the moniker 'Crane Bedi', but what really catapulted her into the spotlight was when a white Ambassador car from the Prime Minister's Office (PMO) was towed away by the traffic police on 5 August 1982.[2] She also sought sponsorships and managed to get jeeps for the traffic police.

She was transferred to Goa as soon as the Asian Games were over. Bedi's term in Goa began in March 1983, months before the prestigious Commonwealth Heads of Government Meeting (CHOGM) scheduled there in November. This transfer was a full seven months after the incident with the PMO's car.[3] At the time, the important Zuari Bridge, which connected Panjim with North Goa, while completed, had not yet been opened to the public because the state government wanted the then Prime Minister, Indira Gandhi, to inaugurate it. During her regular everyday patrol, Bedi saw the huge crowd waiting for the ferry and drove to the bridge, took away the blockades, asked the crowd to move to the bridge and cross over. This action of hers resulted in an uproar.[4]

In November 1983, the CHOGM was a huge challenge, but just having been in charge of the Asian Games in New Delhi the previous year, Bedi was up for it. She was then assigned the position of deputy commandant at the Railway Protection Force in Delhi. After six months, she was reassigned to the Department of Industrial Development in the position of deputy director, working under the Directorate General of Industrial Contingency (DGIC). In 1986, she was made DCP of Delhi's North District.

In 1988, an incident involving a lawyer practising at the Tis Hazari court snowballed when he was arrested and handcuffed. The lawyers protested against his being handcuffed, and Bedi defended this handcuffing.[5] The lawyers led a procession to her office demanding her suspension and were supported by many politicians. The police lathicharged lawyers on strike in Tis Hazari on 21 January, this was followed by a mob running riot at Tis Hazari and smashing car windscreens and destroying the lawyer's chambers in February. This incident would go on to have a major fallout, with the lawyers demanding Bedi's resignation. The Delhi High Court then set up a two-judge committee to investigate this incident, the final report censured Bedi. It was the then Home Minister Buta Singh who acceded to her request to be posted to the Andamans, Arunachal Pradesh or Mizoram.[6]

In April 1990, she took over as deputy inspector general (Range) of Mizoram. Her daughter and her parents moved with her to Mizoram. She would also complete her PhD research during her posting in Mizoram; she received her doctorate in 1993 from IIT Delhi's Social Sciences department for a thesis on drug abuse and domestic violence. A controversy erupted with allegations that she reportedly got her daughter an MBBS seat through the Mizoram quota, leading to protests in the state. She left her position and returned to Delhi under controversial circumstances. She justified her action to NDTV later by saying, 'The rules were that if you've studied in Mizoram [or] living in

Mizoram [and] qualify on merit, then you can get a seat.'[7]

She returned to Delhi in September 1992 and in May 1993, she was appointed as the inspector general of Delhi Prisons. With the charge of Delhi Prisons, she now had to manage the notorious Tihar Jail, a four-jail complex with an original capacity to house around 2,500 prisoners. When Bedi took charge, the prisoners incarcerated numbered around 9,500. Bedi introduced reforms, put hardened criminals into separate barracks, organized vocational training for prisoners, and got the Indira Gandhi National Open University and National Open School to set up their centres right within the prison premises. She set up legal cells in the prison for undertrials and a de-addiction centre. She also brought in a nationalized bank branch on the premises as well as a bakery, a carpentry workshop and a weaving unit.

In May 1994, she organized a health check-up for all the inmates of Tihar. A doctor who visited two of the adolescent wards reportedly claimed that two-thirds of the inmates disclosed that they were indulging in homosexual intercourse and recommended condoms be distributed amongst the inmates to prevent HIV, a suggestion that was endorsed by the then health minister. Bedi however disallowed the distribution of condoms.[8]

Nonetheless, despite this controversy, her work at Tihar got her back into the public eye. The reforms in the infamous Tihar Jail would win her the prestigious Ramon Magsaysay Award in 1994. After a controversy regarding special concessions allegedly given to the serial killer Charles Sobhraj, who was put in Tihar twice, she was removed from the position. In 1999, she was appointed as inspector general of police in Chandigarh.

In 2003, she would become the first Indian woman to be appointed as police advisor to the Secretary General of the United Nations in the Department of Peacekeeping Operations. She came back to Delhi in 2005 after a two-year stint at the

United Nations. She was then appointed as the director general, Home Guards, and then the director general of the Bureau of Police Research and Development. She resigned from the IPS in 2007.

Bedi along with her colleagues launched a campaign against drug abuse, which was renamed Navjyoti India Foundation in 2007. It did commendable work in drug and alcohol rehabilitation and was also involved in the education of street children and slum kids. She established the Navjyoti Community College, which was affiliated with IGNOU in 2010. Back in 1994, Bedi had also set up the India Vision Foundation to work in the space of police and prison reforms, women's empowerment and rural community development. Between 2008 and 2011, she anchored a televised talk show called *Aap Ki Kachehri*. During the anti-corruption movement that swept the nation in 2011, led by Anna Hazare, Bedi joined forces with Arvind Kejriwal and the others who eventually formed the Aam Aadmi Party (AAP). She was part of the AAP for a while, but decided to quit in 2015 and join the Bharatiya Janata Party, where she was given a ticket to contest the 2015 Delhi Assembly Elections. She was pegged as the party's chief ministerial candidate, but unfortunately she didn't win. Post this, in May 2016, she was made the Lieutenant Governor of the Union Territory of Puducherry. When suddenly removed from her position as Lieutenant Governor on 16 February 2021, a few months before her term was due to end, she returned to Delhi.

From the young girl on the tennis court who cropped her hair to the Lieutenant Governor of Puducherry who thought nothing of going around the city on a two-wheeler, Kiran Bedi continues to defy expectations and set new norms. She continues to be a woman who lives by her own rules in a man's world.

NOTES

1. 'In a riot I feel more responsible: DCP Kiran Bedi', *India Today*, 16 March 2015, https://www.indiatoday.in/magazine/indiascope/story/19781130-in-a-riot-i-feel-more-responsible-dcp-kiran-bedi-823419-2014-04-09. Accessed on 19 January 2022.
2. 'I was transferred to Goa for removing Indira Gandhi's car: Bedi', *The Economic Times*, 26 April 2010, https://economictimes.indiatimes.com/i-was-transferred-to-goa-for-removing-indira-gandhis-car-bedi/articleshow/5860410.cms?utm_source=contentofinterest&utm_medium=text&utm_campaign=cppst. Accessed on 19 January 2022.
3. Sandipan Sharma, 'BJP's Delhi CM candidate: Story of Kiran "Crane" Bedi is more myth than fact', *FirstPost*, 29 January 2015, https://www.firstpost.com/politics/bjps-delhi-cm-candidate-story-of-kiran-crane-bedi-is-more-myth-than-fact-2056451.html. Accessed on 19 January 2022.
4. Ibid.
5. 'Why protesting Delhi cops are raising "we need you, Kiran Bedi" cards. Here's what happened 31 yrs ago', IndiaTV, https://www.indiatvnews.com/fyi/story-behind-delhi-police-we-need-you-kiran-bedi-slogan-561465. Accessed on 19 January 2022
6. Sandipan Sharma, 'BJP's Delhi CM candidate: Story of Kiran "Crane" Bedi is more myth than fact', *FirstPost*, 29 January 2015, https://www.firstpost.com/politics/bjps-delhi-cm-candidate-story-of-kiran-crane-bedi-is-more-myth-than-fact-2056451.html. Accessed on 19 January 2022.
7. 'Truth vs Hype: As She Plunges into Politics, the Kiran Bedi Legend Comes under Scrutiny', NDTV, 25 January 2015, https://www.ndtv.com/delhi-news/truth-vs-hype-as-she-plunges-into-politics-the-kiran-bedi-legend-comes-under-scrutiny-731873. Accessed on 19 January 2022.

8. 'Tihar jail bans condoms', *India Today*, 31 May 1994, https://www.indiatoday.in/magazine/indiascope/story/19940531-tihar-jail-bans-condoms-809220-1994-05-31. Accessed on 19 January 2022.

25

MARY KOM

MAGNIFICENT MARY

When she was barely 10 years old, she watched a biopic on a martial arts legend Bruce Lee and this story stayed in some remote corner of her mind. Little did she know then that years later, in 2014, she too would have a movie made on her. The film, *Mary Kom*, had Bollywood superstar Priyanka Chopra Jonas playing the protagonist, immortalizing her story on celluloid.

International boxing champion Mangte Chungneijang Mary Kom wears many feathers in her cap. She is a member of the Upper House of Parliament. She has been bestowed with the Arjuna Award, the Rajiv Gandhi Khel Ratna Award, Padma Shri, Padma Vibhushan and Padma Bhushan. Not just an Olympic medal winner in boxing, she is also the World Amateur Boxing Champion six times over and No. 1 in the AIBA World Women's Ranking Light Flyweight category. She is also the first Indian woman boxer to get a gold medal at the Asian Games 2014 at Incheon, South Korea, the first Indian woman boxer to win gold at the 2018 Commonwealth Games and the only boxer to win the Asian Amateur Boxing Championship five times, a record in itself.

An unlikely international elite athlete, she was born on 24 November 1982, in the remote Kangathei village in the Churachandpur district of rural Manipur. Her parents were tenant farmers who worked in the fields. The poverty she grew up in was real and gritty, circumstances so dire that daily survival itself was a struggle. As a child, Mary helped her parents with the everyday chores around the farm and at home, and later, when she got into sports, she managed her chores alongside her training. In his youth, her father was a wrestler of some repute. She is the eldest child of the family and has a younger sister and brother. She was introduced to athletics in school and took keen interest in training in javelin throw and 400 metres running. She had to leave home and move to Imphal to study at the sports academy. She was barely 15.[1] It was a decision that was destined to change her life. She would eventually graduate from Churachandpur College in Imphal. The return of Dingko Singh from the 1998 Bangkok Asian Games with a gold medal in boxing made him a hero in the state, with many kids in Manipur looking to follow in his footsteps. Mary was one of them.

A friend, Rebika Chiru, who was a national-level boxer, told her that the Sports Authority of India's Imphal Centre was opening slots for women's boxing. Perhaps Mary would like to try her luck. And so she did. She went to the Centre herself, on a hope and a prayer, asking around for coach L. Ibomcha Singh, who agreed to take her on, but felt she wouldn't be able to cope. She would go on to prove him wrong. In 2000, she would continue her training under K. Kosana Meitei in Imphal. Her next coach was the Manipur State Boxing Coach, M. Narjit Singh at Khuman Lampak, Imphal.

There was another battle she had to fight when she decided to take up boxing as a sport: her father's complete resistance to the very idea. He forbade Mary from training in boxing. Mary kept it a secret from him for the longest time. It was when she won the state boxing championship in 2000 and her photograph was splashed across the local newspapers that her father got to know of her training in boxing. He was upset and demanded that she quit the sport. She was determined to continue with or without his support and so she did.

Perhaps the strongest force Mary Kom has behind her is her husband Karung Onkholer, aka Onler. He was at the time the president of the Northeast students' body at Delhi University. They began dating and were married in 2005. They have three children, twin boys born in 2007 and a son who was born in 2013. In 2006, her father-in-law, Reikhupthang Kamang was killed by the Manipur Komrem National Front. He had been a great support to Mary and Onler, and she was devastated by his death, almost giving up boxing, blaming her fame and the ensuing resentment around it as the reason for him being targeted. At the same time, her husband Onler went into a terrible state of mental agitation, to the point of contemplating joining the insurgency to avenge his father's killing. However, when Mary Kom gave birth to twins in 2007, Onler saw this as a sign that his father, who was also one of a pair of twins, was still with them. He abandoned his notion of seeking revenge. Mary returned to training. Onler pushed her to get back to training and sacrificed his own ambitions of becoming a lawyer, totally taking over the care and responsibility of the children, becoming the primary parent.[2]

Mary was back in form and won a silver medal at the 2008 Asian Women's Boxing Championship in India and gold at the AIBA Women's World Boxing Championship in China. She followed both these up with a gold at the 2009 Asian Indoor Games in Vietnam.

In 2010, she won gold at the Asian Women's Boxing Championship in Kazakhstan, as well as at the AIBA Women's World Boxing Championships. This would be her fifth consecutive gold at the AIBA. In the Asian Games that year, she went up to the 51 kilograms class from the 48 kilograms she had competed in at the AIBA and won bronze.

Just before the Asian Cup in 2011, she had a personal crisis. Her son, Khupnievar, was diagnosed with a congenital heart condition and required emergency surgery. He was barely four at the time. The family had a Manipuri friend who was a heart surgeon at the Postgraduate Institute of Medical Education and Research in Chandigarh and they decided to get the surgery done there, given its proximity to the National Institute of Sports (NIS) Patiala, where Mary Kom trained. Onler insisted that Mary fly out to China and compete, he would hold the fort and look after their son. Despite the intense emotional pressure she must have been under, she won gold in the 48 kilograms at the China Asian Women's Cup. She rushed back to India as soon as she could, landed at the airport in Delhi and drove directly to Chandigarh to be with her son in the hospital.[3]

The 2012 AIBA Women's World Boxing Championships were important for her because it wasn't just the title she was competing for but also for a spot in the 2012 Summer Olympics to be held in London. It was the first time ever that women's boxing would be part of the Summer Olympics and Mary was determined to be part of it. She won the bronze in the 51 kilograms semi-finals, defeated by Nicola Adams of the UK, qualifying for the Olympics. Her mother accompanied her to London for the 2012 Summer Olympics; she won an Olympic bronze and made the country proud.

In 2014, she won her first Asian Games gold at Incheon, South Korea, competing in the 51 kilograms category. In 2017, she won a fifth gold medal in the 48 kilograms category at the ASBC Asian Confederation Women's Boxing Championships at Ho Chi Minh City in Vietnam. She made up for the lack of a medal at the Commonwealth Games the next year, when in 2018, she finally won gold the year her category was introduced, competing in the 48 kilograms light flyweight. The very same year, she would make history by winning six world championships and the 10th AIBA Women's World Boxing Championships in New Delhi. In 2019, she was named in the boxing athlete ambassadors group for the 2020 Tokyo Olympic Games by the International Olympic Committee. She has been allowed the use of the post-nominal letters OLY after her name by the World Olympian Association.[4]

In fact, she is the only boxer across male and female categories to win eight World Championship medals.

It had been a tough journey. Tournaments in India were held in places such as Kolkata and Hisar where the athletes travelled by state transport buses and sleeper trains because they wouldn't be able to claim reimbursement on air conditioned compartments. When she won the Olympic medal in 2012, the Manipur government awarded her ₹50 lakh and two acres of land. She failed to qualify for the 2016 Rio Olympics and at Tokyo 2020, held in 2021 due to the pandemic, she lost to Columbia's Ingrit Valencia.

In 2013, author Dina Serto worked with her to co-author her autobiography, *Unbreakable* and in 2014, the movie *Mary Kom*, on her life, with Priyanka Chopra playing the title role was released. She feels the movie, despite everyone's best effort, failed to capture the visceral struggle that her life was, that she worked the fields with her bare hands, like a boy when she was young, no excuses made for her being a girl. No one can capture it, she says, unless they have lived it, understood it, internalized it.[5]

She lives in Delhi now, as a member of the Upper House of Parliament. Her days are hectic. As a Rajya Sabha member she attends the House when in session, she trains twice a day, and she has endorsements and appearances to attend to. She finds solace in religion. Whenever she is in her village in Manipur, she visits their church. On Sundays, she visits the Komrem Baptist Church in Delhi. Her faith is what keeps her going. She even sleeps with a Bible under her pillow.

Now is also time to give back to the sport that gave her so much and this she is doing with her academy. The Mary Kom Academy, occupying 3.3 acres of land in Lamphelpat, Imphal, and with a hostel attached to it, was set up in 2006. It is her attempt to build medal winners from the grassroots. It was a tough battle to start the academy and get it running, supervising it from a long distance given her need to be in Delhi and her own training and competitive schedule. But she shrugs it off. She will just do what she can, the best she can: continue training, possibly for another World Championship title, for another Olympic medal, for more accolades, as magnificently as she can. After all, she *is* Magnificent Mary.

Excerpts from an interview with her.

When you were a young girl, you grew up in very challenging circumstances. How do you think your childhood shaped your determination and grit?

Yes, my childhood was indeed challenging and full of struggles. There was hardly any manual work that I did not do, even those meant for boys and men. I once detested my life as a child as most of my wishes remained unfilled, but I later realized that they were the factors for all the achievements I could make thus far. Those experiences trained my mind and gave me the skills to tolerate hardships. It let me accept all the struggles in my boxing career as normal. It also prepared my physical fitness and endurance.

You were always attracted to sports and athletics. You took to boxing after Dingko Singh returned with his gold medal. Did you face any resistance while taking up boxing as it was not considered a sport for women?

I faced resistance first from my family, especially my father. It took me sometime to convince him. And of course it was harder and impossible for me to convince the society, which talked much about my switching to boxing, saying it is not appropriate for a girl, but I took it as a challenge to prove them wrong.

You were barely 15 when you moved to Imphal to study and train at the Sports Academy. As a young girl, staying away from your family, what were the challenges you faced?

My passion to learn and win was greater than any of the feelings around. The only limitation or challenge was resources. Since I came from a poor family, my parents couldn't support all my requirements in terms of food, nutrition, rent and other financial requirements, for which I had to stay in the house of my relatives, helping them in the household chores. Only those who have gone through this experience will understand how difficult it is to manage time or work. Helping in the household work becomes one of the priorities even though not an obligation or not asked or forced to do. I had to force myself to fulfill both: training and work.

Within yourself, what were the fears you had to overcome when you chose boxing?

I have my inborn strength; I am bold and confident in almost everything except for public speaking (*laughs*). When I chose boxing, I knew I can do great in it.

Given boxing is a sport of aggression yet tactical playing, how did you have to reprogramme yourself to be more aggressive?

My thirst to win! Boxing, by nature, is a game of aggression. You have to be aggressive.

You have a number of firsts and the only woman to have credits to your name. What is the pressure on you to keep living up to the expectations from your own self, not just from those in the fraternity?

It is very natural for a person to live under pressures to maintain or safeguard the status or level of achievement. I too have it but as for me, boxing has become a part of me. I always stay fit and try to give my best. And with the experiences I have acquired for years, there is less pressure.

That first bronze at the Olympics in 2012 put you in the public eye and you became an icon to women and girls all over India at the time. Tell us about your emotions and feelings in the run-up to that bout and on winning.

Human wants are unlimited. People must have envied my achievement and I was also very happy to have won, though not as I wanted and hoped for. Yes, participating in Olympics was my dream but after winning a bronze, I still want to change the colour of the medal. It was such a good feeling that I cried and felt so good for having won the first medal for India in women's boxing.

As a mother, you've never let parenting and motherhood come in the way of your training and performance. They often say, the most important career decision a woman can make is who she chooses to be her husband. How would you say your husband's support kept you going through it all?

My husband is a soft gentleman, who knows how to handle or deal with any situation well. He takes good care of my children and lets me feel that all is well and I need not worry about anything. This is why I could focus on my training without any tension. Not only that, he manages my professional matters. I am so proud of him and have confidence in him.

Another very common factor that professional women and mothers deal with is the guilt of spending work time away from their young children. Did you face it and if yes, how did you deal with it?

I spend most of my days in training camps and competitions. As a mother, there is such a strong longing to be with my family and children. I have had to leave them at one year of age. What I would do is call them and talk to them over the phone, make sure I keep good stock of their requirements during my absence.

Religion is very important to you. How would you say it keeps you focused and centred in your bouts?

Apart from your preparation and effort, when you commit the rest of the bout to God, it is such a good feeling to fight without much pressure. You believe that your sincere efforts and sweat will not be in vain. You rather focus on your bout with calmness.

You've had a biopic made on your story. Do you think the film did your struggle justice or was there a lot that went on behind the scenes that didn't come through in the film?

It is difficult to include everything about me, my life and my struggles in a two-hour-long movie. The movie did its best to portray my life and journey, but there was still a lot more which was not seen in the movie.

As someone who has been in high-pressure bouts globally, what is your routine before you go into the ring to keep yourself in the zone?

I just thank God for another opportunity and commit the rest into His hands. I had done my part in preparing and training well, I will give my best in the bout but the winning and losing part is beyond my control. I just pray to God to help me do my best.

As a member of the Rajya Sabha, how involved are you as a representative of both women sportspersons, as well as the Northeast in the House?

As I am still active in my sports career, my parliamentary responsibility is secondary. As of now, I am just showing my respect to the honour given to me by the government. If time favours me, I hope to be a voice for sports and the Northeast in the future.

What is your daily schedule like, given your multiple responsibilities in sports bodies, being a Member of Parliament, as well as your training?

I start my day by seeing off my kids to school after they have their breakfast. I then set off for the morning session of my training. I train twice a day, morning and evening, for fitness and endurance, which I hardly compromise on unless unavoidable.

Then I quickly freshen up for Parliament session (only during sessions). If I am lucky enough, I get to sleep for an hour or two in the afternoon, which will be followed by my evening session of training. This is my everyday schedule. Besides these, there will be sets of meeting people/visitors, interviews, photo and video shoots, and travelling for events and programmes.

You began the Mary Kom Academy to train youngsters. Tell us your motivation to start this academy and how you manage to run the academy.

There are hundreds of budding athletes and boxers who will definitely face similar hardships that I came across. I don't want to let others experience the same, lest they end up nowhere. This is why I offer all possible support in my academy. They lack nothing and they don't have to worry about anything apart from their training.

My husband, with a team of trustworthy individuals, manages the entire administration. I also have a group of trainers and coaches who train the boxers. When I am home, I am there to assist, observe, correct and motivate them.

On a lighter note, tell us about your tattoos and what motivated you to get them done.

This had been in my mind since 2012, post London Olympics, but did not get a green signal from my husband though he was not against it. I always feel that I deserve to have and carry a piece of Olympic on me as I have already won a medal, therefore I tattooed its logo on my left arm. On the other side, I put on a cross signifying my faith in Jesus Christ, who is the reason of my existence and victory. All the Glory to Him!

NOTES

1. https://sportsmatik.com/hall-of-fame/view/mary-kom-2048. Accessed on 21 January 2022.
2. Sourabh Duggal, 'MC Mary Kom: Unboxed', *Hindustan Times*, 1 October 2014, https://www.hindustantimes.com/brunch/mc-mary-kom-unboxed/story-YxEatSTDqlRdY51Rstmi3O.html. Accessed on 21 January 2022.
3. 'Mary breaks down after seeing sick son,' *Mid-Day*, 12 May 2011, https://www.mid-day.com/articles/mary-breaks-down-after-seeing-ill-son/121647. Accessed on 21 January 2022.
4. Six-time world champion Mary Kom becomes "Mary Kom OLY"', *India Today*, 7 November 2019, https://www.indiatoday.in/sports/other-sports/story/world-champion-mary-kom-mary-kom-thanks-world-olympian-association-woa-oly-title-1616685-2019-11-07. Accessed on 22 January 2022.
5. Gaurav Bhatt, 'Mary Kom on punches, prayers and what still drives her', *The Indian Express*, 10 November 2019, https://indianexpress.com/article/express-sunday-eye/how-does-an-athlete-at-the-pinnacle-of-her-career-motivate-herself-for-more-6111347. Accessed on 19 January 2022.

26

MENAKA GURUSWAMY

BY THE CONSTITUTION

Menaka Guruswamy is imposing in the quiet way that only a woman who is comfortable in her skin is. She can own a room when she walks into it, her gaze is direct, her voice is calm and assured and she is imposing without being overpowering. In her office in New Delhi, the collected works of Dr Bhimrao Ambedkar, a recent gift, bears pride of position along with a photograph of Pandit Jawaharlal Nehru. These are both men who inspire her, men she admires and whose life work she draws strength from. Perhaps this is also why she is among the top constitutional lawyers in not just the country, but the world over, and why she is so passionate about taking up cases that compel one to revisit the Constitution and defend it. Of all the achievements to her name though, Menaka Guruswamy is most identified with her role in the landmark win striking down Section 377, a win that was historic in the decriminalizing of a colonial era law in India, which considered homosexuality as a criminal act. However, it will be unfair to identify her solely on the basis of this victory.

She bears her many accolades lightly. Senior advocate at the Supreme Court of India, B.R. Ambedkar Research Scholar and Lecturer at Columbia Law School and visiting faculty at Yale Law School, New York University School of Law and University of Toronto School of Law, she has to her credit many other landmark cases, including the bureaucratic reforms case, the infamous AgustaWestland case, the Salwa Judum case and the Right to Education legal battle, among others. She's been amicus curiae with the Supreme Court in the case concerning the alleged extrajudicial killings in Manipur, perhaps the first time that the Central Bureau of Investigation (CBI) has filed 41 first person reports (FIRs) against security personnel.[1]

Apart from these achievements, she's worked as an advisor with the United Nations Development Fund and the United Nations Children's Fund (UNICEF) in New York and South Sudan on international human rights law. She's worked with Nepal on the constitution-making process.

Her parents, Mohan Guruswamy, a former advisor to the Ministry of Finance, and Meera Guruswamy, an advertising professional, were far removed from the world of law. But her mother was fascinated by it and steered young Menaka towards the world of legal strategy and the words of legal luminaries. It had a profound effect on Menaka. She had her early education at the Hyderabad Public School, completing high school at Sardar Patel Vidyalaya, New Delhi. In 1992, she was all set to take up economics when serendipitously her mother read about the National Law School of India University (NLSIU) which had been set up a few years ago on the outskirts of Bangalore. She recommended Menaka give law school a shot, stay there for a year and see if she liked it; if she didn't she could always come back to Delhi. Menaka went to NLSIU and loved it.[2]

She found her passion within the Constitution of India and went on to study law further, going on to being awarded the Rhodes Scholarship to read for the Bachelor of Civil Law (BCL) at the University of Oxford in 2000, and the Gammon Fellowship for her Master of Laws (LL.M) at Harvard in 2001. In 2015, she was awarded a DPhil from Oxford for her thesis on constitutionalism in India, Pakistan and Nepal.

She began her professional career in 1997 working with the then Attorney General of India, Ashok Desai, whom she considers a mentor, focusing on litigation and constitutional law. She was just 21 then, the youngest in the office. Everyone around in court were at least twice or thrice her age and women were just about getting into the legal profession. While she was there, she was amongst the juniors on the team who worked on controversial cases like the Jain Hawala case and the fodder scam case, among others.[3]

She went to Oxford a year and a half later to study further. In 2001, after completing her BCL at Oxford, and her LL.M from Harvard, she practised for a while at Davis Polk & Wardwell in New York as an associate. But she came back to India, to New Delhi. Her heart, she says, was in constitutional law, specifically Indian constitutional law and she is most enthused to fight cases around constitutional rights in India. Also, in an interview, she confesses that her favourite thing to do is to walk down the streets of New Delhi in early winter, past heritage structures, with the sun just right—a reminder of what she loves about the country and why she decided to come back home.

Her current practice at the Supreme Court of India covers corporate, constitutional as well as criminal law. She has also represented the Union of India, and the National Capital Region.

What really did shoot her into the limelight was her role in the legal battle to decriminalize homosexuality in India. In April 2016, a team of lawyers filed a landmark petition in the Supreme Court, representing five LGBT (lesbian, gay, bisexual and transgender) petitioners who were challenging Section 377 of the Indian Penal Code, 1860 which criminalized homosexuality. Menaka was part of this team, along with Arundhati Katju. The petitioners were led by Navtej Singh Johar. This was the first time ever petitioners had filed in the Supreme Court that Section 377 violated their fundamental rights. Menaka appeared for these petitioners and also for subsequent petitioners who were students and alumni of the Indian Institutes of Technology (IITs) from all over India. The judgement by the Supreme Court reading down Section 377 as not applicable for consenting adults, was a landmark one, leading to much celebration amongst the LGBTQ community in India, who were finally now, free to love.

After the historic verdict decriminalizing Section 377, Menaka and Arundhati announced on the Fareed Zakaria talk show on CNN that they were in a relationship and this coming out of the duo who had worked on this case created ripples, with their victory in this case now just not only a professional one, but also one that was a huge personal vindication. On the show, she told Zakaria about the sinking moment during the earlier hearing of the case in 2013 when she realized that the verdict would not be in their favour. A senior judge asked a law officer if he personally knew any homosexuals, to which the officer laughed, saying he was not that modern. In that instant, Menaka realized that the judge did not even realize what the concept of being gay in India meant, when she was standing right there, before the Bench. That moment of invisibility to her was the erasure of what she and so many other LGBTQ Indians faced. The battle was personal; decriminalizing Section 377 was reclaiming the rights of so many like her who were denied being equal citizens of the country, thanks to an antiquated colonial era law. In her arguments, she would tell a five-judge Bench, 'How strongly must we love knowing we are unconvicted felons under Section 377? My Lords, this is love that must be constitutionally recognised, and not just sexual acts.'[4]

Among the other high-profile cases that she has been part of are the Salwa Judum case and of *Nandini Sundar versus the State of Chhattisgarh* in 2011 which was about the existent practice of using tribal youths to fight against Maoist insurgency and led to the disarming of the youth. The next year, she was appointed amicus curiae in the case of the alleged 1,528 extrajudicial killings by the armed forces in Manipur. She proposed the setting up of a Special Investigation Team to look into the killings. She represented former Air Chief Marshal S.P. Tyagi before a special CBI court in the AgustaWestland case, a case that had created headlines because of the kickback allegations in a helicopter purchase deal.[5]

In 2019, she was made senior advocate by the Supreme Court of India. Among the many honours she has received, the portrait of her hung at the Milner Hall in Rhodes House at the University of Oxford, is among the most poignant, making her the first Indian and only the second woman ever to receive this honour. She is nostalgic about what it means for a brown person, a woman, who remembers coming to Oxford and seeing only portraits of white men hung in those hallowed halls, to now see her own portrait adorning them. In her acceptance speech, she spoke about what it meant to be a woman from India coming to receive this honour, the awareness of the exploitative colonial legacy that the Rhodes Scholarship was built upon and how future Rhodes scholars had the responsibility to re-imagine the scholarship and to use the legacy to enhance equality and disseminate opportunities.

To quote from her acceptance speech,

> As an Indian, it was even more poignant to come for a post-graduate degree in England, whose history of colonisation and plunder of my country is something we still pay for. And whose lingering colonial remnants include poverty and deep divisions that have not healed.
>
> How it is then that one reconciles moral integrity with the enjoyment of such privilege that the Rhodes Scholarships and an Oxford degree bring? One does so by deploying this privilege to good use: by that, I mean to push the envelope in ways that this privilege allows you to. To ask tougher questions of authority, to attempt to always expand human freedom and be aware when our footsteps contract such freedom, and to practise our professions in

ways that better perpetuate equality, and never to forget that our higher education degrees, our time in this Oxford sunshine and the ability of this extraordinary scholarship to open doors is built on the backs of Africans.[6]

Also in 2019, she was in *Foreign Policy*'s 100 Global Thinkers List, with other names such as Michelle Obama, Kofi Annan and Jeff Bezos, amongst others. The same year, Harvard Law School included her in a portrait exhibition of Women Inspiring Change and she was among *Time* magazine's 100 Most Influential People. *Forbes India* included her in their 2019 list of Women Power Trailblazer.

She also has a number of essays in various publications to her credit and has co-edited *Founding Moments in Constitutionalism* published by Hart/Bloomsbury, UK. She is also working on a book on South Asian Constitutionalism, apart from which she writes extensively for publications like *The New York Times*, *The Hindu*, *The Indian Express* and *Scroll*, to name a few.

If she didn't become a lawyer, she thinks, she would have become a professional chess player; she jokes that one of her childhood aspirations was to become a backup dancer to Madonna, but that her cousins dissuaded her, telling her rather bluntly that she didn't have the talent for it. Chess, her other passion, has a lot in common with law, she feels; one must strategize, see the entire board, anticipate the opponent's moves. Litigation and law were her second option, something she had been fascinated with from an early age. Among her icons, she counts Cornelia Sorabjee, who was the first Indian woman to become a lawyer at a time when only men were admitted to the bar. She was also the first woman to read law at Oxford and Guruswamy sees her as a role model, as someone who set the path that she has now, years later, followed.

Travel is a passion and she's been lucky to have her work take her to different parts of the world as well: Nepal, South Sudan and New York, to name a few. Her favourite book, if you ask her, is something that is definitely not light reading: the Constitution of India. She holds it in high regard, so much so that she chooses to focus on constitutional law. And she continues the battle for the LGBTQIA community, now with her battle to legitimize same-sex marriage in India. As she says, it is a long journey, there's a lot to be done. And she is only just getting started.

Excerpts from a conversation with her:

Growing up, what made you take up law as your chosen career given that in India the tide is generally focused towards medicine or engineering? Was there a turning point or an incident that made you take this decision?

In fact, it was my mother who was super enthusiastic about me becoming a lawyer. My parents were not lawyers. My mother is a copywriter and my father was an economist. She would show me clippings of articles by eminent lawyers like Ram Jethmalani to get me interested in the field. In school, I did participate in many elocution competitions, debates and recitation competitions, and therefore I became comfortable thinking about ideas, with speaking in public, and I thought this is a good career option to pursue. For girls in India, to have supportive parents is a very important thing. We are still very much a patriarchal society, even more so back then. I am 45 now, I went to law school when I was 17, that's over two and a half decades ago. At that time, this law school had just been set up and no batch had graduated yet. It was a big thing to take that call to opt for the five-year law course. I had finished my schooling in Delhi, and had already applied for colleges here. I'd gotten into LSR [Lady Shri Ram] and St Stephen's. It was a risk of sorts I was taking, because at that point, law was traditionally taken up after getting your first degree. The five-year law degree is a recent phenomenon in the last 15 to 20 years. Traditionally law would be a second degree and one went to law school after graduating. But, both my parents have always been so incredibly supportive. I think I fell in love with law at law school, I think it took them by surprise as well about how deeply passionate I was, and am about it.

You said in an earlier interview, you found an approach to teaching law at the National Law School of India University that has been lost. Could you tell us more about your experience as a student there, and how it influenced your career trajectory?

We were the fifth batch at NLS. When I was in the first year, the fifth year hadn't graduated yet. It was an interesting experience, for one it was far removed from the big cities at the time. It was an idea of a few people to have this kind of a five-year programme, it brought back the integrity of the exam system. You had to attend class. I'd get into trouble for not attending class. Being so far from city life, it gave you the time and space to grow into yourself. You had students from all over the country, you made friends across the board. There's something so wonderful about an educational institution that attracts students from all over, you have different educational backgrounds, different cultures, different ethnicities, different religions, and it really taught you about the diversity of the country.

How has this experience at the NLSIU influenced, if at all, your approach to teaching now, as a professor?

I've been to different institutions now since I have a PhD from Oxford. When I joined the National Law School, it was a struggle to stay afloat. I learnt from that struggle, that you pick your own path and often those paths are not easy ones. I learnt this from the institution, from the man who founded it, Madhava Menon, from what a battle it was for him to find land, to find an uninterfering government, to build an institution on merit and to build an institution that said that the law must care about what is happening in the country. Also, by studying abroad you expand your world. You see different legal systems. It teaches you to compare and contrast. Being away from your country gives you time to reflect, and when you go to institutions that are serious about what they teach, they also give you the opportunity to interact with good teachers, motivated teachers, teachers who are generous with the time they give you, the ideas they are willing to discuss with you, it makes all the difference to your own approach.

You have a special interest in constitutional law. What is it about constitutional law that appeals to you?

The constitution of any country is part law and part politics. It is a text made by history and politics. It does two things: one, it tells you what your country is meant to be, what your country must aspire to and two, it is a very important way, when you litigate constitutional law cases, of expanding freedoms. I have a general practice, I do everything from criminal to corporate to constitutional law. I really enjoy doing criminal and constitutional law. Constitutional law is important for exactly this, that you can litigate things for the idea of your country, for those whose freedoms are being compressed, and makes you aware about why it is important to fight for these.

You have, in your legal career, taken up a wide variety of cases. What is it about a case that makes you decide to take it up?

Why to take a case is a decision you make on a daily basis. New cases come in, solicitors bring in new cases, so forth. I take cases that are interesting in criminal and commercial matters. I like representing all kinds of people, corporates, those accused of crimes, as well as those from the most vulnerable sections of society. What makes my job interesting as a lawyer is that you get to meet and interact with an array of people, you learn not to prejudge very quickly, you learn to understand the whole range of what actually motivates human beings. This idea that the guilty mustn't be represented is something I strongly disagree with. As lawyers, we are expected to take up all kinds of cases, we may be more motivated to take certain kinds of cases. In my case, these are cases about freedoms, about an unaccountable state, cases about the right to life. But equally so I find it interesting to represent corporations, to do bankruptcy cases, tax matters, and in the early years of my career, I represented the government and I would prosecute crime. If you practise in Delhi, in the Supreme Court, there is a great joy in getting that array of cases. Also, as a lawyer, you have to read up for your cases, you have to keep reading new things so there is a constant learning that is part of the job. There is something so cerebral and so intellectually satisfying about it. I may sometimes get very excited about some technicality in regulatory laws in a case that has come to me, and I'm very happy to do it, but at the same time, I'm equally happy to do a large rights case where the state has been accused of being unaccountable.

As kids we used to play with the Rubik's cube. I found it fascinating because you had to get a combination of things right. A case is just like that; you have a statute, you have an opposing party, you have a law that has been set or perhaps a law that needs to be overturned, all the things need to be set correctly for everything to fall in place. Two things I really love: Rubik's cube and chess. I played chess very seriously when I was younger and litigation is a lot like chess; you have to strategize, you have to think ahead, you have to know what combination will get you ahead. You have to think of all the pieces on the board, the opposing side's pieces and moves, as well as your own pieces.

You are the first Indian and second woman to have her portrait hung at the Milner Hall in Rhodes House at the University of Oxford. What was your reaction when you heard of this honour, and why do you think it is important to have visible icons across gender, race and orientation in spaces like these in academia?

It was quite surprising. They just send you an email saying this has happened and we'd like to have your portrait painted, and so at first I thought it was a joke. I was travelling for work, so I just ignored the email. After a week I got another message from Rhodes House saying, 'Excuse me, did you get our previous email?' And that's when I realized that this was genuine. When the portrait was unveiled and we had a small ceremony, I did say this at the time, that the legacy of Cecil Rhodes is a pretty dark legacy, it is the legacy of colonisers. The Rhodes scholarship is basically built on the backs of Africans, because Rhodes made his fortune from Rhodesia, now Zimbabwe and the surrounding areas. So in some way, the origin of these scholarships is very dark. So getting these scholarships, it gives you enormous privilege, but the point is—what do you do with this privilege, how do you deploy it? How do you deploy these little platforms of privilege? For me, it was very important to have these difficult conversations, to do the hard cases, to write the hard pieces and to keep pushing. When I went as a young person to Oxford, I was 21 and as I looked around me at the walls of the universities, I saw only white people, only white men. I remember in the orientation programme, the Master of Ceremonies kept calling out the countries the students were from, he went through a list of North American and European countries and left out all of the Global South. The fact is that these institutions have to change, they have to be held accountable and we are part of the process of making that change. Former alumni like me are part of the process of engaging with the institution and making change possible. One small part of that change is about what is hanging on their walls, and another part of that change is who is hanging on those walls and what are they doing about their lives. There are stories there. I hope the young students of colour who go to Oxford now and see these other portraits that have been recently hung, will feel that places are more accessible to them, more friendly to them, that their stories are possible, that they are going to have wonderful lives ahead, where they have the opportunity to do meaningful work, interesting work.

The verdict that struck down Section 377 was a landmark verdict and a long, hard battle that you fought along with the others in the team. Tell us about the moments of despair and struggle when you perhaps were disheartened, and the little moments in the years that it took for the case that kept you going.

It has been a 20-year battle. We got involved a little after 2010, when appeals were filed against the judgement of the Delhi High Court. While it's been a long battle, what were the choices? I'm a queer person who is a lawyer. When we lost this case in 2013, I felt anger. I am not an angry person. But in 2013 to be called a criminal by your own workspace, it left me hugely angry. My instinctive response to this is that this is not okay. What are we going to do about this? What can we do differently? I am not made in that way, I don't know how to walk away. The biggest relief that one gets when a case ends is that the anger ebbs, because anger is not really a productive emotion.

I had a wonderful teacher and mentor, and a senior, Ashok Desai, who was an attorney general. I interned with him while I was at law school and then after I graduated from NLS. He passed away in March 2020. He was Buddhist, and he taught me about being detached and keeping anger at bay. He had been part of this case from 2008, I had taken a brief to him, and so, in a sense we lost together. He called me the next morning after the verdict in 2013 saying, 'Okay, so what are we doing to overturn this?' It meant the world to me that my mentor who was senior counsel, former attorney general, was equally pissed off. I think when you come from that kind of office, with those kind of teachers, it is very difficult to give up. You don't have the skill set to give up. I've made peace with the fact that we will win and lose a lot of battles. And a big thing for young people to consider is in life you will have happiness and disappointment, personally and professionally, that loss will teach you far more than success ever will; the best thing to do is to not get disheartened and keep going on to make things right. What are the good things you have in your life? For me, I have a wonderful family and a wonderful partner, friends and colleagues, a skill set and an occupation that gave me joy. I believe in counting my blessings at times like this. I would say, pick very carefully what you choose to do with your life, your career. That will make all the difference.

Having now won this battle, you are moving on to push for legislation to allow same-sex marriage.

It's a process, we will do anti-discrimination, the transgender act needs to be contested, before we get to same sex marriage. It is a journey. There's a lot to be done. Gay people all over the country just want to lead full lives, and we must do what we can.

Who are your icons? What inspires you about them and their work?

It might seem odd to say this in 2020, but professionally and personally for me, two very big heroes are Bhimrao Ambedkar and Jawaharlal Nehru. They were both lawyers, both picked very different paths. Ambedkar's life meant so much. An untouchable, sitting at the back of the class, not allowed to drink water from the same pot. Knowing and reading about his life, his quest for learning made me realize that knowledge is important, and how his quest for knowledge culminated in our Constitution. I just received a gift from a young solicitor of the collected works of Ambedkar, and I have it in my office, as well as a picture of Nehru and they're both very inspiring. Nehru, the son of the richest lawyer in Allahabad, educated abroad, chooses to give it all up for the freedom struggle, goes to prison for cumulatively nine years, spends his time in prison writing his books. *The Discovery of India* ends abruptly, because he runs out of ink and paper and they don't give him more. They're both human beings who've had hard, difficult and meaningful professional lives and there's so much to learn from their journeys.

Time magazine named you and Arundhati Katju in their list of 100 most influential people of 2019. What would be the ultimate honour that you still hope to achieve? What is the fight you still must fight?

I'm just getting started, honestly. I'm 45 now, I hope to have 25 to 30 years of professional life ahead of me, and I have an enormous amount of work to be done. For me, it is really the small joy of winning a case, and looking at the family's face when a loved one is out of prison, or when a loved one has been killed and justice has been delivered. It is those moments that make it all worthwhile.

Coming out on the Fareed Zakaria show was something that was an act of bravery and also an act of solidarity with the community you fought for so long and hard. What was the response to it, and how liberating was the feeling to finally come out to the world?

It wasn't like our colleagues or our neighbours or our families didn't know that we were partners. People knew. But for me, it boiled down to the conversations when I was growing up, when I was a young law student and I did not know if it was possible for a gay person to be a successful lawyer, I did not know if we could have happy lives. I would like young gay people to know that you will have happy and healthy lives, in as much as it is hard to be a young gay person, I think going through that process will get you to a place of personal happiness. I'd like them to know that they will have an array of role models who will be honest about their sexuality which is what will help young people to have happier lives, less mental health issues. Not just for queer people, but also when it comes to caste and religion, it is so important to have these pictures of strength across the board. Why is Ambedkar so important to all of us, and not just to Dalit Indians? It is because he told us through his life that your dreams are possible. I hope in 20 years we have young queer kids in India growing up with fewer challenges than my generation did, that would be true success for us. That's what it is all about.

NOTES

1. Dipanita Nath, 'The lawyer who wants to get her favourite book: the Constitution', *The Indian Express*, 12 May 2019, https://indianexpress.com/article/express-sunday-eye/and-justice-for-all-5719325/. Accessed on 19 January 2022.
2. Manu Balachandran, 'Menaka Guruswamy: Taking the law into her hands', *Forbes*, 6 March 2019, https://www.forbesindia.com/article/2019-wpower-trailblazers/menaka-guruswamy-taking-the-law-into-her-hands/52721/1
3. Dipanita Nath, 'The lawyer who wants to get her favourite book: the Constitution', *The Indian Express*, 12 May 2019, https://indianexpress.com/article/express-sunday-eye/and-justice-for-all-5719325/. Accessed on 19 January 2022.
4. Ibid.
5. PTI, 'AgustaWestland case: Court to pronounce order on SP Tyagi's bail plea on Dec 26', *The Indian Express*, 23 December 2016, https://indianexpress.com/article/india/agustawestland-case-court-to-pronounce-order-on-sp-tyagis-bail-plea-on-dec-26-4442100/. Accessed on 19 January 2020.
6. M. Guruswamy, 'How can Rhodes scholars reconcile themselves to the moral challenge posed by Rhodes's politics?' *Scroll.in*, 4 October 2017, https://scroll.in/article/851888/how-can-rhodes-scholars-reconcile-themselves-to-the-moral-challenge-posed-by-rhodess-politics. Accessed on 19 January 2022.

27

TESSY THOMAS

THE MISSILE WOMAN OF INDIA

The proud bearer of the titles 'Missile Woman of India' and 'Agni Putri', Dr Tessy Thomas, Director General Aeronautical Systems, Defence Research and Development Organisation (DRDO), has been quietly smashing male bastions. Former President of India and her mentor, Dr A.P.J. Abdul Kalam introduced Tessy Thomas as the Missile Woman of India at a gathering of students. Another moniker she bears with pride is Agni Putri, the daughter of fire. She is, after all, the first woman to lead a missile project with Agni III, and then following that success up with Agni IV, Agni V and more.

It's been a long, hard journey, fraught with challenges, for the young girl from the little town of Alappuzha in Kerala, the Venice of the East, with its picturesque backwater canals and abundant greenery. That she would grow up to become one of the leading names in missile technology and research in India was something her parents would possibly have never imagined. Born in April 1963, into a Syrian Christian family of Alappuzha, she was named Teresa after Mother Teresa, but she would come to be known by the diminutive Tessy that the family called her affectionately. She remembers going off to school every day, playing unconcernedly outside her home after school. When she was in class eight, her father suffered a stroke that left him paralysed. The family went through a financial crisis. Her mother was a homemaker, and had earlier been a teacher, but she could not work out of the house anymore because her father needed constant care. These circumstances made her mother all the more determined that all her children—five daughters and a son—should have good careers of their own. Her parents didn't discriminate between the boy and the girls, ensuring each child got equal opportunities regardless of gender. Tessy would later say in an interview, that in Kerala, even if people don't have enough to eat, they spend the little money they have on educating their children.

They lived close to the Thumba Equatorial Rocket Launching Station. Tessy, with her classmates, went on a school trip to the rocket launching station and stared with wonder at the huge rocket in its launch pad being readied to be test launched a few days later. It fascinated her, the glory and the science behind these magnificent inventions. This was where her love for rockets began.

Both her parents were very particular that all six children focused on their education, and all the six siblings studied hard to get into educational institutions of their choice, and to make their paths in their chosen fields. She was extremely good at maths and science, and her parents encouraged her to pursue the stream, to the best of their limited resources. Young Tessy studied in St Michael's Higher Secondary School and St Joseph's Girl's Higher Secondary School in Alleppey (Alappuzha). It was evident early in her scholastic career that she had a natural affinity as well as ability for both mathematics and physics, scoring 100 per cent in mathematics in her 11th and 12th, and 95 per cent in science. Back in those days, these scores were unthinkable, unlike today when they're the norm rather than the aberration. Back then, anything above 75 per cent was considered a distinction and celebrated. Back in those days, she says, 100 per cent in mathematics and 95 per cent in science was a huge achievement. Her parents were immensely proud of their daughter, and had high hopes from her.[1]

While her parents could give her all the moral support she needed, financial support was tough to come by, given her father's health issues. She had already been awarded a scholarship at the Government Engineering College, Thrissur, that covered her academic expenses and fully funded her tuition. She then applied for an educational loan of ₹100 per month from State Bank of India to cover her living expenses in Thrissur while doing her engineering.

She took an unconventional elective during her engineering—radar systems. Of the entire batch that year, only three students opted for this elective, and Tessy was one of them. Perhaps, somewhere within her, that dream ignited by the glorious sight of the magnificent rockets launching at the Thumba Equatorial Rocket Launch Station still lay dormant, although she had no clue where it was to head or that she would eventually make a career in it. Serendipitously, it was at this point in 1985 that she saw an advertisement for the course offering an M.Tech in Guided Missiles from the Institute of Armament Technology, Pune which is now the Defence Institute of Advanced Technology. The course came with an assurance of a job at the DRDO for those who completed it. At the time, most of her batchmates from her engineering college were applying for jobs at prestigious public-sector companies such as Bharat Heavy Electricals Ltd, Hindustan Aeronautics Ltd, BEML Ltd, etc. but this course was where Tessy wanted to be. She applied for it, gave the written test and was amongst the 10 across the country who made it through the written test and were called for the course. This, she considers the turning point of her life, not just professionally but also personally.

It was during her time in Pune that she would meet her future husband, Saroj Kumar Patel, a naval student from Orissa. They fell in love, and would eventually get married.

Professionally as well, Pune and her stint at the Defence Institute of Advanced Technology would prove to be the launching pad for her immensely inspiring career. Dr Abdul Kalam headed the institution then and was impressed by her work on gyroless navigation. He then had her teach around 50 scientists at the DRDO in Hyderabad. This was perhaps the second turning point in her career when a highly respected scientist like Dr Abdul Kalam took her under his wing. She taught at DRDO for a year.

After she had finished the course in Pune, she came to the DRDO lab in Hyderabad, in 1988. At that point, Dr Abdul Kalam was the director there, he would be director for a couple of years before moving on. He was already known as the Missile Man of India, he would go on to become one of the most loved and respected presidents of our nation later. It was sheer fate that she had planned to join the civil services and had given the exam, but the DRDO interview happened on the same day and she chose DRDO over the Indian Administrative Service (IAS). Dr Abdul Kalam hand-picked her and placed her in the Agni Missile programme when she finished her M.Tech.

She would further go on to supplement her M.Tech with an MBA in Operations Management and a PhD in guidance missile under the DRDO. Being called the 'Missile Woman of India' and 'Agni Putri' is an honour she bears proudly, because her role model and mentor, Dr Abdul Kalam, was himself called the Missile Man of India. She draws inspiration from him, and credits him with bringing in openness and teamwork into the DRDO as an organization. He would stop by the desks of all the juniors, she said, and encourage them all in their work. It was a huge motivator for juniors like her to have someone like Dr Abdul Kalam acknowledge and encourage them.[2]

She was then placed in the design and development department which was to handle Agni, the new-generation indigenously developed ballistic missile. Right from the beginning, they were involved in developing inertial navigation systems. During the first Agni launch in 1989, she was also involved in solid propulsion. She was then made associate project director of the 3,000-km range Agni III missile project. By the time Agni IV came along, she was made project director. Agni IV was tested successfully in 2011. She was also project director of the 5,000-km range Agni V in 2009. It would take her two decades from the start of her journey in missile technology to reach the biggest milestone in her career, the launch of the Agni V missile from Wheeler Island in Orissa in 2012. She brought to the table her expertise on solid propellant systems and was instrumental in developing Agni V's multiple targetable re-entry vehicle.

The journey through the various Agni models hasn't been easy. It has often been fraught with challenges and failures. During the development of the long-range missile Agni IV, she had to come up with a quantum leap in the rocket motor. The earlier models had worked with a metallic rocket motor casing, but with Agni IV, they created a composite rocket motor for the first time ever in India, the result of three years of hard work on designing this. In July 2006, a missile did not meet the required parameters. Tessy and her team had to deal with criticism, which she took head-on and worked 16-hour days to resolve the issues, working through weekends as well. After completing over 10,000 computer simulations, her focus among 2,000-strong team was to get the missile going along the right path to its target, which Agni V achieved with great precision. Agni V was first tested successfully in 2012, and has been tested five times since.

She was appointed as the director general, Aeronautical Systems of DRDO in 2018. The Aero cluster labs that would now be under her command included the Defence Avionics Research Establishment, Gas Turbine Research Establishment, Centre for Airborne Systems, Aeronautical Development Establishment, Centre for Military Airworthiness and Certification, and the

Aerial Delivery Research and Development Establishment. She has never felt that her gender is a barrier in her work, despite the fact that the missile technology space is so male dominated. She says that gender does not matter. You work as a scientist, not as a woman. Women need to be supported and guided to come up.

However, she does admit that as a woman working in defence science, work-life balance is difficult. She not only had to manage a demanding career but, given her husband's postings, had to single-handedly take care of her son. She's once had to take the hard decision of leaving an ill son at home to be at work during the critical time of a missile launch. Interestingly, while it might seem that she has named her son, Tejas, after India's first home-grown Light Combat Aircraft (also developed by DRDO), his name actually comes from a combination of Tessy and Saroj, his parents' names.

She has received multiple prestigious awards for her work. These include the DRDO Scientist of the Year in 2008, DRDO Performance Excellence Award for 2011 and 2012, India Today Woman of the Year in 2009, Lal Bahadur Shastri National Award for Excellence in Public Administration in 2012, CNN-IBN Indian of the Year 2012, Sir Mokshagundam Visvesvaraya Award in 2016, Outstanding Woman Achiever Award by Women in Science and Engineering (WISE) and FLO Icon Award (2018) from FICCI, among others. She has been awarded the Doctorate of Science from five universities and is a fellow of the Indian National Academy of Engineering (INAE), The Institution of Engineers-India (IEI) and Tata Administrative Service (TAS). She has also received honorary doctorates from five universities.

The work she does might be in the space of warfare and weapons, but she calls missiles weapons of peace. To quote her, 'Strength respects strength, so you need to have systems that show our country's strength.' Ambition is not something she subscribes to. She believes in doing one's work to the best of one's capability, the results and the recognition, she says, will follow. Words we would all do well to pay heed.

NOTES

1. https://www.youtube.com/watch?v=6l9tM3G2AGs. Accessed on 19 January 2022.
2. 'We watched breathlessly, praying for inner strength as the missile took off', *Telegraph India,* https://www.telegraphindia.com/7-days/we-watched-breathlessly-praying-for-inner-strength-as-the-missile-took-off/cid/427290. Accessed on 19 January 2022.

28

APARNA SEN

FROM IN FRONT OF THE CAMERA TO BEHIND IT

There's a fascinating story behind how Aparna Dasgupta, whom we now know as Aparna Sen, got her debut role. It was summer vacation and her mother had just convinced a 14-year-old Aparna to read Rabindranath Tagore's short stories. She read 'Samapti', one of the short stories in the collection, and thought that if it were to be adapted into a movie, she would be perfect to play Mrinmoyee, the child bride in the story.

Just then the telephone rang, and even before answering it, she knew who it was. To quote her, 'I don't know how I knew it, but I just did. And there he was, saying to me in his booming voice, *"Ami Satyajit Ray bolchhi. Chidu achhe?"* ("This is Satyajit Ray speaking. Is Chidu home?").[1] Chidu was what Ray called her father Chidananda Dasgupta. Ray was making a film based on the short story 'Samapti', and he was toying with the idea of casting Aparna in the role of Mrinmoyee. She would go on to act in her debut film, *Teen Kanya* (1961). It would be the start of a lifetime of mentorship in the art and craft of cinema, first as an actress and then as a screenwriter and a director under the internationally acclaimed Oscar-winning director Satyajit Ray. She would also have another life-changing moment at this point, she would be clicked by the famous photographer Brian Blake for his 1960 series titled 'Monsoon'. This photograph would make it to the cover of *Life* magazine. At barely 15, Aparna Sen, or Dasgupta as she was then known, was already destined for greatness.

Born on 25 October 1945, in pre-Independence Calcutta, into an illustrious family, she grew up in an atmosphere steeped in art and culture. Her family originally came from Cox's Bazar, now in the Chittagong district of Bangladesh. Her father was the veteran critic and filmmaker, Chidananda Dasgupta and her mother Supriya, a costume designer of repute. Theirs was a household which revolved around discussions on books, cinema, and art and culture. Her early education was at Modern High School in Kolkata and she would go to college to the prestigious Presidency College, in Kolkata for a Bachelor in Arts.

Teen Kanya was also a lesson in how a master director elicits the best performance from the actors. She particularly remembers the final close up in the movie which needed to show Mrinmoyee's emotional transition from a carefree girl to a married woman. To get the expression he wanted, Ray simply told her to put the tip of her thumb in her mouth and to think of lovely, wonderful things. It taught Aparna that to get a desired response from an actor, the director must explain the scene in a manner that the actor understands it and can relate to it.[2]

While her debut *Teen Kanya* came out in 1961, it took her many years to establish herself firmly as an actor of stature in Bengali cinema. In 1965, she acted in Mrinal Sen's *Akash Kusum*, and later in his film, *Mahaprithibi* (1991), which would win her the Best Actress at the Moscow Film Festival. In her Bengali movies, she was often paired with the heartthrob Soumitra Chatterjee and also with Uttam Kumar. Another important long-term creative association in her career began in 1969, when she acted in the Merchant Ivory production, *The Guru*. This would be the first of a long creative association with Ismail Merchant and James Ivory and their production banner. She would go on to make more films with them: *Bombay Talkie* in 1970 and *Hullabaloo Over Georgie and Bonnie's Pictures* in 1978.

Her acting career was going great guns when she began feeling the stirrings of discontent. This would culminate in 1981, 20 years from her debut as an actress, when she directed her first movie *36 Chowringhee Lane*. One day, waiting in the make-up room for her shot to be ready, she wondered if this was all that she was destined to do. This random urge resulted in her writing a short story, which she later showed to Satyajit Ray. Ray insisted she write the screenplay for it and suggested she connect with Shashi Kapoor to produce the movie. When she'd completed the movie, Ray asked her, 'Have you created any moments?' She realized that film-making was not only about the continuum of the narrative, but also about creating little moments within the movie. 'There was a lesson learnt that very day. A film is not just a series of technically perfect shots without any mistakes. It is about moments that will touch the viewers' heart, moments that they will take back with them,' she said at a lecture organized by the Society for the Preservation of Satyajit Ray Films, popularly known as Satyajit Ray Society or just Ray Society.[3]

The story of a lonely, retired Anglo-Indian school teacher in Kolkata, Violet Stoneham, brilliantly played by theatre veteran Jennifer Kendall Kapoor, who is manipulated by an ex-student to use her home for illicit romantic trysts, won Sen the Best Director at the Indian National Film Awards as well as the Grand Prix at the Manila International Film Festival. This was also the year she worked again with Satyajit Ray in his short film, *Pikoo*, where she played an adulterous woman. In *Pikoo*, the narrative was condensed into a day in the life of a six-year-old, shown from the child's perspective. Interestingly, it was during the making of this film that she had a strong difference of opinion with the renowned director as to how one should perceive adultery and the person committing it. This resulted in Sen directing *Paroma*

(1984), starring actress Rakhee Gulzar in the lead role. This film looks at the act of adultery from the unapologetic gaze of a woman.[4] *Paroma* won the Silver Lotus at the National Awards for the Best Bengali Film.

Her film *Sati*, made in 1989, won the National Award for Best Original Screenplay and *Yugant*, made in 1995, got the National Award for Best Bengali Film. What is notable about Sen's directorial efforts is that her movies looked at the human experience through the female and the feminist gaze. Her film *Paromitar Ek Din*, made in 2000, was much acclaimed critically and would win the National Award for the Best Bengali Film, as well as a number of international awards. Her movie, *Mr and Mrs Iyer*, released in 2002, won Sen a National Film Award for direction. The film would also win awards at Locarno, Hawaii and Manila. Her next directorial venture, *15, Park Avenue*, made in 2005, also had Konkona Sen Sharma as part of the cast along with veterans Shabana Azmi, Dhritiman Chatterjee, Waheeda Rehman, Soumitra Chatterjee and Rahul Bose. This film won the National Award for Best English Film.

Through her directorial ventures, she continued to dabble in acting. The movies in which she has acted include *Mohonar Dike* (1984), *Ekanto Apon* (1987) and *Swet Patharer Thala* (1992), among others. Her performance in *Indira*, released in 1984, saw her garner much critical acclaim. She was also seen in the movies *Kari Diye Kinlam* (1989), *Ek Din Achanak* (1999), *Mahaprithibi* (1991), *Unishe April* (1995), *Paromitar Ek Din* (2000), *Titli* (2001), *Antaheen* (2009) and *Chatushkon* (2014). Her role in *Antaheen* (2009) with Sharmila Tagore and Rahul Bose was much lauded and the film won four National Film Awards.

Her next movie as a director was *The Japanese Wife* (2010), starring Raima Sen, Rahul Bose and Chigusa Takaku. The film won her the Ammonite Award for Best Director at The Hidden Gems Film Festival in Canada that year. It also won the audience award at the Kerala Film Festival.

Her 2013 film *Goynar Baksho* told the story of three generations of women, and won both audience appreciation as well as critical acclaim. In 2015, she made *Arshinagar*, an adaptation of *Romeo and Juliet*. The same year, she also directed *Saari Raat*, the only Hindi film she has made. It premiered at the London International Film Festival. In 2017, she made *Sonata*, adapted from a play by Mahesh Elkunchwar, it looked at middle-aged friendship between women and Sen acted in it, along with Shabana Azmi and Lillete Dubey. In 2019, she released *Ghawre Bairey Aaj*, which is a contemporary take on the classic 1984 movie by Satyajit Ray *Ghare Baire*, an adaptation of Rabindranath Tagore's novel. The night she heard about the shooting of Gauri Lankesh, she couldn't sleep, the seed of what would eventually become *Ghawre Bairey Aaj* was sown. To quote her, 'It is the responsibility of a director to introduce their politics in their films, and whether you like it or not your politics will be reflected unless you are an opportunist which some directors are.'[5]

Her politics has always been a part of her oeuvre, and it is essential for her as an artist to take a stand in her creative work. To quote her from her interview with PTI, 'I had also been shaken after the demolition of Babri Masjid in 1992. I mean, I feel I should talk about the right or wrong step committed by any party or organisation whenever I feel there is such need.'[6]

She has received eight Bengal Film Journalists' Association Awards, commonly referred as BFJA Awards, for best actress, best supporting actress and one for lifetime achievement. She has won nine National Film Awards and nine international film festival awards for direction. In 1987, the Government of India awarded her the Padma Shri, the nation's fourth-highest civilian award, in commendation of her work in the field of films. In an interview with *Scroll.in*, she says, 'I was given a Padma Shri and several national awards, but I never lobbied for them. I have never accepted or asked for anything of any government anywhere. I have earned everything with my hard work as an actor and filmmaker. Which is why I never had the need to fear a power. The only thing I am afraid of is the Central Board of Film Certification interfering with my storytelling.'[7]

She has always been very vocal about the political situation in the country, and especially, West Bengal and the politics of the state. In an interview to PTI, she says, 'I was not born with political consciousness, and my political consciousness has slowly evolved during my life's journey.'[8]

It was also her stint as the editor of the popular Bengali magazine for women *Sananda* that made her more politically aware and involved. Unlike other celebrity editors, she was completely hands-on with the content that went into the magazine and wrote the editorial herself for each and every issue. To quote her, 'I am basically a radical humanist, a believer in secular ideals. But I have never come to the support of any particular party or group because I am a believer in issue-based politics only.'[9]

Her personal life has largely been out of the public glare, and that's how she prefers it. Fiercely private, she has lived life on her own terms. Her first marriage, to ad filmmaker Sanjoy Sen, ended in separation. Sanjoy died soon after they were separated and Aparna brought up their little daughter on her own. She later married journalist Mukul Sharma and had another daughter, Konkona Sen Sharma, who is an acclaimed actress herself today. They too would separate eventually.

Love returned to her life in the early 1990s, when she went to the US as part of the team performing two commercial plays: *Pannabai* (1989) and *Bhalo Kharap Mcye* (1991). It was during these tours that she would meet US-based literature professor, Kalyan Roy Choudhury and they would get married.

Her latest movie *The Rapist* won the prestigious Kim Ji-seok award at 26th Busan International Film Festival in 2021. The initial seed idea for the film came to Sen 15 years ago. She told *Variety* magazine, 'I began to wonder about why men rape.

No one is born a rapist. They go through infancy, through the toddler stage and through boyhood in all innocence. When and how do these persons then become rapists?'[10]

She is a woman of our times—fiercely outspoken, an independent auteur, politically conscious and an inspiration to many.

NOTES

1. Arshia Dhar, 'Aparna Sen and Madhabi Mukherjee on Satyajit Ray, the man, and his enduring legacy', *FirstPost*, 2 May 2021, https://www.firstpost.com/long-reads/aparna-sen-and-madhabi-mukherjee-on-satyajit-ray-the-man-and-his-enduring-legacy-8322451.html. Accessed on 19 January 2022.
2. 'Satyajit Ray's advice to Aparna Sen: Create moments that touch viewers' heart', *Mid-Day*, https://www.mid-day.com/articles/bollywood-news-satyajit-ray-advice-aparna-sen-touch-viewers-heart/18213161. Accessed on 19 January 2022.
3. Ibid.
4. Arshia Dhar, 'Aparna Sen and Madhabi Mukherjee on Satyajit Ray, the man, and his enduring legacy', *FirstPost*, 2 May 2021, https://www.firstpost.com/long-reads/aparna-sen-and-madhabi-mukherjee-on-satyajit-ray-the-man-and-his-enduring-legacy-8322451.html. Accessed on 19 January 2022.
5. 'Aparna Sen interview: 'Going against any one party does not mean going against the country', *Scroll.in*, 29 September 2019, https://scroll.in/reel/938500/aparna-sen-interview-going-against-any-one-party-does-not-mean-going-against-the-country. Accessed in 19 January 2022.
6. 'I am a radical humanist, says Aparna Sen', http://www.millenniumpost.in/kolkata/i-am-a-radical-humanist-says-aparna-sen-382939. Accessed on 19 January 2022.
7. 'Aparna Sen interview: 'Going against any one party does not mean going against the country', *Scroll.in*, 29 September 2019,

https://scroll.in/reel/938500/aparna-sen-interview-going-against-any-one-party-does-not-mean-going-against-the-country. Accessed in 19 January 2022.
8 'I am a radical humanist, says Aparna Sen', http://www.millenniumpost.in/kolkata/i-am-a-radical-humanist-says-aparna-sen-382939. Accessed on 19 January 2022.
9 Ibid.
10 Naman Ramachandran, 'Busan: Aparna Sen on Kim Ji-seok Award Contender "The Rapist", 28 September 2021.

29

KIRAN MAZUMDAR-SHAW

POWER LISTER

At a time when entrepreneurship was not an option for most ambitious Indians, let alone women, she not only became an entrepreneur, but did so in a space that was totally male dominated. However, at every step of her rather unconventional journey, Kiran Mazumdar-Shaw has been dogged about carving out her own path.

Born in Pune, on 23 March 1953, into a Bengali family, she studied at the Bishop Cotton Girls High School and then at Mount Carmel College in Bangalore when her family relocated there. She had set her heart on going to medical school, but missed out on getting a seat. She had expected her father to pay the capitation fee as most of her friends' parents were doing, but he refused. He had provided for her education and if she had missed out, she hadn't worked hard enough. Her father, Rasendra Mazumdar, was the managing director and master brewer at United Breweries. He told the young Kiran that perhaps an option for her was to study fermentation science, train to be a brewmaster. This was way back in the 1970s when no women entered the field, let alone a woman from India.

She applied to Australia's Ballarat College in Melbourne to study malting and brewing.[1] She was accepted and was then the only woman enrolled in the brewing course at the college in 1974. Being in a minority didn't intimidate her at all; in fact, she topped her class. What her stint at Ballarat College taught her was that gender is never a handicap, women can do anything and even do it better than their male counterparts if they are capable and willing to put in the effort required.

A year later, in 1975, she was a qualified Master Brewer. Her first positions were as trainee brewer in Carlton & United Breweries, Melbourne, and as a trainee maltster at Barrett Brothers, in Australia. For a while, she also worked at Jupiter Breweries in Calcutta as a consultant, and as a technical manager at Standard Maltings in Baroda, between 1975 to 1977. But she found herself hitting a glass ceiling and this drove her to look for opportunities abroad and she finally found a position in Scotland.

For Kiran Mazumdar-Shaw, the first turning point would be when she decided to go to Australia to study, a radical decision that set her on an unconventional career path. The second turning point came at this juncture of her life. She happened to meet Leslie Auchincloss, the founder of the company Biocon Biochemicals in Cork, Ireland. His company made enzymes that were used in the brewing industry as well as in food packaging and the textile industry. Coincidentally, at the time he was looking for an Indian partner to help him set up a presence in India and asked Mazumdar if she would be interested. The thought of being an entrepreneur had never crossed her mind, but his confidence in her compelled her to think about changing tracks to entrepreneurship. She contemplated the offer and decided to take it up, on one condition. If six months down the line, she did not wish to continue, she said, she wanted a job as a brewmaster, the same as the one she would have to let go to take up his offer. He agreed to her conditions and she returned to India, after training for a bit at Biocon in Cork. And this was how in 1978, a young woman of barely 25, with no experience of entrepreneurship, set up Biocon India in the garage of her rented home in Bangalore. Her seed capital was a humble

₹10,000. Biocon India was set up with a 30 per cent stake from the international company, because of Indian laws which at that point restricted foreign direct investment to only 30 per cent in the Indian subsidiary. Consequently, the majority 70 per cent stake belonged to Kiran Mazumdar-Shaw.

It wasn't easy. No bank would lend her money. They wanted her father to be her guarantor on paper. It was a chance meeting with a banker at a social function that helped her get her foot in the door with the capital she required for her project. Her next challenge was to find staff to join. Those who came for job interviews assumed she was the secretary and looked around for the man who would be interviewing them. They had their reservations. Her first employee was a retired garage mechanic. She forged on nonetheless. With the financing she received, she set up her first factory in a 3,000 sq. ft shed.

The fledgeling company began with the extraction of the enzyme papain from papaya which was used to tenderize meat and isinglass, an enzyme from tropical catfish used to clarify beer. In its very first year, Biocon was able to not just manufacture enzymes, but had also begun exporting them to the United States and Europe. With this, it became the first Indian company to do so. Within the first year itself, Mazumdar-Shaw was able to buy a 20-acre property with the profits, with an eye on future expansion. There were other challenges too. She was willing to take risks. She did things that people didn't expect a young girl to do, such as travel the length and breadth of the country on a bus or a train alone, as she couldn't afford airfare everywhere. It was a time of unrest in Punjab, and Mazumdar-Shaw would think nothing of travelling in state transport buses in North India. Often, she recalls, she would be the only woman on the bus. All the men on the bus would stare at her. The drivers would very considerately stop the bus right at the gate of the industrial complex she wanted to go to.[2] Those days had their own charm, she recollects in retrospect.

Slowly but surely, Mazumdar was able to convert Biocon into a completely integrated biopharmaceutical company, with a business portfolio that offered both products as well as research focused on diabetes, oncology and autoimmune diseases. She set up two subsidiaries: Syngene, in 1994, to provide early research and development support services to companies on a contractual basis and in 2000, Clinigene, to focus on clinical research trials as well as developing generic and new medicines. She merged both companies later.

What set Mazumdar-Shaw apart was her vision and drive in the field and her willingness to take risks and look into the future. These might seem like clichés, but she set up a research and development team at Biocon, as far back as 1984, sensing the potential in the discovery of novel enzymes and development of novel techniques in the technology for solid substrate fermentation. The company got its lucky break in 1987, when ICICI Ventures, led by Narayan Vaghul, created a venture capital fund of $250,000. This venture capital fund helped Biocon to expand its research and development facilities. With the funds received, Mazumdar built a new plant with proprietary solid substrate fermentation technology based on a semi-automated tray culture process, which in turn was influenced by Japanese techniques. Barely two years after this, in 1989, Biocon got US funding for proprietary techniques making it the very first Indian biotech company to do so. She also incorporated Biocon Biopharmaceuticals Private Limited (BBLP) to produce and sell biotherapeutic products under a joint venture with the Cuban Center of Molecular Immunology. In 1989, Unilever acquired Biocon Biochemicals from Leslie Auchincloss. Unilever then sold its speciality chemicals division, and with it Biocon to Imperial Chemical Industries (ICI). At this time, Mazumdar-Shaw's husband, John Shaw, raised, on his personal strength, $2 million to purchase the Biocon shares from ICI. John Shaw, who was till then the chairman of Madura Coats, quit his job to join Biocon and became the company's vice chairman in 2001. Three years later, Mazumdar-Shaw decided to list the company on the stock exchange. She took this step after consulting with Narayana Murthy of Infosys on what he felt was the path forward for Biocon. Her aim in doing this was to raise enough capital to help Biocon move forward on their research programmes. This made Biocon the first biotechnology company in India to go in for an initial public offering (IPO). Astoundingly, the IPO was oversubscribed 33 times, and closed its first day with a market value of $1.11 billion, becoming the second Indian company to cross $1 billion on the very first day of it being listed.

What has helped her in her journey to this day is the advice given to her by her father: that to be a good manager one has to find and bring out the good in people.

Mazumdar-Shaw also firmly believes in giving back to society. Interestingly, she doesn't quite like the term 'philanthropy', preferring to use 'compassionate capitalism' instead. In 2004, Biocon set up a corporate social responsibility (CSR) division called the Biocon Foundation to focus on health, education and infrastructure in rural Karnataka. She went a step further by joining The Giving Pledge in 2015, promising at least half her wealth to philanthropy. She teamed up with Padma Shri-awardee Dr Devi Shetty of Narayana Hrudayalaya to establish clinics offering critical care, generic medicines and tests for those who might not be able to afford them. Losing her best friend, Nilima Rovshen, to cancer, spurred her towards supporting cancer research as well as treatment. In 2009, she set up the 1,400-bed cancer care centre called the Mazumdar Shaw Medical Foundation in Bengaluru.

Apart from all these initiatives, she is also actively involved in the welfare of the city of Bengaluru and is part of the Bangalore City Connect Foundation, a non-profit organization that works with both the government and urban stakeholders to discuss civic issues. She partners with the Jana Urban Space

Foundation and the local government to improve the roads in the city. She is also actively involved in the Bangalore Political Action Committee, which reviews and recommends candidates contesting the city elections.

She's been part of many important lists too. In 2010, she was named in *Time* magazine's 100 most influential people in the world. In 2011, *The Financial Times* put her in the list of top 50 women in business across the world. In 2021, she was listed at number 72 on the Forbes list of Power Women, 53 on their list of India's richest and 727 on their worldwide billionaires list.[3]

In May 2015, the Federation University Australia (formerly the University of Ballarat) named a road in its Mt Helen campus after her, honouring their former student, calling it Mazumdar Drive. In 2019, the United States's National Academy of Engineering elected her as a member for her contribution to the development of affordable biopharmaceuticals and the biotechnology industry in India, making her the first Indian woman to receive this honour. Apart from these recognitions internationally, the Government of India has awarded her the Padma Shri in 1989 and the Padma Bhushan in 2005. *The Economic Times* gave her the Businesswoman of the Year in 2004. In 2012, she was named the Global Indian Woman of the Year by the Pharmaleaders Pharmaceutical Leadership Summit. In 2009, she was awarded the Express Pharmaceutical Leadership Summit Award for Dynamic Entrepreneur. Her alma mater also conferred an honorary doctorate on her in 2004, in honour of her contributions to biotechnology. Apart from this, she has received several honorary doctorates from universities in India and abroad. Most recently, Ernst & Young named her its EY World Entrepreneur of the Year for 2020.

What next, one might wonder. She herself has said, there is never an end to an entrepreneur's journey. It is the milestones on the way that matter.

Excerpts from an interview:

Your career and the unconventional path it took came about quite through serendipity. Opting to take up brewing because you missed getting into medical college, in retrospect do you feel that that one miss was providential for you? Has serendipity played a role in how your career shaped out further?

I call myself an 'accidental entrepreneur' because I never really planned to start a business. I went to brewing school in Australia and graduated with a Master Brewer certification. I was India's first woman brewmaster and intended to pursue a career as a brewer. However, I was in for a rude shock when I discovered the gender discrimination that was rampant in the brewing industry in India. It did not take me long to realize that I would never become a brewmaster in India because that was a male bastion.

For some time after coming back from Australia I consulted along with my father, helping several breweries in India to run their business, troubleshooting for them and aligning them with the best international practices of brewing. However, this is not what I wanted from life, my heart was set on being in the driving seat as the Master Brewer. I wanted to challenge this concept that women can't do certain roles. After several job rejections, I realized that I was in the wrong country with the right credentials. I finally gave up and began to look for work abroad.

Very quickly, I landed a very interesting position at a brewery in Scotland. I was about to move to Scotland to take up the job, when serendipitously I met Leslie Auchincloss, an Irish biotech entrepreneur and promoter of speciality chemicals company Biocon Biochemicals.

Leslie was in India looking for a partner to develop a papaya-based enzyme, papain. He persuaded me to give up my job in Scotland and replace it with a dream of being a biotechnology entrepreneur in India. Amidst apprehensions and with great persuasion from Leslie, I accepted the challenge to be his Indian partner and started Biocon India as an enzymes company.

I was 25 at that time, with no business background and only

limited financial resources. When I applied for loans at several banks, I was turned down because the bankers were sceptical about my business acumen as I was a woman. After several failed attempts, the breakthrough came when at a wedding reception, I met a branch manager of Canara Bank, who agreed to sanction Biocon's first loan.

I again needed money when we were trying to scale up our proprietary solid state fermentation technology, which we had frugally developed to pilot plant level. Encouraged by the initial success of this home-grown technology, we decided to upgrade it to commercial scale but realized it would cost us over a crore of rupees, a huge amount in the early '80s. When I approached the Karnataka State Financial Corporation (KSFC) and the Karnataka State Industrial Investment and Development Corporation (KSIIDC) for a loan to scale up the technology, I hit a hurdle because they wanted access to the intellectual property (IP) in order to validate it. I obviously refused as this was proprietary technology and the IP needed to be guarded closely. I was even advised to licence an imported technology to get the loan sanctioned. I was refused a loan as nobody understood that the whole point of biotechnology was not about licencing technology but about developing your own IP and innovation-led technology.

It was a chance breakfast meeting with Mr Narayan Vaghul, the visionary chairman of ICICI, which proved serendipitous. Mr Vaghul was keen on initiating the concept of funding first-generation entrepreneurs through equity rather than debt financing, and my enzyme business fit his criteria perfectly. Biocon's technology and ethos appealed to him and he became our first-ever investor.

Around the same time, Unilever acquired our Irish parent's business. This event taught me a lot about IP and what it takes to be a player on the global stage. With this new-found support, I started thinking strategically about where I wanted Biocon to go next.

It occurred to me that we could expand our horizons, so we spent the next 20 years developing and diversifying our enzyme technologies to serve a range of industries before ultimately ending up in biopharma.

After Biocon had pivoted to researching, developing and manufacturing biopharmaceuticals, I visited the Center of Molecular Immunology (CIM), Cuba, in 2001 and there serendipitously I spotted a molecule that showed promise in treating autoimmune diseases. We in-licenced this early stage R&D [research and development] asset from CIM. This novel monoclonal antibody, Itolizumab, was developed by scientists at Biocon and launched in India in 2013 to treat acute psoriasis.

During the ongoing novel coronavirus pandemic, we realized that Itolizumab's unique mechanism of action might work against the cytokine release syndrome (CRS), which has been found to be one of the causes of mortality in COVID-19 patients. Working on this hypothesis, we decided to repurpose this novel drug and conducted a Phase II clinical trial in leading hospitals in major cities across India with the hope that Itolizumab would benefit patients suffering from COVID-19 complications. At the same time, our partner in Cuba also started using Itolizumab for COVID-19 patients and saw promising results. The results of the clinical trials in India were positive and the Indian regulator granted Itolizumab an emergency use approval for treating CRS in acute respiratory distress syndrome (ARDS) patients due to COVID-19 in July 2020.

Your father pushed you to study brewing which was at that point an unconventional career choice. Could you tell us about how he influenced you in your career path going forward and what were the lessons you imbibed from him? Who are the other mentors and persons who have positively impacted your journey?

My late father, R.I. Mazumdar, was one of the most influential figures in my life. He kept encouraging me during those initial years of struggle. He made me believe that nothing was impossible and that as a woman I could achieve just as much if not more than any man. He also believed that good leadership was built on giving people the freedom to discover their own capabilities. His lessons have always resonated with me, and I've tried my best to apply them to my own companies: giving my colleagues the space to tackle issues using their own initiative. Though I was always there to guide them, I wanted my team to feel confident in their own decision-making skills. Another important lesson my father taught me was to always give back. He always said, 'Money is not a currency to buy favours, but a means to make a difference.' As my companies grew, I was able to extend a hand where there was a need. From the arts to healthcare organizations to R&D, both at home and abroad, I seek out opportunities to help.

I also owe my success to Mr Narayan Vaghul, who had started India's first venture capital fund TDICI or Technology Development Investment Corporation of India (later re-christened ICICI Ventures) with the primary objective of providing seed capital to technology-led start-ups. He helped me access venture funding from TDICI when I failed to get conventional lending institutions such as the KSFC and KSIIDC. Thanks to him, Biocon was one of the first recipients of venture funding in the biotech sector, which was a turning point in our business as it enabled financial resourcing in an accretive way and we no longer had to worry about servicing debt.

My husband, John Shaw, has also been a pillar of strength. In 1998, when Unilever sold its speciality chemicals business, of which Biocon was a part, to ICI, I wanted to buy back Unilever's stake in Biocon as we had the first right of refusal. That was also the time when John and I got married, and then we got Arthur Andersen to broker the deal with Unilever. They came up with the valuation where I could buy out Unilever's stake in Biocon for about $2 million. So, John sold his prime and prized possession—a house in Chelsea (London)—and bought out Unilever's stake and thus backed my venture.

As a young woman in a very male-dominated industry, starting at college itself, was the sexism you faced overt or subtle? How did you deal with it, and what would you tell young women today looking to enter and make their mark in fields considered 'off limits' because of gender?

I often joke, 'Do you know that India's largest biopharmaceutical company was founded because of a gender bias?' I decided to turn entrepreneur because of the gender bias I faced in the brewing industry. On turning entrepreneur, I came across some other facets of gender bias.

In those days, women were not perceived as good entrepreneurs. Banks and financial institutions were reluctant to fund me and some even suggested that my father should be the guarantor for any loans. I refused to allow him to stand guarantee and it took several failed attempts before I managed to meet bankers who had the confidence of lending to a woman-led enterprise.

My being a woman also made it difficult for me to hire people. Potential recruits felt working for a woman entrepreneur—or for a woman-led company—was not going to provide them job security. So I had a tough time trying to find people to work for me. Some even assumed I was the secretary to the managing director (MD), and not the MD, when they came for interviews. Finally, I got two retired tractor mechanics to be my first employees, and rented a shed to house the enzyme-extraction machinery I had purchased, and Biocon was born.

Moreover, my suppliers were reluctant to give me credit because they did not have confidence in my business abilities. When I negotiated business, many of them would feel very uncomfortable dealing with a woman and suggested they discuss prices with my 'manager'. It took a sustained effort on my part to educate these patriarchal people who were completely unfamiliar in dealing with women.

It is my firm belief that knowledge makes no distinction of gender. As a woman, all you need is the self-belief that you can excel in whichever field you choose to make a mark in. Courage of conviction and perseverance to overcome disappointments and failures are the hallmarks in this journey of endurance. Women need to believe in their goals and aspirations and attain them with confidence!

Setting up Biocon was an act of faith and determination. You have called yourself an accidental entrepreneur. What drove you back then to set up something of your own at a time when entrepreneurship was not the buzzword it is now, and people preferred secure jobs? What were the challenges of being a young woman in a highly specialized field as an entrepreneur?

After setting up Biocon, I was single-minded in my determination to see my venture succeed. I believed that by focusing on one step at a time, I could make things happen if I adopted a sensible and adaptable approach. I have never been one to give up easily, which is why, when I faced the initial hiccups that any start-up in India faced during the pre-liberalization period, I simply became more determined to make it work.

I started by making eco-friendly speciality enzymes for the first time in India. These enzymes helped several industries replace some of the polluting chemicals used in their processes.

Having attained success in enzymes, I leveraged my knowledge of biotechnology to try and disrupt the healthcare industry by introducing affordable biopharmaceuticals for patients who needed them the most. What spurred me on this mission of making a difference to global health was the realization that a significant proportion of the world's population does not have access to essential medicines and, where healthcare does exist, it is unaffordable.

From wanting to 'green the world' through eco-friendly enzyme technologies, my mission changed to 'heal the world' by developing affordable, life-saving drugs for patients across the globe. In the course of my journey, I leveraged innovation, differentiated technologies and a talented scientific pool to create a world-class, agile organization. In doing so, Biocon was able to scale great heights and emerge as a credible global biopharmaceuticals player.

As a young woman in a highly specialized field, the biggest challenge I faced was that of building credibility not only for myself but also for the nascent field of biotechnology that I had decided to pioneer. Getting people to change their mindset was by far the toughest challenge I faced.

You decided to invest in research and development at a time when companies were content to just be producers. You have consistently believed in going beyond what is expected at Biocon, so how important is it, you would say, for an entrepreneur to think innovatively?

I believe innovation is not just about doing different things but also doing things differently. As a first-generation entrepreneur, I have learnt that innovation creates value and differentiation builds competitive advantage. I created a business that leveraged science for the benefit of society through affordable innovation.

In India, Biocon pioneered the development of biotech drugs, which are difficult to make, and complex and expensive therapies that fight chronic, life-threatening conditions. However, we chose to do this through a model of affordable innovation that could deliver these life-saving therapies to the maximum number of patients.

We addressed the relatively unmet needs of patients by bringing advanced biopharmaceuticals against diabetes and cancer at price points that made them affordable and thus accessible. Biocon thus made a significant impact on global health by rationalizing healthcare spends and enhancing access to affordable biotherapeutics.

Giving back to society has been a constant with your growth story. What makes you choose the causes you do, and what compels you to be a proactive citizen? Given your work with Bangalore city, and the health- and education-related initiatives you have funded and driven, what have been the most rewarding initiatives?

Having grown up in a middle-class family in India, I was brought up by my parents to believe that wealth creation is about making a difference to society. As a first-generation entrepreneur, I built my company Biocon on these guiding principles. My success with Biocon has given me the wherewithal to pursue my overarching commitment to social inclusiveness.

I bring my expertise as a scientist and entrepreneur to my philanthropic efforts. My passionate pursuit of science to target cancer led me to set up the Mazumdar Shaw Medical Center in partnership with internationally renowned cardiac surgeon Dr Devi Shetty. This centre aims to create a sustainable and affordable cancer-care model that leverages advanced technologies, state-of-the-art diagnostics and best-in-class talent to address the challenges associated with this fatal disease. I have also set up the Mazumdar Shaw Center for Translational Research, which has developed a number of advanced yet affordable genomics-based cancer diagnostics including liquid biopsies that are enabling early diagnosis and better treatment outcomes.

My most recent venture in the field of cancer is Immuneel Therapeutics, a start-up co-founded with Pulitzer prize-winning author, cancer and stem cell biologist Siddhartha Mukherjee, and Boston-based 5AM Ventures founder and life-sciences professional Kush Parmar. Immuneel plans to bring the promising CAR-T [chimeric antigen receptor T-cell] therapy to cancer patients in India at a fraction of the cost charged in the US and Europe.

My philanthropic initiatives are also directed at making a difference to the lives of marginalized communities. Through Biocon Foundation's primary healthcare centres, telemedicine initiatives, health-awareness programmes, public-health initiatives and preventive screenings for oral and cervical cancer, I am attempting to make public-health delivery more efficient and effective in India.

My long-held belief in the power of entrepreneurship to drive change has led me to support start-ups, especially in the area of healthcare. I have played the role of an angel investor for start-ups such as UE LifeSciences, which has developed an affordable breast cancer screening device, Oncostem Diagnostics, which analyses the tumour cells of cancer patients to determine the need of chemotherapy for treatment and Embrace Innovations, which manufactures low-cost infant warmers targeted at premature and low birth-weight babies.

I was inspired to join Bill and Melinda Gates and the growing Giving Pledge fraternity in their philanthropic efforts to make this world a better place. In 2016, I became the second Indian to take the Giving Pledge to contribute a majority of my wealth towards philanthropy.

You are accessible on social media, very vocal and responsive to those who tweet to you. You also post on your blog to get your thoughts across directly to people. How important is it for you to have a direct connection with people who might want to reach out to you?

I took to social media because I realized that digital platforms such as Twitter and blogs enable you to share your views with the world at large. Social media gives me an opportunity to engage with people in real time. It empowers me to play the role of a global citizen effectively. I share my opinions on a wide variety of global and local issues. I counsel entrepreneurs and professionals seeking guidance and I sometimes address the concerns of Biocon's shareholders.

The problem of 'fake news' is a huge concern and it is affecting science and scientific research as well, especially in the context of the COVID-19 pandemic. As members of the scientific community, I believe we have an ethical and social obligation to stop the spread of fake news and I often use my social media presence to do so.

You have received several honours and awards throughout your career. Of these, are there any that are the most precious to you, and what makes them so? How emotional a journey was it to have a road named after you in your erstwhile university in Australia?

The most precious honours are the Padma Shri and the Padma Bhushan. In 1989, I became one of the youngest recipients of the Padma Shri, which made it special. I received the Padma Bhushan in 2005 from our then President and one of India's greatest scientists, Dr A.P.J. Abdul Kalam, which made it much more special.

I have many happy memories of the Ballarat College of Advanced Education (one of Federation University, Australia's predecessor institutions), which played a significant role in my education and development. So, I felt really gratified and happy when Federation University decided to generously name a road as 'Mazumdar Drive' in my honour.

What still drives you after all the laurels you have received? What keeps you motivated? How do you keep yourself passionate about the work you do as an individual, and as a team leader, a leader of industry? Are there any decisions you would have taken differently in retrospect?

I have a mission, which is to make an impact on global healthcare by ensuring affordable access to life-saving therapies for chronic diseases such as diabetes and cancer.

I am appalled by the ugly and unethical divide between the billion who have health security in the developed world and the nearly seven billion others who are vulnerable to disease and death because of little or no access to health protection. Non-communicable diseases (NCDs) kill over 40 million people each year, a majority of those living in the developing world. These deaths could have been prevented if only they had access to essential and life-saving medicines. For the vast majority in the developing world, life is about survival and we need to throw them a lifeline by developing disruptive new technologies that can provide affordable access to drugs for chronic and life-threatening diseases. I believe with all my heart that the healthcare industry has a special humanitarian responsibility to provide life-giving care.

It is this global healthcare challenge that drives my life's work of building a new model of innovation that adds the condition of affordability to ensure accessibility.

As a woman who is a self-made billionaire in the country, you are an icon to many. What would you tell young girls who look up to you to keep in mind as they set out to achieve their goals?

In my entrepreneurial journey, my ability to face and learn from failure and move on has helped me a great deal in achieving success. It is a trait that every girl needs to have in order to be successful. Failures provide the experience that no amount of success can. I am not suggesting one must seek failure, but when it does come your way, take it as a learning experience. I often say failure is temporary but giving up is permanent. We should never feel defeated in the face of failure, but should take it in our stride, learn from it and move on.

NOTES

1. 'From entrepreneur to MIT Board Member: The inspiring story of Kiran Mazumdar-Shaw', *Reliance Money*, https://www.reliancemoney.co.in/from-entrepreneur-to-mit-board-member-the-inspiring-story-of-kiran-mazumdar-shaw. Accessed on 21 January 2022.
2. Shradha Sharma, 'The unstoppable walk of an Indian woman, inspiration and Kiran Mazumdar Shaw', Your Story, 19 November 2014, https://yourstory.com/2014/11/kiran-mazumdar-shaw/amp. Accessed on 21 January 2022.
3. '#72 Kiran Mazumdar-Shaw', https://www.forbes.com/profile/kiran-mazumdar-shaw/?sh=1fe2c9b359ad. Accessed on 21 January 2022.

30

MAHARANI GAYATRI DEVI

THE QUEEN OF HEARTS

The Second World War had ended. In London, Indira Devi of Cooch Behar, who was pregnant at the time, was reading Rider Haggard's Gothic fantasy *She, A History of Adventure,* about an immortal queen and was much taken by the protagonist, Ayesha. On 23 May 1919, she gave birth to a baby girl, whom she named Ayesha. We would know the child as the ethereally beauteous Gayatri Devi.

Hers was an immensely privileged childhood. She recalls in her memoir, *A Princess Remembers: The Memoirs of the Maharani of Jaipur,* an unsupervised shopping spree at Harrods in London, as a very young child with the store manager available at her command. Her father, Prince Jitendra Narayan became the king of Cooch Behar when his elder brother passed away. She recalls, 'A mental picture of him (her father) standing in front of the fire in the drawing-room at Hans Place. He was wearing his dressing-gown and held a glass of whisky in his hand. He was very tall—nearly all the men in the Cooch Behar family are over six foot—and extremely handsome.' Some years later, he passed away as well, at barely 36. She remembers travelling back on a ship when this unfolded, '(I) have confused memories of my mother, dressed entirely in white, crying a lot and shutting herself in her cabin.'[1] Indira Devi took complete charge upon her husband's death, governing the state until her son came of age to become the regent. She was beautiful and formidable, with impeccable style. Gayatri Devi had inherited not just her mother's sense of style and panache, but also her exquisite features, huge limpid eyes and flawless skin.

Her childhood, along with that of her siblings, was as cosmopolitan and eclectic as it could get. She studied at the Glendower Preparatory School in London, Nobel laureate Rabindranath Tagore's Visva-Bharati University at Shantiniketan and at Lausanne in Switzerland where she did her finishing school. In 1932, His Royal Highness, Sawai Man Singh II of Jaipur visited her family in Calcutta on the invitation of her mother, Indira Devi. He was a polo player of formidable repute. The young, impressionable Gayatri was completely smitten by him.

In an interview with *Outlook*, she states, 'It was the year I had a huge crush on Jai (Maharaja Sawai Man Singh). I'd first met him when I was 12; he came to Calcutta to play polo and stayed with us. He cut such a dashing figure and although he was eight years older, I felt an instant connection with him.'[2]

Sawai Man Singh was 21 at the time, but already had two wives, both political alliances. He was entranced by Gayatri Devi; they had a courtship that spanned continents, away from the watchful eyes of those supervising her. Once she came of age, Man Singh proposed to her in a car while they were circling Hyde Park in London. She married Sawai Man Singh II on 9 May 1940 in a lavish wedding, against her mother's wishes. Her brother warned her that Jai liked girls and she should be prepared for it. She retorted tartly that given Jai was marrying her and not the other way around, he would have no further need for 'girls'. The marriage would be a blissful one. They had a son, Jagat Singh of Jaipur, born on 15 October 1949, who was granted his uncle's fief as a subsidiary title.

She went straight into a zenana of over 400 women of the royal household but later would make her home in Rambagh Palace, getting it lavishly redecorated by London-based designers.

She lived to the hilt, having her portraits clicked by Cecil Beaton, throwing extravagant parties for the who's who from around the world and summering at Knightsbridge in London. In her garages, there weren't just many imported cars but also a private aircraft, one that she is infamously reported to have flown to Delhi just to get her hair done. While she threw lavish parties, she also maintained a tight hold on the palace kitchens, much to the consternation of the palace staff. She could be generous to a fault, and pecuniary too. Tennis player Akhtar Ali recounts of her generosity in an interview. He says, 'She asked me if I would like to compete at the Junior Wimbledon that year. I candidly told her that I didn't have the financial strength to compete in London. A couple of days later, she declared at a party that I would be going to Junior Wimbledon. I lost in the semis and broke down. Gayatri Devi was watching the match. She consoled me and sponsored my trip the next year too! She used to say, "Money can't buy everything, but money can buy what money can buy".[3]

She was on *Vogue* magazine's list of the Ten Most Beautiful Women in the World. Her short, coiffed bob, her bare eyes and pale skin accentuated by just a dash of lip colour and gossamer light French chiffons with pearls set a trend the world over, but she claimed to never be overly concerned about her appearance. On the episode of *Rendezvous with Simi Garewal* (1998), she said, 'I never thought so much about myself, I was raised with brothers.'[4] In fact, she was teased by her siblings and called a broomstick because she was so excessively thin.

She drew a lot of her fashion inspiration from her mother Indira Devi, who was a style icon across continents. To quote her, 'Ma was very fussy about her clothes. Did you know she was the first person to start wearing saris made of chiffon? But her greatest passion was for shoes. She had hundreds of pairs and still went on ordering them from Ferragamo in Florence.'[5]

While the luxe life could have been comfortable enough, there was a very strong social conscience that saw her throwing herself wholeheartedly into social causes. She set up many schools in Jaipur, the most famous of which was the acclaimed Maharani Gayatri Devi Girls' Public School, established back in 1943, set up to encourage the nobility of Rajasthan to send their daughters to school.

Independence in 1947 caused a sea change in the lives of the royals. Jaipur was amongst the first princely states to sign the instrument of accession to India upon Independence. Jai converted Rambagh, their residence, into a palace hotel with a great deal of foresight, before palace hotels became popular in India.

By the late 1950s and the early 1960s, Maharani Gayatri was disillusioned with how nepotism and corruption had made their way into Indian politics. The Congress party asked her to contest for elections from Jaipur. It was then that she came across the Swatantra Party, an independent (as the name suggests) political party founded by the reformist leader C. Rajagopalachari. She found her views aligning with the principles of this party and decided to join it. She wanted to help with fundraising and canvass for the candidates from the party, but the party asked her to contest the elections and so she did. She campaigned for over two months, travelling in jeeps, in the heat and dust of Rajasthan. The bare necessities that she had always taken for granted—a clean bed and a bathroom—became luxuries for her on the road.[6]

However, she was soon able to anticipate the kind of questions the locals would have for her, and she answered them as realistically and honestly as she could. She writes, 'Seeing and meeting the people of Jaipur, as I did then, I began to realise how little I really knew of the villagers' way of life. I found that most villagers, despite the cruel experiences of famine and crop failure, possess a dignity and self respect that are striking and have a deep security in an inclusive philosophy of life that made me feel admiration and...almost envy.'[7]

She won by a landslide victory, with 1,92,909 votes out of

2,46,516 cast. It was a record victory at the time, making it to the *Guinness Book of World Records*, and she held onto the Lok Sabha seat in the 1967 elections as well as in 1971, as a member of the Swatantra Party.[8] Three terms as a Member of Parliament was an achievement by itself. She was a vocal parliamentarian, taking on then Prime Minister Pandit Jawaharlal Nehru in the course of a debate on the Indo-China War. She famously said to Pandit Nehru in Parliament, 'If you knew anything about anything, we wouldn't be in this mess today.'[9]

The dark shadow of tragedy struck in 1970, when her beloved Jai had a terrible accident on the polo fields in Circenster, England, resulting in fatal head injuries. He passed away the same day. Gayatri Devi was devastated. Upon his death, his son Bhawani Singh, Gayatri Devi's stepson, was crowned Maharaj of Jaipur and she became the Rajmata of Jaipur. To add to her woes, the royalty had to contend with the termination of the privy purses in 1971 the very next year after Sawai Man Singh II's death.

The state of Emergency declared by Indira Gandhi in 1975 saw Mrs Gandhi ruthlessly stifle all dissenting voices by jailing them. There was an income tax raid at Gayatri Devi's home situated on Aurangzeb Road in Delhi and she was arrested under the COFEPOSA (Conservation of Foreign Exchange and Prevention of Smuggling Act), for alleged undeclared gold and wealth.[10] The amount that got her arrested? A measly sum of nine pounds sterling in change found on her dressing table.

She would spend six months in Tihar Jail and have the Rajmata of Gwalior as her cellmate. Gayatri Devi bore the incarceration in good spirit. She wore her French chiffons and pearls, and perfumed herself and is even said to have poured perfume in the drains of the infamous jail when the stench got unbearable.

She would later make light of her experience. 'It wasn't too bad. In Tihar, I had my own bedroom with a veranda and my own bathroom. We were well looked after, except we were not free.' She kept herself busy. She recalled, 'There was a lot to do. I looked after people, started a school for children. There was a badminton court where we used to play badminton.'[11] At the end of the year in jail, she wrote to Mrs Gandhi, 'May I take this opportunity to assure you, Madam, of my support to you in person and your programme in the interest and betterment of our country.' She added, 'I have decided not to join any political party. In view of what I have stated above, as well as my deteriorating health, in spite of the medical facilities allowed and provided to me, may I request you for gracious considerations that I may be released.'[12] She was released in January 1976, after spending a solitary Christmas and New Year in confinement. She did have more personal tragedy to deal with. Her only son, Jagat Singh, was married on 10 May 1978 to Mom Rajawongse Priyanandana Rangsit of Thailand, and had two children, Rajkumari Lalitya Kumari and Maharaj Devraj Singh, Raja of Isarda. Jagat Singh died young, in 1997. He had long been estranged from his wife, and his two children grew up in Bangkok, away from their paternal grandmother. The loss of her son was compounded by the estrangement from her grandchildren. She said, 'Really, the toughest thing in life is to live without people you love. It was tough when I had to be on my own after I lost my mother, brother and husband, Jai.'[13]

She lived out the rest of her days in her cottage Lilypool on the grounds of the Rambagh Palace or at her home in Knightsbridge, London, during the summers. She had never quite recovered from the damage her stint at Tihar Jail had caused. In 2009, when she was in London, her gastric issues got so serious that she had to be admitted to King Edward Hospital. She requested to be flown back to her beloved Jaipur from London via an air ambulance. She passed away on 29 July 2009, in hospital. She was 90. Her estranged grandson was by her bedside when she passed away. She was cremated with state honours in the royal funeral ground. On her demise, beauty and elegance that had lit up our world with its incandescence was lost forever.

NOTES

1. Maharani Gayatri, *A Princess Remembers: Memoirs of the Maharani of Jaipur*, Rupa, 1995.
2. Gayatri Devi, 'I Had Shot My First Panther Before I Turned Thirteen', *Outlook*, 20 October 2008, https://magazine.outlookindia.com/story/i-had-shot-my-firstpanther-before-i-turned-thirteen/238724. Accessed on 20 January 2022.
3. Hemchhaya De, 'Maharani Gayatri Devi: Iron fist, velvet glove', *Femina*, 30 May 2019, https://www.femina.in/celebs/maharani-gayatri-devi-iron-fist-velvet-glove-124859.html. Accessed on 20 January 2022.
4. Taran Deol, 'Gayatri Devi, princess-politician and Indira Gandhi critic who was jailed during Emergency', *ThePrint*, 23 May 2020, https://theprint.in/features/gayatri-devi-princess-politician-and-indira-gandhi-critic-who-was-jailed-during-emergency/426887/. Accessed on 19 January 2022.
5. Kashika Saxena, 'The Life and Times of Maharani Gayatri Devi', Vagabomb, 6 January 2016, https://www.vagabomb.com/The-Life-and-Times-of-Maharani-Gayatri-Devi/. Accessed on 19 January 2022.
6. Maharani Gayatri, *A Princess Remembers: Memoirs of the Maharani of Jaipur*, Rupa, 1995.
7. Hemchhaya De, 'Maharani Gayatri Devi: Iron fist, velvet glove', *Femina*, 30 May 2019, https://www.femina.in/celebs/maharani-gayatri-devi-iron-fist-velvet-glove-124859.html. Accessed on 20 January 2022.
8. Taran Deol, 'Gayatri Devi, princess-politician and Indira Gandhi critic who was jailed during Emergency', *ThePrint*, 23 May 2020, https://theprint.in/features/gayatri-devi-princess-politician-and-indira-gandhi-critic-who-was-jailed-during-emergency/426887/. Accessed on 19 January 2022.
9. Hemchhaya De, 'Maharani Gayatri Devi: Iron fist, velvet glove', *Femina*, 30 May 2019, https://www.femina.in/celebs/

maharani-gayatri-devi-iron-fist-velvet-glove-124859.html. Accessed on 20 January 2022.
10. Taran Deol, 'Gayatri Devi, princess-politician and Indira Gandhi critic who was jailed during Emergency', *ThePrint*, 23 May 2020, https://theprint.in/features/gayatri-devi-princess-politician-and-indira-gandhi-critic-who-was-jailed-during-emergency/426887/. Accessed on 19 January 2022.
11. 'Nehru loved India, but the things he did were not right for India — Gayatri Devi in 2006', *ThePrint*, 29 July 2020, https://theprint.in/walk-the-talk/nehru-loved-india-but-the-things-he-did-were-not-right-for-india-gayatri-devi-in-2006/470459/. Accessed on 19 January 2022.
12. John Zubrzycki, 'How Indira Gandhi made Maharani Gayatri Devi grovel during the Emergency', *Live Mint*, 16 August 2020, https://www.livemint.com/mint-lounge/features/how-indira-gandhi-made-maharani-gayatri-devi-grovel-during-the-emergency-11597510186056.html. Accessed on 19 January 2022.
13. Prakash Bhandari, 'Rajmata and the dark days of Emergency', *The Times of India*, 30 July 2009, https://timesofindia.indiatimes.com/city/jaipur/Rajmata-and-the-dark-days-of-Emergency/articleshow/4835809.cms. Accessed on 19 January 2022; John Zubrzycki, *The House of Jaipur: The Inside Story of India's Most Glamorous Royal Family*, Juggernaut Books, 2020.

ACKNOWLEDGEMENTS

This book would not have happened without the lovely Saswati Bora, who commissioned me to write it, and was immensely patient through all my dithering and dathering and COVID-19-induced slacking. Deepest gratitude to Manali Das for her eagle eye over the content and references. Thanks to Rupa Publications for reposing their trust in me for this work.

To my agent, Suhail Mathur of The Book Bakers, thank you for all your support through the process.

To all those who graciously responded and agreed to speak with me for the select interviews in this book, gratitude for taking time out of your schedules for this book. Sonal Mansingh, Kiran Mazumdar-Shaw, Karnam Malleswari, Menaka Guruswamy, Naina Lal Kidwai and Mary Kom, I am immensely grateful for your kindness and generosity of spirit.

To all the women who are in this book; I am honoured and humbled to learn from their lives and the challenges they faced. Researching into their lives has made me even more acutely aware of how we take the rights and privileges we have for granted because so many women before us have fought battles all their lives to get them.

Thanks due to Yasser Usman for his insights into Rekha for the chapter on the stunning, evergreen actress.

For the lovely cover, thanks due to Amrita Chakravorty.

And to all my readers, I hope you get from this book the sense of awe and wonder that I did while researching it. Stories of women we know, some women we've grown up hearing about, some women who are no longer in our midst, but all women who, through their lives, have becoming shining examples of fortitude and courage, regardless of whatever life, society and misogyny put in their paths. They have struggled, they have suffered, but over it all, they have forged new paths—paths we must all acknowledge for having put down for the next generations to follow.

www.ingramcontent.com/pod-product-compliance
Lightning Source LLC
Chambersburg PA
CBHW030104170426
43198CB00009B/484